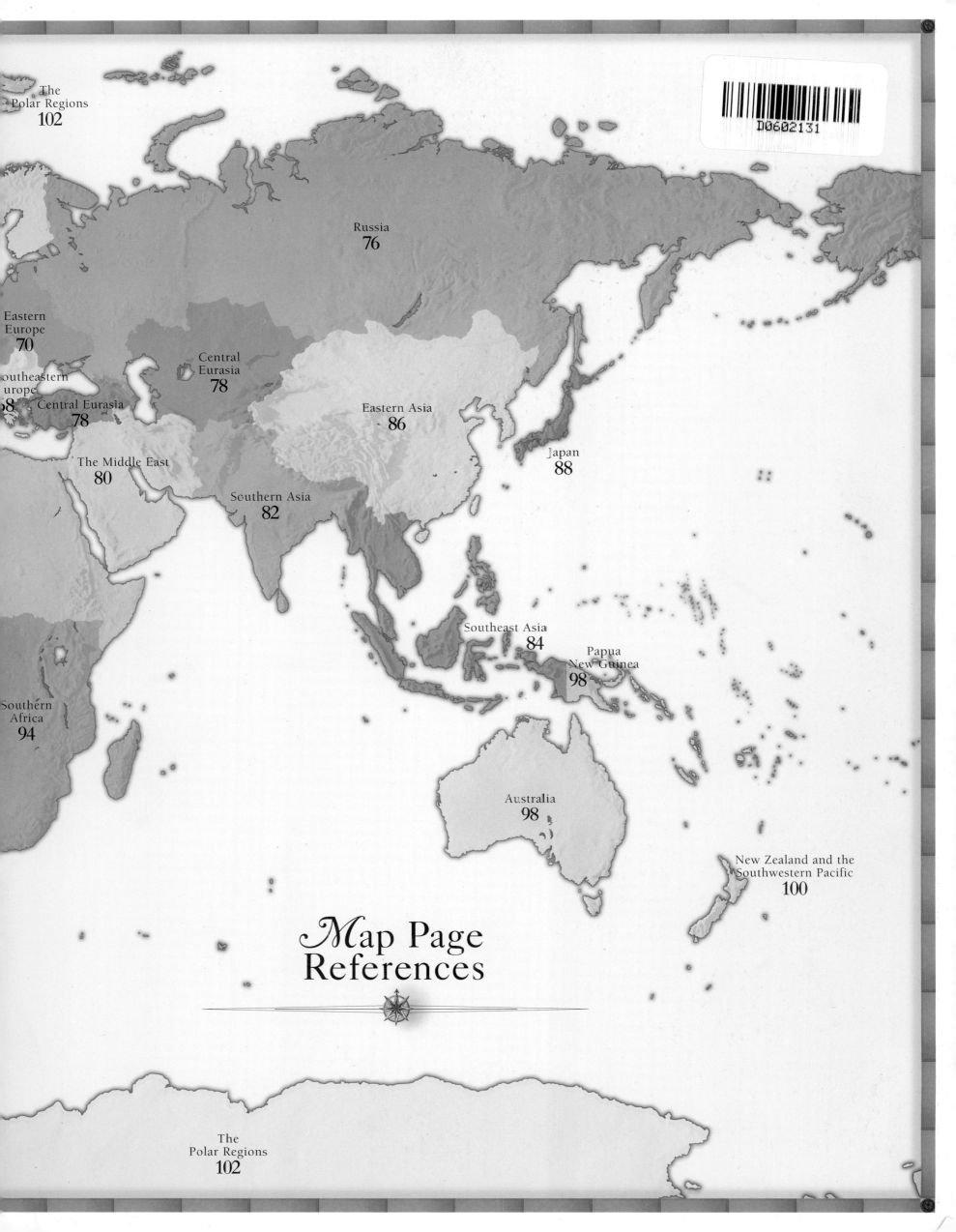

Map Page References

Children's Atlas of the World

Children's Atlas of the World

Published by Fog City Press
Conceived and produced by Weldon Owen Pty Limited
61 Victoria Street, McMahons Point, NSW, 2060, Australia

Copyright © 1998 Weldon Owen Pty Ltd
This edition copyright © 2007 Weldon Owen Pty Ltd

WELDON OWEN PUBLISHING
Group Chief Executive Officer: John Owen
Chief Executive Officer and President: Terry Newell
Publisher: Sheena Coupe
Creative Director: Sue Burk
Vice President International Sales: Stuart Laurence
Vice President, Sales and New Business Development: Amy Kaneko

Design Concept: John Bull
Managing Editor: Ariana Klepac
Project Editor: Scott Forbes
Consulting Editor: Colin Sale
Text: Scott Forbes
Editorial Coordinator, Third Edition: Jessica Cox
Senior Designer: Hilda Mendham
Designer, Thematic Spreads: Lena Lowe
Pre-press Co-ordinator: Jocelyne Best
Computer Production: Laura Sassin, Amanda Woodward
Computer Graphics: Stuart McVicar
Cover Design: John Bull
Senior Picture Researcher: Anne Ferrier
Picture Researcher: Peter Barker

Production Director: Chris Hemesath
Production Manager: Todd Rechner

Illustrators: Susanna Addario, Andrew Beckett/illustration, André Boos, Anne Bowman, Greg Bridges, Danny Burke, Martin Camm, Fiammetta Dogi, Simone End, Giuliano Fornari, Chris Forsey, John Francis/Bernard Thornton Artists, U.K., Jon Gittoes, Ray Grinaway, Terry Hadler/Bernard Thornton Artists, U.K., Tim Hayward/Bernard Thornton Artists, U.K., David Kirshner, Frank Knight, Mike Lamble, James McKinnon, Peter Mennim, Nicola Oram, Tony Pyrzakowski, Oliver Rennert, Barbara Rodanska, Claudia Saraceni, Michael Saunders, Peter Schouten, Stephen Seymour/Bernard Thornton Artists, U.K., Marco Sparaciari, Sharif Tarabay/illustration, Steve Trevaskis, Thomas Trojer, Genevieve Wallace, Trevor Weekes, Rod Westblade, Ann Winterbotham

Maps: Digital Wisdom Publishing Ltd
Flags: Flag Society of Australia

All rights reserved. No part of this publication may be reproduced, stored in a retrieval system or transmitted in any form or by any means, electronic, mechanical, photocopying, recording or otherwise, without the permission of the copyright holder.

Color reproduction by Colourscan Co Pte Ltd
Printed by Tien Wah Press
Printed in Singapore

ISBN-10: 1-74089-614-9
ISBN-13: 978-1-74089-614-6

This edition first printed in 2007
1 3 5 7 9 10 8 6 4 2

A WELDON OWEN PRODUCTION

Children's Atlas of the World

Consulting Editor: Colin Sale

FOG CITY PRESS

CONTENTS

NORTH AMERICA 32

SOUTH AMERICA 48

EUROPE 54

ASIA 74

AFRICA 90

AUSTRALIA AND OCEANIA 96

How to Use This Atlas

THE READER'S DIGEST CHILDREN'S ATLAS OF THE WORLD takes you on a fascinating tour of our extraordinary world. Before you set off, read the sections called Maps and Mapmaking and How to Read a Map. There you will find out about different kinds of maps and how they are made, and learn how to read and use maps. The remaining introductory pages are a guide to our planet, Earth. They show you where it is located in space, what it is made of, how its landscapes have been shaped, and how weather, wildlife and peoples vary around the world. The atlas maps are divided into seven parts—one for each of the continents of North America, South America, Europe, Asia, Africa, and Australia and Oceania, and one for the polar regions. Each part begins with a continent map that includes country lists and shows the most important features of the landscape. The continent map is followed by a series of illustrated maps which are packed with facts, pictures and activities. The sample maps and notes on these two pages explain the features on both types of map. At the back of the atlas you will find the World Fact File. This provides useful information on all of the world's countries and major territories. Finally, there is a glossary of terms used in this book, as well as a gazetteer—a geographical index that helps you to find places on the maps.

ILLUSTRATED MAP

Country list This is a list of the countries or states on the map, their populations and capital cities.

France

FRANCE, THE LARGEST COUNTRY in western Europe, has a varied climate and landscape. In the north, the weather is mild and wet, and much of the land is flat. As you travel south, the climate becomes warmer and the land more mountainous. Three-quarters of the population live in towns and cities, but most of the country is farmland, and France is Europe's leading farming country. The northern plains are covered in fields of wheat and sugar beets, and in central and southern France vineyards dot the hillsides—more wine is produced in France than in any other country except Italy. The area around Paris, the capital, is the most densely populated place. It is home to one-fifth of the country's population and most of its industries. Several great rivers, including the Seine and the Loire, cross France's northern and western plains. These waterways were once the country's main transportation routes, and their banks are lined with historic villages and magnificent castles known as châteaus. In the south, the mountains of the Pyrenees and the Alps separate France from Spain and Italy. Among their snow-capped peaks lie popular ski resorts and national parks that are home to eagles, marmots and goatlike antelopes called chamois. Along the Mediterranean coast there are many busy beach resorts. Near the Italian border lies Monaco, the second-smallest country in the world. Monaco is famous for its casinos and its annual Grand Prix motor race.

FRANCE
POPULATION: 59,765,983 • CAPITAL: Paris
MONACO
POPULATION: 31,987 • CAPITAL: Monaco

Amazing Fact
This box contains fascinating facts about the area on the map.

❖ AMAZING FACT ❖

France is now connected to Great Britain by an undersea rail link known as the Channel Tunnel. The tunnel took seven years to build and includes two rail tracks. Trains take 35 minutes to pass through the tunnel. Travelers can journey from London to Paris in about three hours.

Continent Facts This includes the size of the continent, its population and the names of its countries.

CONTINENT MAP

Records This is a list of the tallest, longest and largest features of the continent.

Size comparison These pictures show how the continent's most important mountains and rivers would look if you could see them side by side.

Political map This map shows all the countries in the continent.

Physical map This map shows the main features of the landscape.

Colored border
Each part of the atlas has a different colored border.

Map reader's grid The letters and numbers on the border help you find places on the map. See page 10 to find out how to use the grid.

Projects By trying out these activities and experiments, you can learn more about a topic or a part of the world.

KEY TO **M**AP **S**YMBOLS

country border

regional (state) border

disputed border

CHANNEL ISLANDS (U.K.)

territory and country to which it belongs

France – See World Fact File page 107

• PROJECT: *Cave Painting* •

The cave paintings at Lascaux were created about 15,000 years ago. Here's how you can create your own painting that will look thousands of years old.
❶ Stuff a strong paper bag with crumpled newspaper and then staple the bag closed.
❷ Mix some glue and sand and use this to paint the whole bag. When it dries it will look like a rock.
❸ Collect three or four different-colored soils. Sift out the lumps and then mix each color with glue to make earth paints (add water if the paints are too thick). Now you are ready to paint. Like the artists who created the Lascaux cave paintings, you can paint animals living in your area.

• LOOK AGAIN •
• Which cathedral lies southwest of Paris?
• Name a horned animal found in the Pyrenees.
• What kind of food is produced in Dijon?
• Which small country is located east of Nice?

FRANCE

TOUR DE FRANCE
France's most famous sporting event, this cycle race around the entire country covers about 2,500 miles (4,000 km).

Look Again
To answer these questions, you'll need to take a close look at the information on the map.

Locator globe
This globe shows where the area on the map is located.

•Baltimore
⊛ANNAPOLIS
✪WASHINGTON, D.C.

✪ national capital
⊛ regional capital
● city or town

Arno

river

Lake Ontario

lake

▲Ben Nevis
4,406 ft (1,343 m)

▲ major mountain

Ⓔ African elephants

Ⓔ endangered animal

Illustrations These show the people, places, wildlife and activities in the area on the map.

Feature illustrations These pullout features provide extra information on some of the map illustrations.

Scale The scale bar helps you to calculate distances on the map. To find out how to do this, see page 10.

Compass The compass helps you find north. To find out how to use the compass, see page 10.

KEY TO **M**AP **C**OLORS

Desert and semidesert

Forest and grassland

Tundra

Ice cap

Maps and Mapmaking

A MAP IS A PICTURE that shows you what an area of land looks like from above. Any area, no matter how large or small, can be drawn as a map. Some maps show small areas such as a town; others show the whole world. Because maps usually show areas that are much larger than the page they are printed on, objects have to be drawn much smaller than they really are. This is called drawing to scale. The bigger the area of a map, the smaller the real objects have to be drawn. Maps that show a small area and a large amount of detail are called large-scale maps. Maps that show a large area and a small amount of detail are called small-scale maps. On most maps, real objects are represented by lines, colors and symbols. For example, on a map of a town, black outlines may indicate streets, and colored shapes may show buildings. On a map of a country, towns may appear as simple black dots, and rivers as blue lines. A book of maps—like the one you are reading now—is called an atlas. An atlas usually contains maps of the whole world as well as maps of countries and continents.

◆ AMAZING FACT ◆

In Greek mythology, Atlas was a man who led a rebellion against the gods. As a punishment for this act, he was made to support the world on his shoulders. When the first books of maps were published in the 16th century, many had an illustration of Atlas carrying a globe on their covers. As a result, a book of maps soon became known as an atlas.

MAPPING THE WORLD

Each of these maps shows the location of Riverford School, but each is drawn at a different scale.

In this map of Riverford School, lines, colored shapes and labels are used to show the school, nearby streets and other features. Maps of small areas like this are often called plans.

This is a map of Riverford town. Because the area of the map is larger, less detail can be shown. You can now see that the school is near houses, a park and a river, but you can no longer see the school parking area or playing field.

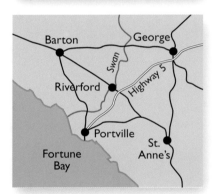

This map shows the region around Riverford. The town is now represented by a simple black dot, so you can no longer see the school or the streets. But you can see that Riverford is near water, and that it is linked to other towns by major and minor roads.

◆ PROJECT: *Mapping Your Neighborhood* ◆

You can draw a map of your neighborhood. To do this you will have to think about where places are, how far apart they are, and what shape they are. You may need to go for a walk and make a list of the things you want to show on your map.

❶ Once you have decided what you are going to include, draw in the streets.

❷ Then add shapes to represent features such as buildings, parks and rivers. Label the streets.

❸ Now color your map. Use one color for houses, one for streets, and so on. Draw a key to show what the colors represent. Finally, add labels for important places such as your home and school.

Arctic
Circle
(66.5°N)

Tropic of
Cancer
(23.5°N)

Equator
(0°)

Tropic of
Capricorn
(23.5°S)

Antarctic
Circle
(66.5°S)

180°   Greenwich meridian (0°)   180°

MAKING MAPS

People who make maps are known as mapmakers or cartographers. Before airplanes and spacecraft were invented, mapmakers used information supplied by travelers and explorers to make maps. Nowadays, most maps are based on surveys and on photographs taken by satellites positioned in space, high above Earth. Mapmakers face one major problem: Earth is round, but most maps have to be flat. A globe is the most accurate kind of map because it is the same shape as Earth. But if you tried to create a flat map by simply peeling the surface of a globe, you would end up with a world map made up of pieces, or segments. You can test this for yourself by carefully peeling an orange and trying to flatten out the skin. You will find that it is impossible to make the peel lie flat without breaking it. In order to create a flat map, mapmakers have to stretch and squash the segments of the globe. The different ways in which they do this are known as projections. There are many types of projections, and each creates a slightly different map.

A FLAT EARTH

As shown above, the surface of the globe can be divided into segments. To create a flat, rectangular map like the one on the left, mapmakers must fill in the gaps between the segments. To help them do this and plot locations, mapmakers use lines of latitude (horizontal lines) and longitude (vertical lines).

LINES AROUND THE WORLD

Mapmakers use a grid system to plot locations on the globe. Lines of longitude are drawn between the North Pole and the South Pole and are measured in degrees east or west of the Greenwich meridian (0°). Lines of latitude are drawn in a west-east direction and measured in degrees north or south of the equator (0°). The equator divides the world into the Northern and Southern hemispheres. The Greenwich meridian and the 180° line separate the Eastern and Western hemispheres.

How to Read a Map

MAPS ARE PACKED WITH INFORMATION. They tell you where places are, what size and shape they are, and how far and in what direction they lie from each other. Maps can also tell you about a region's climate, landscape, vegetation, towns and cities, and transportation routes. Once you have learned how to read maps, you can use an atlas to find out many things about countries all around the world.

FINDING PLACES

Most maps and atlases use a gazetteer and grid system to help you find places. You look for the place name in the gazetteer— an index of place names which usually appears at the back of the atlas—and then use the grid reference to find the location on the relevant map. Normally, a map grid consists of a series of letters along the top and bottom of the page and a series of numbers down the sides. Take a look at the map of Australia on the right. The grid reference for the city of Melbourne is H8. To find Melbourne, look at the letters on the top or bottom border and find H. Then find 8 on the left- or right-hand border. Imagine a line running down the page between the two Hs and another running across the page between the two 8s. (You can use a ruler to help you line up the numbers.) You will find Melbourne near the intersection of these lines.

USING THE MAP GRID

In the gazetteer of this book, each place name is followed by a grid reference. The grid reference for the city of Nashville, Tennessee, in the United States is 41 L4. To locate Nashville, turn to page 41 and find L and 4 on the grid. Trace a line down from L and another across from 4. Nashville is near the intersection of the two lines.

DESCRIBING DIRECTION

A map usually has a compass symbol, which indicates the direction of north (N) on the map. Sometimes, as on the map above, it also shows the directions of south (S), east (E) and west (W). You can use the points of a compass to describe where places are. For example, on the map above we can say that Sydney is east (E) of Adelaide and that Brisbane is north (N) of Sydney. Brisbane is both north and east of Adelaide, so we can use a combination of compass points and say that Brisbane is northeast (NE) of Adelaide. But Brisbane is farther to the east of Adelaide than it is to the north of it. So, if we want to be even more accurate, we can describe Brisbane as being east-northeast (ENE) of Adelaide. The compass above left shows all the combinations of compass points that you can use to describe direction.

dry
land

river

forests and
grasslands

mountains

G H I J

RALIA

Lake
Eyre Cooper Creek

Darling

Lachlan

Murray

Adelaide

● Brisbane

5

6

7

● Sydney

■ CANBERRA

8

● Melbourne

9

● Hobart

G H I J K

COLOR KEYS

On this map of Australia, dark shading indicates mountains. Green represents forests and grasslands, and orange shows desert and other dry land. Areas of water such as oceans, lakes and rivers are all colored blue.

THE LAY OF THE LAND

The colors of a map may tell you something about a region's landscape, vegetation and climate. Often, shading is used to show mountain ranges, and colors are used to represent different kinds of vegetation. Green normally represents forests or grasslands, while yellow or orange indicates an area of dry land such as desert. On many maps, a special symbol, such as a square or star, is used to indicate a capital city. Most maps and atlases have a key that explains these features. In this atlas, you will find the key on page 7.

MEASURING DISTANCE

Most maps have a scale. This shows how distance on the map compares with real distance. Many scales appear as a bar that is divided into sections, as do the ones used in this book. In the scale shown on the map above, each section on the top part of the bar is equal to 250 miles, and each section on the bottom of the bar represents 400 kilometers. The project on this page shows you how to use this type of scale to measure distances on a map. Scales can also be written like this:

1:1,000,000

This shows that the map has been reduced 1,000,000 times. Distances on the ground are therefore 1,000,000 times greater than they are on the map. Thus 1 inch on the map is equal to 1,000,000 inches, or 15¾ miles, and 1 cm on the map is equal to 1,000,000 cm, or 10 km. Other scales are written like this:

1 inch = 10 miles

This shows that 1 inch on the map corresponds to 10 miles in real distance.

◆ PROJECT: *Using a Scale* ◆

To measure the distance between Perth and Sydney on the map at left, follow these steps:

❶ Place the straight edge of a piece of paper on the map so that it lines up the dots of the two cities. Mark their positions on the paper.

❷ Place the paper next to the scale so that one of the dots lines up with zero. The scale is shorter than the distance, so mark the paper where the scale ends and note the distance it represents.

Place the mark back at zero and repeat these steps as often as necessary. Add the figures to calculate the distance between the cities.

You can also use the scale to measure distances along curved lines.

❶ Place a piece of string on the map along the Darling River, bending it to match the course of the river.

❷ Grasp the string at each end of the river, then straighten it out and measure it against the scale. You can then calculate the length of the river.

N

Planet Earth

WE LIVE ON A SMALL PLANET in a tiny part of a vast universe. Our part of the universe is called the solar system. There are nine planets in the solar system, and they move around, or orbit, a star that we call the Sun. Enormous groups of stars are known as galaxies. Our galaxy is called the Milky Way and it is made up of at least 100 billion stars! There are many millions of galaxies in the universe and each one is surrounded by a vast, empty space. The solar system formed about five billion years ago from a large, swirling cloud of dust and gases. The hot, central part of the cloud became the Sun, while farther out, rocks and gases combined to form the planets. Other rock fragments became asteroids, or minor planets.

◆ AMAZING FACTS ◆

- Our galaxy looks like this. The faint, glowing arms of this galaxy are clouds of stars. Each of these stars is like our Sun and may have its own system of planets.

- Jupiter is bigger than all the other planets, moons, comets and asteroids put together. Yet, it is still only about a hundredth as large as the smallest star.

ROUND AND ROUND
As each planet orbits the Sun, it also spins, or rotates, on its axis—an imaginary line through its center. Earth rotates once every 24 hours, and takes one year to orbit the Sun. Planets near the Sun orbit more quickly than those farther away. Asteroids also orbit the Sun. Most are located between Mars and Jupiter, in an area known as the asteroid belt. The planets and asteroids are all held in their orbits by gravity, a powerful force that pulls them toward the Sun. Without this force, they would fly off into space.

THE PLANETS IN PERSPECTIVE
The illustration below shows the relative distances between the planets, as well as how long the planet takes to orbit the Sun (a year on that planet) and how long it takes to spin on its axis (a day on that planet).

Sun

Mercury Year: 88 Earth days. Day: 59 Earth days.

Venus Year: 225 Earth days. Day: 243 Earth days.

Earth Year: 365.25 days. Day: 24 hours.

Mars Year: 1.9 Earth years. Day: 24.6 hours.

Asteroid Belt

Jupiter Year: 11.9 Earth years. Day: 9.8 hours.

Saturn Year: 29.5 Earth years. Day: 10.2 hours.

Uranus Year: 84 Earth years. Day: 17.9 hours.

◆ PROJECT: *Space Mobile* ◆

You can make your own mobile of the solar system to hang up in your bedroom or in your classroom at school.

❶ First, collect some paper, colored pens, string or cotton thread, scissors and a coat hanger.

❷ Draw the Sun and each of the planets and color them. Make sure you copy the colors and relative sizes of the planets as shown in the illustrations on these pages.

❸ Carefully cut out each planet using a pair of scissors.

❹ Make a small hole in the top of each planet with the point of a pen or pencil and thread a length of string through the hole.

❺ Tie the Sun and the planets to the bottom of the coat hanger. Place the Sun in the middle and arrange the planets on either side of it in the order shown in the illustration on these pages. Don't forget that some planets are closer together than others.

❻ When all the planets are in place, the mobile is ready to hang.

WORLD IN MOTION

As Earth turns on its axis, we move in and out of the Sun's light. Day begins as we move into the light. As we turn away from the Sun, night falls. Because Earth is tilted at an angle, the amount of sunlight reaching different parts of the world varies throughout the year. When part of Earth is tilted toward the Sun, it is summer there. When it is tilted away from the Sun, it is winter.

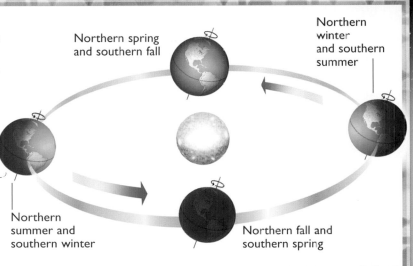

Northern spring and southern fall

Northern winter and southern summer

Northern summer and southern winter

Northern fall and southern spring

FIT FOR LIFE

Some planets are surrounded by a layer of gases called an atmosphere. As far as we know, Earth is the only planet in the solar system with an atmosphere that contains sufficient water and oxygen for life to flourish. Our atmosphere is so thin that if the planet were the size of an apple, the atmosphere would be only as thick as the peel.

Neptune Year: 165 Earth years. Day: 19.2 hours.

Pluto Year: 248 Earth years. Day: 6.4 Earth days.

An Ever-Changing Planet

EARTH IS SHAPED LIKE a large ball. Inside are several layers made of different materials. As Earth formed, heavy minerals such as iron and nickel sank to the center, while lighter materials rose to the middle and upper levels. At first, the upper levels consisted entirely of hot, liquid rock, but as Earth cooled, the outside solidified to form a thin, hard crust. This crust broke into several pieces, known as lithospheric plates. These plates float on the liquid, molten rock—or magma—underneath and are constantly moving, although you cannot feel the movement. Energy from Earth's core creates powerful convection currents that force the plates together and apart. This happens extremely slowly, but over millions of years these movements shape and shift the surface of Earth, causing earthquakes and volcanic eruptions and forming mountains and islands.

- Inner core
- Outer core
- Lower mantle
- Asthenosphere
- Lithosphere
- Upper mantle
- Ocean crust
- Continental crust
- Convection currents

INSIDE EARTH
Our planet's solid iron inner core is surrounded by an outer core of liquid iron and nickel. Above this is a layer of solid rock called the lower mantle and a wide band of liquid rock known as the asthenosphere. Earth's outer layer is called the lithosphere. It consists of the solid rock of the upper mantle, and the crust. Crust under the land (continental crust) is usually thicker than crust under the sea (ocean crust). In Earth's core, temperatures reach an amazing 5,400°F (3,000°C). This heat creates strong convection currents that push the crust in different directions.

◆ PROJECTS: *Folding the Crust* ◆

❶ Cut a paper plate in half. These halves represent two of Earth's lithospheric plates.

❷ Using adhesive tape, attach a sheet of paper to the plate halves. The paper represents Earth's crust.

❸ If you slide one half of the plate under the other, the paper buckles. Similarly, when two of Earth's plates collide, their crusts fold, forming mountains.

❶ Take a sheet of paper, fold it in half and continue to fold it.

❷ After six folds, it becomes difficult to fold the paper any further. In the same way, the thicker Earth's crust, the greater the force required to fold it.

Hot-spot volcanoes

Spreading plates

Coastal collisions

WORLD IN MOTION
Convection currents cause Earth's plates to collide, separate and slide past each other. The effects of these movements are shown in the illustration above and in the photographs on the right.

Coastal Collisions
When thin ocean crust meets thick continental crust, the thin crust slides under the thicker crust. Magma rises to the surface and forms a line of volcanoes. This process formed Mount St. Helens in the United States.

Hot-Spot Volcanoes
Weaknesses in the middle of plates, known as hot spots, allow magma from the asthenosphere to burst through the crust and form volcanoes. The Hawaiian Islands were created by hot-spot volcanoes.

Spreading Plates
Circulating magma may force plates apart. Where the plates separate, magma rises through the gap and cools and hardens to form a ridge. Normally this happens under the sea, but in Iceland it can be seen on land.

200 million years ago

90 million years ago

Present

60 million years from now

ON THE MOVE

Over millions of years, plate movements have joined and divided Earth's landmasses. Two hundred million years ago, there was a single "supercontinent." It split into two landmasses, which then broke up to form the continents we know today. Further changes to these landmasses will occur as Earth's plates continue to drift.

PLATE MOVEMENTS

Earth's plates fit together like the pieces of a jigsaw puzzle, but the plates are constantly moving. This map shows the direction in which each plate moves. Most volcanoes and earthquakes occur where plates meet. This means that countries in the center of plates, such as Australia, have few earthquakes and volcanoes, whereas countries at the edges of plates, such as Japan, have many.

← Direction of movement

▲ Volcanoes

Earthquake zones

• AMAZING FACTS •

- When the volcano on the island of Krakatoa in Indonesia erupted on August 27, 1883, the explosion was heard 3,000 miles (4,800 km) away!
- More than 500,000 earthquakes occur every year. Fortunately, most of these are too weak to cause any damage.

Sliding plates

Folding crust

Undersea collisions

Sliding Plates

A fault line forms where two plates slide past each other. The friction between the plates creates earthquakes. These occur regularly along the San Andreas fault in California as part of the coastline slides northward.

Folding Crust

When two plates with crusts of similar thickness collide, the edge of one plate slides under the other, and the crusts buckle and fold to form mountains. This process created the massive Himalayas mountain range in Asia.

Undersea Collisions

When two plates with ocean crust collide, one may sink beneath the other, forming a deep trench. In places, magma bursts through the crust to form volcanic islands. The islands of Japan formed in this way.

• LOOK AGAIN •

- What is Earth's inner core made of?
- What kind of volcanoes formed the Hawaiian Islands?
- Where are earthquakes most likely to occur?

Weather and Climate

OUR WEATHER MAY CHANGE from day to day, but we usually experience the same kind of weather from year to year. The pattern of weather that occurs in a region over a long period is known as the climate. The climate of an area depends on three main factors: how far north or south of the equator it is (its latitude), how high it is (its altitude), and how close it is to the sea. As a result of Earth's orbit and its round shape, sunlight warms areas near the equator more than areas near the poles. Tropical regions are therefore hot year-round, and the poles are always cold. Areas between the tropics and the poles are temperate. This means that they have warm summers and cool winters. Mountains are colder than lowland areas because as you climb higher the atmosphere becomes thinner and retains less heat. In coastal regions, sea breezes and ocean currents prevent the weather from becoming too hot or too cold, so these areas have a milder climate than inland areas. Where winds blow inland from the sea, they are usually moist and bring high rainfall.

WIND PATTERNS

Because hot air rises and cold air sinks, the Sun's uneven heating of Earth's surface causes air to circulate as shown in the large diagram below. These patterns of air circulation are deflected by the planet's rotation, and form the major wind systems shown on the globe below right. These winds carry warm or cold, moist or dry air, and are an important influence on Earth's climates.

Air Circulation

Cold easterly winds blow from the poles.

Warm and cold air meet, creating a belt of stormy, wet weather.

Air flows poleward from the southwest

Air flows toward the equator from the northeast

60°N

30°N

Equator

WORLD CLIMATES

The world can be divided into eight major climate zones, which are shown on this map and described on these pages. Ocean currents influence many of these climates. For example, northwestern Europe has a mild climate as a result of the warm waters of the Gulf Stream.

warm currents   cool currents

Cold Temperate

These regions have long, bitterly cold and snowy winters. Their summers are usually mild and damp.

Mountain

Mountains are normally colder, wetter and windier than neighboring regions that lie nearer sea level.

Polar

The polar regions are extremely cold for most of the year. Although snow falls regularly, the poles are relatively dry.

Upper air cools and sinks, creating dry conditions.

Warm, moist air rises at the equator, clouds form and rain falls.

Wind Systems

Polar easterlies

Westerlies

Trade winds

Westerlies

Polar easterlies

Wet Temperate
Wet temperate regions have four distinct seasons, with cool, wet winters and warm, wet summers.

Dry Temperate
Rainfall is relatively low in these regions. Most areas have mild, wet winters and hot, dry summers.

Desert and Semidesert
These are dry, barren areas with very low rainfall. They are usually hot by day, but may be cold, or even frosty, at night.

Subtropical
In summer, these regions are hot and wet like tropical areas. In winter, they are dry and mild like deserts.

Tropical
The tropics are hot and wet. In some areas, it rains all year round. In others, most of the rain falls in summer.

◆ AMAZING FACT ◆

Thunderstorms are most common in tropical areas, but occur all over the world. At least 20,000 storms occur each day, and at any one time about 2,000 may be taking place. Lightning from these storms strikes the ground as frequently as 100 times every second.

ENERGY FROM THE SUN
Because Earth is shaped like a ball, the Sun strikes it more directly near the equator than at the poles. This is why tropical areas are hot and the polar regions are cold.

◆ PROJECT: *Why the Poles Are Colder Than the Equator* ◆

❶ In a dark room, hold a lighted flashlight a few inches above, and at right angles to, a flat surface such as a tabletop. Observe the shape and brightness of the patch of light.

❷ Tilt the flashlight and note how the light changes. When the light strikes the surface from directly overhead, the patch of light is small and intense. When the light strikes the table at an angle, the patch is larger and weaker.

In a similar way, sunlight is most intense at the equator, where it strikes the ground from directly overhead. At the poles, the light strikes Earth at an angle and is spread across a wider area, making it much weaker.

The Living World

ALMOST EVERY PART OF OUR PLANET is inhabited by an amazing variety of living things. So far, scientists have named about two million kinds, or species, of plants and animals, but there may be between 10 and 100 million species on Earth! All living things inhabit the biosphere, which is made up of the land, oceans and atmosphere. Within the biosphere, there are many kinds of environments. Over millions of years, plants and animals have gradually altered their bodies and behavior to suit their particular environments. This process is known as adaptation. Together, an environment and its inhabitants form an ecosystem. The members of each ecosystem depend on each other for food and other resources. For example, vegetation provides food for plant-eating animals (herbivores) which may in turn be eaten by meat-eating animals (carnivores). These close relationships mean that damage to one part of an ecosystem is likely to affect every other part of it.

GLOBAL ECOSYSTEMS
Each of Earth's environments has its own community of plants and animals. This illustration shows how ecosystems change between the tropical rain forests (far left) and the polar ice caps (far right).

Oceans
The oceans contain a huge variety of species that have adapted to life under water. Marine plants include many kinds of seaweed. Animals include sea mammals such as seals and whales, coral, and thousands of fish species.

Tropical Rain Forests
The hot, humid weather of the tropics creates dense forests that are home to more species than any other environment. Monkeys and birds live high in the trees, while jaguars and other mammals prowl the forest floor.

Subtropical Savannas
With rain falling only in summer, subtropical areas have few trees. The African savanna grasslands support herds of herbivores such as zebras, which are hunted by lions and other carnivores. Vultures and other scavengers eat the leftovers.

Deserts and Semideserts
Desert species have adapted to drought. Some plants, such as cacti, store water in their stems. Others have long roots that reach water far underground. In hot deserts, many animals come out only at night, when it is cooler.

WORLD ENVIRONMENTS

Because the weather determines the types of plants that grow, Earth's environments are closely related to its climate zones.

- Tropical rain forests
- Subtropical savannas
- Deserts and semideserts
- Temperate grasslands and shrub woodlands
- Temperate forests
- Coniferous forests
- Mountains
- Polar ice caps and tundra

AMAZING FACT

The world's largest flower, the rafflesia, is found in the rain forests of southeast Asia and can measure up to three feet (1 m) in diameter. It gives off a smell like rotting flesh which attracts insects.

Mountains

The higher the land, the less vegetation there is and the colder and windier it gets. Thick fur coats keep many mountain animals warm. Some species, such as mountain goats, have special hooves that help them climb rocky slopes.

Polar Ice Caps and Tundra

The ice caps are bitterly cold and offer little shelter. Some animals have fur and a thick layer of fat to keep them warm. Tundra is treeless land that surrounds the Arctic ice cap. Its low shrubs feed hares, lemmings and other herbivores.

Temperate Grasslands and Shrub Woodlands

Moderate rainfall creates grasslands and shrub woodlands. Grasslands attract herbivores such as bison and are ideal hunting grounds for birds of prey. There is little shelter, so some animals live in burrows.

Temperate Forests

Trees grow well in wet temperate regions. In areas with cold winters, most of the trees are deciduous, which means that they shed their leaves in fall. Some animals migrate in winter; others survive on food stored during summer.

Coniferous Forests

Cold temperate regions are covered by forests of evergreen trees called conifers. Shaped so that snow slides off them, these trees are well adapted to the cold winters. Many animals have thick fur, and some hibernate for the winter.

LOOK AGAIN

- Name a plant-eating animal that lives on the African savanna.
- Which plants store water in their stems?
- How have animals adapted to mountain environments?

Our Natural Resources

EARTH PROVIDES US with everything that we need to live. Its atmosphere, rivers and lakes supply fresh water which, with sunshine and soil, enables plants to grow. In turn, plants produce vital supplies of oxygen and provide us and other animals with food. Animals supply humans with meat, wool and dairy products. Plants also provide timber, fuel, and textiles such as cotton. All these resources—water, plants, crops, animals—are renewable. This means that if we manage them carefully they will never run out. Other resources are nonrenewable. They do not regrow or replenish themselves and will eventually be used up. They include minerals, precious stones and fossil fuels (coal, oil and gas). Minerals—such as clay, chalk and many metals—and precious stones—such as diamonds and emeralds—have a wide range of uses, particularly in industry. Coal, oil and gas supply most of the energy we need for lighting and heating our homes and for fueling our cars. They are known as fossil fuels because they are the remains of animals and plants buried deep underground. Some of these nonrenewable resources may run out within the next 50 years. Because of this, and because burning fossil fuels creates pollution, scientists are trying to find ways of using renewable resources to supply more of the energy we need.

ENERGY SUPPLIES

The illustration below shows our principal sources of energy. As the chart on the right indicates, coal, oil and gas still supply most of our fuel. But alternative energy supplies such as wind and solar power are being developed in many parts of the world. As reserves of fossil fuels run out, these sources will become increasingly important.

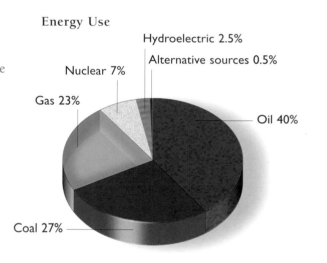

Energy Use

- Hydroelectric 2.5%
- Alternative sources 0.5%
- Nuclear 7%
- Gas 23%
- Oil 40%
- Coal 27%

EARTH'S RESOURCES

The map above shows how land is used in different parts of the world, and where major fuel reserves are located.

- Major gas field
- Major coal field
- Major oil field
- Urban areas: towns, cities and industries
- Areas with large farms where people grow crops and raise animals for sale

Oil
Oil and gas are found together in rock layers in Earth's crust. They are extracted by drilling from sea- or land-based rigs.

Coal
Coal is more plentiful than other fossil fuels. It can be collected by digging at the surface or by mining deep underground.

Uranium
Radioactive elements such as uranium emit high-energy particles that are converted into electricity at nuclear power plants.

Geothermal Power
In some parts of the world, ground water is heated by hot volcanic rocks, creating steam that is used to generate power.

A process known as the water cycle provides us with a regular supply of fresh water. Water in oceans, lakes and rivers is constantly evaporating into the air, where it exists as water vapor. The warmer the air, the more water vapor it can hold. When air cools, its ability to hold water decreases, and some of the water vapor turns, or condenses, into tiny water droplets or ice crystals. These droplets or crystals form clouds. If the droplets or crystals combine and become heavy enough, they fall as rain or snow. Water that falls on land drains into rivers, lakes and underground channels. It then flows into the sea, replenishing the oceans and completing the water cycle.

◆ PROJECT: *Create a Water Cycle* ◆

This simple experiment will show you how the water cycle works.

❶ Cool a long, metal spoon or ladle by placing it in a freezer for a few minutes. Choose a spoon with a wooden handle.

❷ Ask an adult to help you boil some water in a kettle or saucepan.

❸ As the water boils, the warm air above the water rises. As it starts to cool, it condenses and forms clouds of steam.

❹ Hold the cold spoon over the steam, being careful not to burn yourself. The cooling effect of the cold metal causes the water vapor to condense more quickly and form droplets of water on the underside of the spoon.

❺ The droplets grow in size until they become heavy enough to fall, just like rain. Some of the droplets may fall back into the kettle or saucepan, replenishing the water supply.

Areas with small farms where people grow crops and raise animals mainly for their own use

Grassland areas used for grazing large numbers of animals

Deserts, dry grasslands and tundra used for grazing small numbers of animals

Forested areas with some farming, hunting and mining

Areas that are too cold or dry for farming, but include some mining and hunting

Major fishing grounds

Hydroelectric Power
Hydroelectric power is created when water is passed through electricity-generating turbines at the bottom of a dam.

Wind Power
Windmills convert the power of the wind into electricity. The wind turns the windmills, which drive electrical generators.

Solar Power
Clusters of mirrorlike solar panels reflect the Sun's rays onto a solar furnace, where the intense heat is converted into electricity.

Sea Power
At a tidal dam or barrage, waves pass through narrow tunnels, driving huge turbines that produce power.

The Human Family

OUR PLANET IS HOME to about 6 billion people. This population is not spread evenly over Earth's landmasses. Instead, people are concentrated where resources are plentiful, or can be easily obtained by trade. Therefore, few people live in deserts or polar regions, but many live in fertile areas, close to energy sources, and near rivers and coasts. The world's population is now growing more quickly than ever before. In the time it takes you to read this sentence, more than 20 babies will have been born. Since 1950 the number of people on Earth has more than doubled. This growth is the result of a longer life expectancy due to improved medical services, and a high birth rate in some parts of the world. The most rapid population growth occurs in developing countries—poorer countries with little industry or technology. It is difficult for these countries to feed and take care of their growing populations, so many of them are urging their people to have fewer children.

NATIONAL POPULATIONS
This diagram shows the 10 countries with the world's largest populations. China has by far the biggest population—in fact, one in every five people in the world lives in China!

WHERE PEOPLE LIVE
The dots on this map show the world's most densely populated areas.

Developed countries
Developing countries

China	India	U.S.A.	Indonesia	Brazil	Pakistan	Russia	Bangladesh	Nigeria	Japan
1.28 billion	1.05 billion	281 million	231 million	176 million	148 million	145 million	133 million	130 million	127 million

CROWDED COUNTRIES
Some countries are densely populated—a large population lives in a small area. Others are sparsely populated—a small population occupies a large area.

The Netherlands:
1,000 people per square mile
(400 per sq. km)

Australia:
6 people per square mile
(2 per sq. km)

GROWING CITIES
As countries develop, people move to cities to look for work in factories and businesses. As shown by this comparison of the populations of Paris, France, and Jakarta, Indonesia, cities in developing countries are now growing more rapidly than those in developed countries.

Paris   Jakarta

1970		1990		2010	
8.5 million	3.9 million	9.3 million	9.3 million	9.6 million	19.2 million

◆ AMAZING FACTS ◆

- Every second, three babies are born.
- If the world's population were spread out evenly over its landmasses, each person would occupy an area larger than four football fields.
- Standing side by side, everyone in the world could fit onto the island of Jamaica.

POPULATION GROWTH

Every four days, one million children are born. If the world's population continues to grow at this rate, it will have reached 10 billion by the year 2100. The populations of developing countries are expanding rapidly while those of developed countries are growing slowly or decreasing.

- Developing countries
- Developed countries

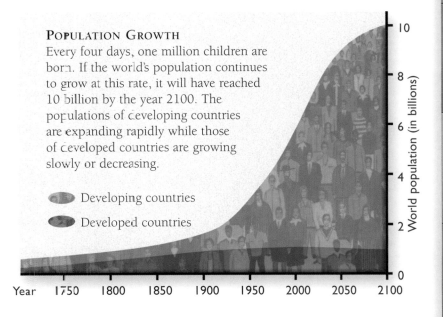

World population (in billions)

Year 1750 1800 1850 1900 1950 2000 2050 2100

RICH AND POOR

Countries with large industries and high levels of technology are called developed countries. People in these parts of the world are generally wealthy and have many possessions. In countries with little industry and technology, people are poorer and have few possessions. These countries are known as developing countries. Although they are home to far fewer people, developed countries are much richer and use a much larger proportion of the world's resources than developing countries.

◆ PROJECT: Languages ◆

More than 3,000 languages are spoken around the world, but more than one-third of the world's population speaks one of the following six languages. So you can learn to say "hello" to more than two billion people!

hello
English
(350 million speakers)

你好
ni hao
Chinese
(1 billion speakers)

مرحبا
mar-ha-ban
Arabic
(150 million speakers)

¡holà!
o-la
Spanish
(250 million speakers)

नमस्ते
na-ma-stay
Hindi
(200 million speakers)

npuвem!
pree-vyet
Russian
(150 million speakers)

Developed countries:
make up 20% of the world's population
own 80% of the world's wealth
use 70% of the world's energy

Developing countries:
make up 80% of the world's population
own 20% of the world's wealth
use 30% of the world's energy

Planet in Peril

THE FUTURE OF OUR PLANET is at risk, now more than ever before. In the last 200 years, rapid population growth and the development of industry and technology have magnified the effect of our activities on the environment. Supplies of fossil fuels and other nonrenewable resources are running out. We are overusing the soil, forests and fishing grounds, and no longer giving these renewable resources a chance to recover. Waste from our homes and industries is poisoning water supplies, and gases from our cars and factories are polluting the air we breathe. Increasing air pollution may even be changing the climate. Scientists all over the world are trying to find ways to preserve resources and limit the damage we are doing to Earth. Through simple activities such as recycling, using our cars less and buying environmentally friendly products, we can all play a part in protecting Earth and preserving its resources for future generations.

A GLOBAL CRISIS

This map shows that environmental problems affect almost every part of Earth. The most serious problems are described and illustrated on these pages.

- Existing deserts
- Areas at risk of becoming deserts
- Existing rain forest
- Cleared rain forest
- Cities with severe air pollution
- Areas affected by acid rain
- Polluted waterways
- Heavy oil slicks created by shipping
- Light oil slicks created by shipping
- Major nuclear accidents
- Major oil tanker disasters
- Major oil rig explosions

AMAZING FACTS

- An acre (0.4 ha) of Brazilian rain forest is destroyed every nine seconds.
- Every day, more than 50 species become extinct. This is mainly the result of human activities such as forestry and hunting.

Holding Back the Desert

In dry parts of the world, overgrazing and clearing the land of its natural vegetation can turn fertile areas into desert. To keep deserts from spreading farther, we need to better manage the land we farm and replant trees and shrubs.

Saving the Forests

Vast areas of natural forest are being cleared to supply timber, fuel and paper, and to make way for towns and farms. You can help protect the world's forests and reduce the need for more wood by recycling paper. Replanting trees also helps.

Reducing Air Pollution

Cars and factories fill the air with grime and poisonous gases. Industries and car manufacturers are trying to reduce such pollution. You can also help by walking, cycling or using public transportation instead of traveling by car.

Oil Spills
Oil and other pollutants spilled by ships are a threat to wildlife. In 1989, oil spilled by the tanker *Exxon Valdez* off the coast of Alaska, in the United States, killed thousands of animals, including 350,000 seabirds.

Nuclear Accidents
Nuclear accidents occur rarely but can be devastating. In 1986, an accident at the Chernobyl nuclear power plant in the Ukraine released a cloud of radioactive gas across Europe, poisoning land, crops and people.

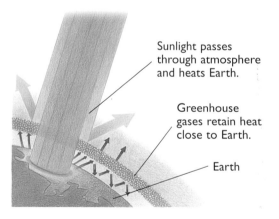

Oil Well Explosions
Accidents on oil and gas rigs can cause major environmental problems. During the Gulf War in Kuwait in 1992, hundreds of oil wells were set on fire, causing serious water and air pollution throughout the region.

Eliminating Acid Rain
Air pollution can turn rain into a strong acid. Acid rain kills trees, pollutes rivers and even damages buildings. The only way to stop acid rain is to reduce air pollution.

Saving the Ozone Layer
A layer of ozone in the upper atmosphere filters out harmful radiation from the Sun. This layer is being damaged by chlorofluorocarbons (CFCs)—chemicals found in some aerosols and refrigerators. Always buy CFC-free products.

Keeping Our Water Clean
The world's rivers and oceans are being poisoned by waste from factories and shipping, and sewage from homes and offices. To help protect water supplies, support local cleanup programs, and never dispose of garbage in or near waterways.

Sunlight passes through atmosphere and heats Earth.

Greenhouse gases retain heat close to Earth.

Earth

GLOBAL WARMING
Gases in the atmosphere, known as greenhouse gases, keep Earth warm by trapping some of the energy that comes from the Sun. But the burning of fossil fuels is raising the levels of these gases, causing the planet to warm too much. If this continues, some fertile land may turn into desert, and ice caps may melt, causing flooding in lowland areas. Most countries are trying to reduce greenhouse gas emissions.

◆ LOOK AGAIN ◆

- How can we prevent acid rain?
- What gases keep Earth warm?
- How can you help protect the ozone layer?

The Physical World

WE CALL OUR PLANET EARTH, but more than two-thirds of its surface is covered by salt water. Large areas of salt water are called oceans, and smaller areas are known as seas. There are four oceans—the Pacific, Atlantic, Indian and Arctic—and many seas. The Pacific Ocean alone is larger than all of Earth's landmasses combined. Land covers only 29 percent of our planet's surface. Its shape and the kind of soil and vegetation that cover it vary enormously from place to place. Throughout the world there are hills, mountains and areas of flat land called plains. Trees and other plants cover many parts of Earth, but some places have almost no vegetation. Deserts—very dry areas with sparse vegetation—cover about one-fifth of the world's land. The polar regions and many mountaintops are covered in ice and snow. The seas, too, have their mountains and valleys. Deep trenches are found in most oceans, and mountains on many islands are actually the tops of undersea mountains. For instance, Mauna Kea, on the island of Hawaii in the Pacific Ocean, is 33,480 feet (10,205 m) high, measured from the sea floor to its highest point. That's far taller than Mount Everest, the highest mountain on land.

Physical Facts

Circumference of Earth around the equator: 24,902 miles (40,067 km)
Area of sea: 139,433,000 square miles (361,132,000 sq. km)
Area of land above sea level: 57,156,000 square miles (148,940,000 sq. km)
Largest ocean: Pacific Ocean, 60,061,000 square miles (155,557,000 sq. km)
Largest landmass: Eurasia (Europe and Asia), 20,733,000 square miles (53,698,000 sq. km)
Deepest ocean trench: Mariana Trench, Pacific Ocean, 35,840 feet (10,924 m)
Largest island: Greenland, 840,000 square miles (2,175,000 sq. km)

· Amazing Fact ·

Almost all of the water on Earth—97.3 percent—is salt water. Less than 3 percent is fresh water, and two-thirds of this is locked up in icecaps and glaciers. That leaves less than 1 percent in rivers, lakes and underground channels.

ARCTIC OCEAN

2

SEVERNAYA ZEMLYA

FRANZ JOSEF LAND

Spitsbergen

SVALBARD

NOVAYA ZEMLYA

Greenland Sea

Barents Sea

Kara Sea

Laptev Sea

NEW SIBERIAN ISLANDS

East Siberian Sea

Chukchi Sea

3

Jan Mayen Island

Iceland

Norwegian Sea

Doina

CENTRAL SIBERIAN PLATEAU

Bering Strait

FAEROE ISLANDS

SCANDINAVIA

WESTERN SIBERIAN PLAIN

Ob'

Yenisey

Yenisey

Lena

Bering Sea

ALEUTIAN ISLANDS

4

Ireland

North Sea

BRITISH ISLES

EUROPE

Volga

Ob'

Irtysh

Angara

S I B E R I A

Amur

Sea of Okhotsk

ALEUTIAN TRENCH

CHANNEL ISLANDS

CARPATHIAN MTS.

Dnieper

ASIA

Lake Baikal

Kuril Islands

KURIL TRENCH

ALPS

Danube

THE STEPPE

Lake Balkhash

GOBI DESERT

Sea of Japan (East Sea)

Hokkaidō

AZORES

Black Sea

Caspian Sea

Aral Sea

TIAN MTS.

Honshū

NORTHWEST PACIFIC BASIN

5

MADEIRA

Mediterranean Sea

Tigris

HINDU KUSH

KUNLUN MTS.

PLATEAU OF TIBET

Huang (Yellow)

PACIFIC

CANARY ISLANDS

ATLAS MTS.

Euphrates

ZAGROS MTS.

HIMALAYAS

Indus

Chang (Yangtze)

East China Sea

MIDWAY ISLANDS

OCEAN

E VERDE ISLANDS

SAHARA DESERT

NUBIAN DESERT

ARABIAN PENINSULA

Nile

Red Sea

Arabian Sea

DECCAN

Gang es

Mekong

Taiwan

PHILIPPINE BASIN

Wake Island

MARIANA ISLANDS

MID-PACIFIC MOUNTAINS

6

N

SAHEL

Niger

S A H E L

AFRICA

Bay of Bengal

LACCADIVE ISLANDS

Luzon

South China Sea

Guam

Philippine Sea

MARIANA TRENCH

MARSHALL ISLANDS

CENTRAL PACIFIC BASIN

Johnston Atoll

Gulf of Guinea

Ubangi

Uele

Congo

Sri Lanka

ANDAMAN ISLANDS

NICOBAR ISLANDS

PHILIPPINE ISLANDS

PHILIPPINE TRENCH

Palau

CAROLINE ISLANDS

M I C R O N E S I A

CONGO BASIN

Kasai

Lake Victoria

GREAT RIFT VALLEY

MALDIVES

Nauru

GILBERT ISLANDS

7

Ascension

SEYCHELLES

MID-INDIAN RIDGE

MID-INDIAN BASIN

Sumatra

Borneo

M E L A N E S I A

New Guinea

SOLOMON ISLANDS

OCEANIA

MARTIN VAZ ISLANDS

St. Helena

Zambezi

Mayote

Madagascar

Mauritius

NINETYEAST RIDGE

INDIAN

Christmas Island

COCOS (KEELING) ISLANDS

Java

JAVA TRENCH

Tuvalu

Tokelau

SAMOA ISLANDS

NAMIB DESERT

KALAHARI DESERT

Orange

Réunion

OCEAN

WHARTON BASIN

Coral Sea

Vanuatu

FIJI ISLANDS

Niue

8

MID-ATLANTIC RIDGE

WALVIS RIDGE

SUNDA ISLANDS

GREAT SANDY DESERT

SIMPSON DESERT

New Caledonia

Tonga

TONGA TRENCH

Tristan da Cunha

CAPE OF GOOD HOPE

SOUTHWEST INDIAN RIDGE

Amsterdam Island

AUSTRALIA

GREAT VICTORIAN DESERT

Lake Eyre

Norfolk Island

KERMADEC ISLANDS

KERMADEC TRENCH

Gough Island

St. Paul Island

Darling

Murray

Tasman Sea

9

SOUTH SANDWICH ISLANDS

CROZET ISLANDS

KERGUÉLEN ISLANDS

Great Australian Bight

Tasmania

NEW ZEALAND

North Island

CHATHAM ISLANDS

PRINCE EDWARD ISLANDS

SOUTHEAST INDIAN RIDGE

HEARD AND McDONALD ISLANDS

Macquarie Island

AUCKLAND ISLANDS

South Island

Bouvet Island

ATLANTIC-INDIAN BASIN

SOUTH INDIAN BASIN

10

ANTARCTICA

Ross Sea

Countries of the World

APART FROM ANTARCTICA, which has no permanent population, all the land on Earth is divided into countries. There are almost 200 countries in the world, and each country has its own government and its own laws. The world's smallest country, the Vatican City, measures only one-fifth of a square mile (0.44 sq. km). That's about the size of 100 football fields. The largest country in the world, Russia, is 39 million times bigger! The lines that separate countries are called borders. On this world map, the countries are shown in different colors so that you can see the borders clearly. Borders may be straight or curved. Some are formed by rivers or mountain ranges; others cross lakes or seas. The sizes of countries and the shapes of their borders often change. Sometimes a large country divides into smaller countries because groups of people want to form separate countries. Neighboring countries often disagree about where a border ought to be. Such disputes have led to wars in many parts of the world. In this atlas, disputed borders are shown by a dotted line. Many countries govern areas of land in other parts of the world. These are called territories. On a map, the name of the governing country usually appears in parentheses after the name of the territory.

POLITICAL FACTS

Number of countries: 193
Number of territories: 65
Largest countries:
Russia, 6,592,812 square miles (17,075,383 sq. km)
Canada, 3,851,809 square miles (9,976,185 sq. km)
China, 3,705,386 square miles (9,596,960 sq. km)
Smallest country: Vatican City, 0.17 square miles (0.44 sq. km)
Longest border: U.S.-Canada, 3,987 miles (6,416 km)

◆ LOOK AGAIN ◆

The following shapes represent countries shown on the world map on the right. Can you find and name them?

KEY TO NUMBERED COUNTRIES

1 THE NETHERLANDS	9 CROATIA	16 YUGOSLAVIA
2 BELGIUM	■10 ANDORRA	17 ALBANIA
■3 LUXEMBOURG	■11 MONACO	18 MACEDONIA
4 CZECH REPUBLIC	■12 SAN MARINO	■19 GIBRALTAR (U.K.)
5 SLOVAKIA	■13 VATICAN CITY	20 ARMENIA
6 SWITZERLAND	14 BOSNIA-	21 AZERBAIJAN
■7 LIECHTENSTEIN	HERZEGOVINA	22 UNITED ARAB
8 SLOVENIA	15 MOLDOVA	EMIRATES

ARCTIC OCEAN

SVALBARD
(NORWAY)

JAN MAYEN ISLAND
(NORWAY)

ICELAND

FAEROE ISLANDS
(DENMARK)

SWEDEN

NORWAY

FINLAND

ESTONIA

DENMARK

LATVIA

LITHUANIA

UNITED
KINGDOM

RUSSIA

IRELAND

POLAND

BELARUS

GERMANY

RUSSIA

UKRAINE

KAZAKHSTAN

MONGOLIA

FRANCE

AUSTRIA

HUNGARY

ROMANIA

ORES
(UGAL)

PORTUGAL

SPAIN

ITALY

BULGARIA

GEORGIA

UZBEKISTAN

KYRGYZSTAN

MADEIRA
(PORTUGAL)

GREECE

MALTA

TURKEY

TURKMENISTAN

TAJIKISTAN

CHINA

NORTH
KOREA

SOUTH KOREA

JAPAN

CYPRUS

SYRIA

LEBANON

IRAN

AFGHANISTAN

MOROCCO

ISRAEL

IRAQ

JORDAN

CANARY ISLANDS
(SPAIN)

ALGERIA

LIBYA

EGYPT

KUWAIT

BAHRAIN

PAKISTAN

NEPAL

BHUTAN

TAIWAN

WESTERN SAHARA
(MOROCCO)

QATAR

SAUDI
ARABIA

BANGLADESH

MYANMAR
(BURMA)

LAOS

MAURITANIA

MALI

NIGER

CHAD

OMAN

INDIA

ANDAMAN
ISLANDS
(INDIA)

THAILAND

VIETNAM

DE
DS

SENEGAL

SUDAN

ERITREA

YEMEN

LACCADIVE
ISLANDS
(INDIA)

CAMBODIA

PHILIPPINES

GAMBIA

BURKINA
FASO

NIGERIA

DJIBOUTI

NICOBAR
ISLANDS
(INDIA)

GUINEA-BISSAU

GUINEA

SIERRA
LEONE

CENTRAL
AFRICAN
REPUBLIC

ETHIOPIA

SRI
LANKA

MALDIVES

BRUNEI

MALAYSIA

LIBERIA

CÔTE D'IVOIRE
(IVORY COAST)

EQUATORIAL
GUINEA

CAMEROON

KENYA

SOMALIA

SINGAPORE

SÃO TOMÉ
AND PRÍNCIPE

GABON

DEMOCRATIC
REPUBLIC OF
THE CONGO
(ZAIRE)

UGANDA

RWANDA

BURUNDI

BRITISH INDIAN
OCEAN TERRITORY (U.K.)

INDONESIA

EAST TIMOR

ASCENSION
(U.K.)

CONGO

TANZANIA

SEYCHELLES

CHRISTMAS ISLAND
(AUSTRALIA)

COCOS (KEELING) ISLANDS
(AUSTRALIA)

PAPUA
NEW
GUINEA

ST. HELENA AND DEPENDENCIES
(U.K.)

ANGOLA

ZAMBIA

MALAWI

COMOROS

MAYOTTE
(FRANCE)

SOLOMON
ISLANDS

IN VAZ ISLANDS
(BRAZIL)

NAMIBIA

ZIMBABWE

MOZAMBIQUE

MADAGASCAR

MAURITIUS

RÉUNION (FRANCE)

BOTSWANA

TRISTAN DA CUNHA
(U.K.)

SWAZILAND

LESOTHO

SOUTH
AFRICA

INDIAN

OCEAN

AUSTRALIA

NORFOLK ISLAND
(AUSTRALIA)

ATLANTIC

OCEAN

AMSTERDAM ISLAND
(FRANCE)

ST. PAUL ISLAND
(FRANCE)

GOUGH ISLAND
(U.K.)

PRINCE EDWARD ISLANDS
(SOUTH AFRICA)

CROZET ISLANDS
(FRANCE)

KERGUÉLEN ISLANDS
(FRANCE)

HEARD AND McDONALD ISLANDS
(AUSTRALIA)

NEW
ZEALAND

CHATHAM ISLANDS
(N.Z.)

AUCKLAND ISLANDS
(N.Z.)

SOUTH
SANDWICH ISLANDS
(U.K.)

BOUVET ISLAND
(NORWAY)

MACQUARIE ISLAND
(AUSTRALIA)

CAMPBELL ISLAND
(N.Z.)

PACIFIC

OCEAN

PACIFIC

OCEAN

MIDWAY ISLANDS
(U.S.A.)

WAKE ISLAND
(U.S.A.)

NORTHERN
MARIANA
ISLANDS
(U.S.A.)

MARSHALL
ISLANDS

JOHNSTON
ATOLL (U.S.A.)

GUAM (U.S.A.)

PALAU

FEDERATED STATES
OF MICRONESIA

NAURU

KIRIBATI

TUVALU

TOKELAU
(N.Z.)

WALLIS AND
FUTUNA
(FRANCE)

SAMOA

AMERICAN
SAMOA
(U.S.A.)

VANUATU

NIUE
(N.Z.)

NEW
CALEDONIA
(FRANCE)

FIJI

TONGA

KERMADEC ISLAND
(N.Z.)

ANTARCTICA

The Power of Politics

EXACTLY HOW DID countries form? Early on, people lived in small family groups and their ways of life, or cultures, were shaped by the physical demands of the regions they lived in. Eventually, as the family groups grew larger, relations between the groups helped form the regions into countries—a fact that has created many of the conflicts we've recently seen. Africa, for example, was divided into countries by outside colonial powers, splitting up many ethnic groups and mixing others together. Today, more than 60 borders or territories are causing conflict within and between countries, and disputes that start as local affairs can soon escalate into something bigger. For instance, when the Serbian leader Slobodan Milosevic tried to purge Kosovo of ethnic Albanians, the United States, United Kingdom, and other NATO countries stepped in and launched air strikes to stop him. In the midst of so much conflict, many people keep working for peaceful solutions. The United Nations was established in 1945 to preserve peace through international cooperation, and almost every country in the world is now a member. It encourages fighting sides to negotiate and can send in peacekeeping forces to maintain order.

KASHMIR

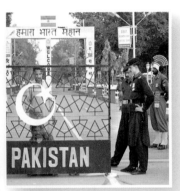

In 1947, when British India was divided into India—a state populated mostly by Hindus—and Muslim Pakistan, both countries claimed Kashmir. The United Nations drew the "Line of Control" and most of Kashmir went to India. Many Muslim Kashmiris have since rebelled against Indian rule. And now that India and Pakistan both have weapons of mass destruction, nuclear war is a possibility.

Hot spot
Peacekeepers

• AMAZING FACT •

On achieving independence, countries often change their names: Belize used to be called British Honduras, Sri Lanka was Ceylon, and Botswana was Bechuanaland.

GLOBAL HOT SPOTS

Wars can be internal disputes, such as civil wars and independence struggles, or conflicts involving two or more countries, often caused by disagreements over borders or territory. Since September 11, we've seen a new kind of war appear—a global war on terrorism, rather than against a country.

SEPTEMBER 11, 2001

When terrorists hijacked passenger planes and flew them into the World Trade Center and the Pentagon, the United States declared war on terrorism. The hijackers were linked to Osama bin Laden's al Qaeda organization, an international terrorist network run largely from Afghanistan. The United States led a military attack that helped to bring down Afghanistan's Taliban regime, and continues to pursue networks of terrorists throughout the world.

World Trade Center, New York
The Pentagon, Arlington, Virginia

ISRAEL AND PALESTINE

Palestinians, a people displaced by the formation of Israel, have long hoped to establish their own state in the West Bank and Gaza Strip, lands held by Israel since a 1967 war. But in 2000, after a series of failed negotiations, the Palestinians launched an "Intifada," or uprising, and suicide bombers began targeting Israeli civilians. Israel has responded with military force to try to root out terrorists.

Areas occupied by
Israel since 1967

NEW COUNTRIES

The number of countries in the world has nearly tripled since the end of the Second World War. In 1946, there were just 74 countries, while today there are 193 countries. The world map above shows the new countries created since 1990. Most of these appeared when Communism collapsed in the Soviet Union and people in Eastern Europe and the Balkans formed their own governments. Some countries, such as East Timor and Palau, achieved independence from other nations. Others, such as Yemen and Germany, formed when two countries reunited.

FORMER U.S.S.R.
ARMENIA
AZERBAIJAN
BELARUS
ESTONIA
GEORGIA
KAZAKHSTAN
KYRGYZSTAN
LATVIA
LITHUANIA
MOLDOVA
RUSSIAN FEDERATION
TAJIKISTAN
TURKMENISTAN
UKRAINE
UZBEKISTAN

FORMER YUGOSLAVIA
BOSNIA AND HERZEGOVINA
CROATIA
MACEDONIA
SLOVENIA

OTHERS
CZECH REPUBLIC
EAST TIMOR
ERITREA
FEDERAL REPUBLIC OF GERMANY
FEDERATED STATES OF MICRONESIA
MARSHALL ISLANDS
NAMIBIA
PALAU
REPUBLIC OF YEMEN
SLOVAKIA

North America

THE CONTINENT OF NORTH AMERICA extends from just south of the North Pole to just north of the equator. It includes almost every kind of environment, from ice caps to forests, mountains, deserts and jungles. In the west, an almost unbroken chain of mountains stretches from Alaska to Costa Rica and includes the Rocky Mountains, one of the world's most famous mountain ranges. The United States (often called the U.S.A. or America) and Canada are the largest of the continent's 23 countries. The United States is made up of 50 states. Canada is divided into ten provinces and three territories. North America includes some of the world's biggest cities, but also vast areas of wilderness. Most North Americans are the descendants of European immigrants, but there are also many people of African origin as well as groups of native peoples.

Continent Facts

Regional land area: 8,522,127 sq. miles (22,078,049 sq. km)
Regional population: 486,069,988
Independent countries: Antigua and Barbuda, The Bahamas, Barbados, Belize, Canada, Costa Rica, Cuba, Dominica, Dominican Republic, El Salvador, Grenada, Guatemala, Haiti, Honduras, Jamaica, Mexico, Nicaragua, Panama, St. Kitts–Nevis, St. Lucia, St. Vincent and the Grenadines, Trinidad and Tobago, United States of America

World Records

WORLD'S LARGEST GORGE
GRAND CANYON, U.S.A., 277 MILES (446 KM) LONG, 10 MILES (16 KM) WIDE, 1 MILE (1.6 KM) DEEP

WORLD'S LARGEST FRESHWATER LAKE
LAKE SUPERIOR, U.S.A.-CANADA, 31,800 SQ. MILES (82,350 SQ. KM)

WORLD'S LONGEST CAVE SYSTEM
MAMMOTH CAVES, U.S.A., 351 MILES (565 KM)

WORLD'S LARGEST ACTIVE VOLCANO
MAUNA LOA, HAWAII, U.S.A., 13,680 FT (4,170 M) HIGH, 75 MILES (120 KM) LONG, 31 MILES (50 KM) WIDE

WORLD'S LONGEST BORDER
U.S.-CANADIAN BORDER, 3,987 MILES (6,416 KM)

WORLD'S TALLEST ACTIVE GEYSER
STEAMBOAT GEYSER, YELLOWSTONE NATIONAL PARK, U.S.A., 380 FT (115 M)

WORLD'S LARGEST THEME PARK
WALT DISNEY WORLD, U.S.A., 47 SQ. MILES (122 SQ. KM)

Continent Records

HIGHEST MOUNTAIN
MOUNT MCKINLEY (DENALI), U.S.A., 20,320 FT (6,194 M)

LOWEST POINT
DEATH VALLEY, U.S.A., 282 FT (86 M) BELOW SEA LEVEL

LONGEST RIVER
MISSISSIPPI-MISSOURI, U.S.A., 3,740 MILES (6,020 KM)

LARGEST COUNTRY BY AREA
CANADA, 3,851,809 SQ. MILES (9,976,185 SQ. KM)

LARGEST COUNTRY BY POPULATION
UNITED STATES OF AMERICA, POPULATION 280,562,489

LARGEST CITY BY POPULATION
MEXICO CITY, MEXICO, POPULATION 18,330,000

Major Mountains and Rivers

Mount McKinley (Denali), U.S.A. 20,320 ft (6,194 m)
Mount Logan, Canada 19,524 ft (5,951 m)
Orizaba, Mexico 18,700 ft (5,700 m)
Mount St. Elias, U.S.A.-Canada 18,008 ft (5,489 m)
Popocatépetl, Mexico 17,887 ft (5,450 m)
Mount Whitney, U.S.A. 14,495 ft (4,418 m)

Mississippi-Missouri 3,740 miles (6,020 km)
Mackenzie 2,630 miles (4,240 km)
Mississippi 2,350 miles (3,780 km)
Missouri 2,350 miles (3,780 km)
Yukon 1,980 miles (3,185 km)
Rio Grande 1,880 miles (3,030 km)

Political Map

ALASKA (U.S.A.)

CANADA

UNITED STATES OF AMERICA

HAWAII (U.S.A.)

MEXICO

CUBA

THE BAHAMAS

BERMUDA (U.K.)

DOMINICAN REPUBLIC

JAMAICA
BELIZE
HONDURAS
HAITI
GUATEMALA
NICARAGUA
EL SALVADOR
COSTA RICA
PANAMA

SOUTH AMERICA

TRINIDAD and TOBAGO

ANGUILLA
VIRGIN ISLANDS (U.S.A./U.K.)
ANTIGUA and BARBUDA
ST. KITTS–NEVIS
GUADELOUPE (FRANCE)
PUERTO RICO (U.S.A.)
DOMINICA
MARTINIQUE (FRANCE)
ST. LUCIA
ST. VINCENT and THE GRENADINES
BARBADOS
GRENADA

*P*HYSICAL MAP

ASIA

ARCTIC OCEAN
× NORTH POLE

Chukchi
Sea

Ellesmere
Island

QUEEN
ELIZABETH
ISLANDS

Greenland

EUROPE

Bering
Sea

Beaufort
Sea

Banks
Island

Baffin
Bay

BROOKS RANGE

Yukon

Victoria
Island

Baffin
Island

ALEUTIAN ISLANDS

Mt. McKinley □
(Denali)

Mt. Logan

Mackenzie

Great
Bear
Lake

Arctic Circle

Labrador
Sea

Mt. St. Elias

Gulf of
Alaska

C A N A D I A N

Great Slave
Lake

Hudson
Bay

LABRADOR

Newfoundland

QUEEN
CHARLOTTE
ISLANDS

COAST MTS.

ROCKY MOUNTAINS

G R E A T

S H I E L D

Lake
Winnipeg

Vancouver
Island

Missouri

Lake
Nipigon

Lake
Superior

Lake
Huron

Lake
Ontario

St. Lawrence

PACIFIC OCEAN

WAIIAN
LANDS

COAST RANGES

GREAT
BASIN

Great
Salt
Lake

P L A I N S

Mississippi

Lake
Michigan

Lake
Erie

ATLANTIC OCEAN

Mt.
Whitney

Colorado

Missouri

Ohio

APPALACHIAN MOUNTAINS

Bermuda

SIERRA MADRE OCCIDENTAL

SIERRA MADRE ORIENTAL

Rio Grande

Mississippi

THE
BAHAMAS

Gulf of California

Tropic of Cancer

Gulf of
Mexico

GREATER ANTILLES

LESSER ANTILLES

Popocatépetl

Bay of
Campeche

Caribbean Sea

Orizaba

Lake
Nicaragua

SOUTH AMERICA

9

10

Equator

GALÁPAGOS
ISLANDS

11

Western Canada and Alaska

CANADA, THE WORLD'S SECOND-LARGEST country, covers more than half of North America. Northern Canada is a vast wilderness where bears fish icy rivers for salmon, and wolves hunt caribou across snow-covered plains. The new Arctic territory of Nunavut, occupying the eastern mainland of the Northwest Territories and most of the Arctic islands, came into existence in 1999. Nunavut means "our land" in the language of its Inuit inhabitants. Few people live in this cold environment. Eighty percent of Canada's residents live within 185 miles (300 km) of the southern border, where the climate is milder and the land is more fertile. The prairie grassland that covers parts of Alberta, Manitoba and Saskatchewan is one of the world's most productive farming regions. These provinces also supply most of Canada's oil and gas. West of the towering Rocky Mountains is the Pacific coastline, a maze of islands and narrow waterways. In the Gulf of Alaska, glaciers creep down the mountains toward the shore, while seals and whales swim in the bays. Alaska is the biggest of the United States, but it is separated from the rest of the country by Canada. More than half of Alaska's lands are wildlife refuges, and the state contains some of North America's largest oil fields.

ALASKA (U.S.A.)
POPULATION: 634,900 * CAPITAL: JUNEAU

ALBERTA
POPULATION: 3,064,200 * CAPITAL: EDMONTON

BRITISH COLUMBIA
POPULATION: 4,095,900 * CAPITAL: VICTORIA

MANITOBA
POPULATION: 1,150,000 * CAPITAL: WINNIPEG

NORTHWEST TERRITORIES
POPULATION: 40,900 * CAPITAL: YELLOWKNIFE

NUNAVUT
POPULATION: 28,200 * CAPITAL: IQALUIT

SASKATCHEWAN
POPULATION: 1,015,800 * CAPITAL: REGINA

YUKON TERRITORY
POPULATION: 29,900 * CAPITAL: WHITEHORSE

♦ AMAZING FACT ♦

The United States bought Alaska from Russia in 1867 for $7.2 million. At the time, many people thought that this was a waste of money. But once the state's large reserves of gold and oil were discovered, the deal seemed like a bargain.

ALASKAN BROWN BEAR
At 9 ft (2.7 m) long, these huge bears are the largest meat-eaters living on land. They often fish for salmon in rivers and streams.

Bering Strait · Nome · Walrus · Iditarod musher and dog team · BROOKS RANGE · Trans-Alaskan oil pipeline · Beaufo[rt] · ALASKA (U.S.A.) · Alaskan brown bear catching salmon · Mt. McKinley (Denali) 20,320 ft (6,194 m) · Fairbanks · Yukon · Log cabin · Caribou · Gold · MACKENZIE MTS. · Canada goose · Mackenzie · ALASKA RANGE · Oil · Dall sheep · Dawson · YUKON TERRITORY · ALEUTIAN ISLANDS · Harbor seals · Anchorage · Timber · Snowmobile · Humpback whale · Fishing boat · Kodiak Island · Gulf of Alaska · Mt. Logan 19,524 ft (5,951 m) · Mt. St. Elias 18,008 ft (5,489 m) · WHITEHORSE · Zinc · PACIFIC OCEAN · JUNEAU · Salmon · Tlingit totem pole · Grizzly bear · BRITISH COLUMBIA · Natural gas · Williston Lake · Daws[on] Cree[k] · ROCKY MOUNTAINS · QUEEN CHARLOTTE ISLANDS · Prince Rupert · Timber · Prince George · COAST MOUNTAINS · Fraser · Bald eagle · Vancouver Island · Kwakiutl ceremonial mask · Skiing · Vancouver · VICTORIA

◆ PROJECT: *Inuit Finger Masks* ◆

In ceremonies and rituals, the Inuit (Eskimos) use tiny finger masks to represent their spirit ancestors. The masks are often carved from wood or stone, but you can make yours out of cardboard.

❶ Cut out a circle about four inches (10 cm) in diameter. Cut two small holes at the bottom of the circle large enough for your fingers to poke through.

❷ Draw a face in the center of the circle and color it. Cut a fringe in the cardboard or glue feathers or beads around the face.

❸ To perform with the mask, move your hand slowly from side to side to the beat of a drum.

Narwhal

ARCTIC OCEAN

Ellesmere Island

Musk ox

QUEEN ELIZABETH ISLANDS

Polar bears

Arctic fox

PARRY ISLANDS

Banks Island

Snow goose

Somerset Island

Prince of Wales Island

Baffin Bay

GREENLAND

Davis Strait

Arctic hare

Victoria Island

Inuit building igloo

Baffin Island

Prince Charles Island

Traditional church

Inuit fishing through ice

Kittiwake

Harp seals

IQALUIT

eat Bear Lake

Silver

Wolf

NUNAVUT

Igloo-shaped houses

Southampton Island

Hudson Strait

LOCATION

ORTHWEST TERRITORIES

YELLOWKNIFE

Great Slave Lake

Gold

Gray jay

QUÉBEC

Moose

Hudson Bay

Ⓔ Beluga whale

CANADA

Slave

Zinc and lead

Lake Athabasca

Uranium

Reindeer Lake

Churchill

• Churchill

Belcher Islands

LBERTA

Edmontonia dinosaur fossils

Beaver

Nelson

Nickel and copper

N

W — E

S

ley

Mountie

MANITOBA

SCALE

MILES

0   100   200   300

EDMONTON

SASKATCHEWAN

Saskatchewan

Gold

ONTARIO

0   100   200   300   400   500

KILOMETERS

Oil

Natural gas

Wheat

Lake Winnipeg

• Saskatoon

REGINA

Grain elevators

WINNIPEG

• Calgary

Calgary Stampede

Legislative Building

ROYAL CANADIAN MOUNTED POLICE (MOUNTIES)
Canada's national police force was founded in 1873 to prevent disputes between native tribes and European traders.

UNITED STATES OF AMERICA

J   K   L   M   N   O   P   Q

Eastern Canada

ABOUT 60 PERCENT OF THE POPULATION of Canada live along the shores of the St. Lawrence River and the Great Lakes, an area that occupies only 2 percent of the country's land area. From the early 17th century onward, European immigrants settled here because the land was fertile and the waterways provided transportation routes. Today, the region is home to many of Canada's biggest cities, including the two largest, Toronto and Montréal. Canada has two main languages—English and French. The majority of French speakers live in the province of Québec, which was once a French territory. The forests, lakes and rivers that cover most of Québec and Ontario provide a wealth of resources. Québec's forestry industry produces about 12 percent of the world's pulp and paper. Hydroelectric power stations create so much electricity that Québec and Ontario can export energy. The climate of eastern Canada ranges from temperate in the south to arctic in the north. For nine months of the year, Hudson Bay remains frozen, allowing polar bears to prowl the pack ice in search of food. Off Newfoundland's north shore float huge icebergs measuring up to 150 feet (45 m) high. Farther south, enormous tides surge in and out of the bays. In the Bay of Fundy, the sea can rise 50 feet (15 m) at high tide—high enough to cover a four-story building!

NEW BRUNSWICK
POPULATION: 757,100 * CAPITAL: FREDERICTON

NEWFOUNDLAND
POPULATION: 533,800 * CAPITAL: ST. JOHN'S

NOVA SCOTIA
POPULATION: 942,700 * CAPITAL: HALIFAX

ONTARIO
POPULATION: 11,874,400 * CAPITAL: TORONTO

PRINCE EDWARD ISLAND
POPULATION: 138,500 * CAPITAL: CHARLOTTETOWN

QUÉBEC
POPULATION: 7,410,500 * CAPITAL: QUÉBEC

◆ LOOK AGAIN ◆

- Which city is Canada's national capital?
- Which endangered sea mammal swims off the east coast of Newfoundland?
- What kind of mineral is mined in Newfoundland?

Hudson Bay

Icebreaker ship

MANITOBA

Severn

Muskrat

Hiking

Kayaking

Lumberjack

Timber

Common loons

Uranium

Freight train

Harbor seals

BELCHER ISLANDS

James Bay

Albany

ONTARIO

Lake Nipigon

Blue jay

Red foxes

Moosonee

Nipigon

Hearst

Zinc

Thunder Bay

Hydroelectricity

Silver

Lake Superior

UNITED STATES OF AMERICA

Lake Huron

Farmhouse

Ice hockey

Sault Ste. Marie

Lake Michigan

Uranium

Sudbury

The Big Nickel

CN Tower

Maple forest

Parliament building, Ottawa

Pigs

London

TORONTO

Lake Ontario

Windsor

Lake Erie

Niagara Falls

Arctic tern

THE BIG NICKEL
The Sudbury, Ontario, area is rich in nickel. As a symbol of the metal's importance to the community, a giant Canadian five-cent piece, or nickel, stands outside the town.

ICE HOCKEY
This fast-moving game was first played in 1855 by British soldiers based in Ontario and Nova Scotia. It is now Canada's national sport.

Ivujivik

Polar bears

PÉNINSULE D'UNGAVA
(UNGAVA PENINSULA)

Wolverine

Snowy owl

Furs

QUÉBEC

Hydroelectricity

Réservoir de la
Grande Deux

Black bear

ac
akami

old

Cross-country
skiing

Lac
Mistassini

Paper

Zinc and
copper

Lac
Saint-Jean

Saguenay

Statue of
De Maisonneuve,
founder of
Montréal

Château
Frontenac

St. Lawrence

Québec

Food processing

TTAWA

Montréal

UNITED STATES
OF AMERICA

Hydroelectricity

FREDERICTON

Saint John

NEW
BRUNSWICK

Bay of Fundy

HALIFAX

Fishing
port

HARP SEALS
Each year in March, more than a
quarter of a million of these seals
travel to the islands in the Gulf
of St. Lawrence to give birth to
their young.

Hudson Strait

Ungava Bay

Feuilles

Orca
(killer
whale)

Moose

Beaver

Iron
ore

Raccoon

Timber

Cross-country
skiing

Camping

Hydroelectricity

Cap-des-Rosiers
Lighthouse

PÉNINSULE
DE LA GASPÉSIE
(GASPÉ PENINSULA)

Iceberg

Puffins

Labrador Sea

Hooded seal

Nain

Gannet

LABRADOR

Smallwood
Reservoir

Churchill

Happy Valley-
Goose Bay

Canada
geese

Harp seals

Île d'Anticosti
(Anticosti Island)

Gulf of St. Lawrence

PRINCE
EDWARD
ISLAND

CHARLOTTETOWN

Anne of Green
Gables's House

NOVA
SCOTIA

Lobster

ATLANTIC OCEAN

NEWFOUNDLAND

Ⓔ Blue whales

Zinc

Beaver

Traditional church

Newfoundland

ST. JOHN'S

ST-PIERRE AND
MIQUELON (FRANCE)

AMAZING FACT

The Canadian National (CN)
Tower in Toronto is the tallest
freestanding structure in the world.
Completed in 1976, it stands
1,816 feet (553 m) high—the
equivalent of a 150-story building!
On a clear day, you can see for
more than 75 miles (120 km)
from the top of the tower.

LOCATION

N
W E
S

SCALE

MILES
0   50   100   150   200

0   100   200   300   400
KILOMETERS

Northeastern United States

THE NORTHEAST is home to 70 million people—more than one-quarter of the population of the United States. From Boston in the north to Washington, D.C. in the south, a line of great cities stretches for over 400 miles (640 km) along the Atlantic shore. Including its suburbs, New York City is home to almost 20 million people. It is the largest city in the U.S.A. and the third largest in the world. New York is one of the world's leading centers of trade, industry and culture. The heart of the city is the island of Manhattan, where giant skyscrapers, including some of the world's tallest, tower over long, straight streets packed with people and traffic.

The Appalachian Mountains separate the cities of the coast from the Great Lakes and the plains of the interior. They stretch for more than 1,600 miles (2,600 km) from northern Alabama, in the southern United States, to northern Maine. In the south, these mountains are rich in minerals—Kentucky produces more coal than any other state. Farms occupy many Appalachian valleys, but large areas of the mountains are covered by deciduous forests where black bears forage for blueberries and otters swim in the streams. In fall, these forests provide spectacular displays of color, as their leaves change from green to brilliant shades of orange, red and gold.

CONNECTICUT
POPULATION: 3,425,000 ◆ CAPITAL: HARTFORD

DELAWARE
POPULATION: 796,200 ◆ CAPITAL: DOVER

DISTRICT OF COLUMBIA
POPULATION: 571,800 ◆ CAPITAL: WASHINGTON, D.C.

KENTUCKY
POPULATION: 4,065,600 ◆ CAPITAL: FRANKFORT

MAINE
POPULATION: 1,286,700 ◆ CAPITAL: AUGUSTA

MARYLAND
POPULATION: 5,375,200 ◆ CAPITAL: ANNAPOLIS

MASSACHUSETTS
POPULATION: 6,379,300 ◆ CAPITAL: BOSTON

NEW HAMPSHIRE
POPULATION: 1,259,200 ◆ CAPITAL: CONCORD

NEW JERSEY
POPULATION: 8,484,400 ◆ CAPITAL: TRENTON

NEW YORK
POPULATION: 19,011,400 ◆ CAPITAL: ALBANY

PENNSYLVANIA
POPULATION: 12,287,200 ◆ CAPITAL: HARRISBURG

RHODE ISLAND
POPULATION: 1,058,900 ◆ CAPITAL: PROVIDENCE

VERMONT
POPULATION: 613,100 ◆ CAPITAL: MONTPELIER

VIRGINIA
POPULATION: 7,187,700 ◆ CAPITAL: RICHMOND

WEST VIRGINIA
POPULATION: 1,801,900 ◆ CAPITAL: CHARLESTON

◆ PROJECT: *Iroquois Beads* ◆

According to the custom of the native Iroquois people, a person saying something important must give the listener a gift to confirm the truth of the statement. This gift is often a string of white and purple shell beads known as wampum. Try making your own Iroquois friendship beads. Thread some colored beads onto pieces of string and attach the strings to a length of yarn. Remember to explain the meaning of your gift to the receiver.

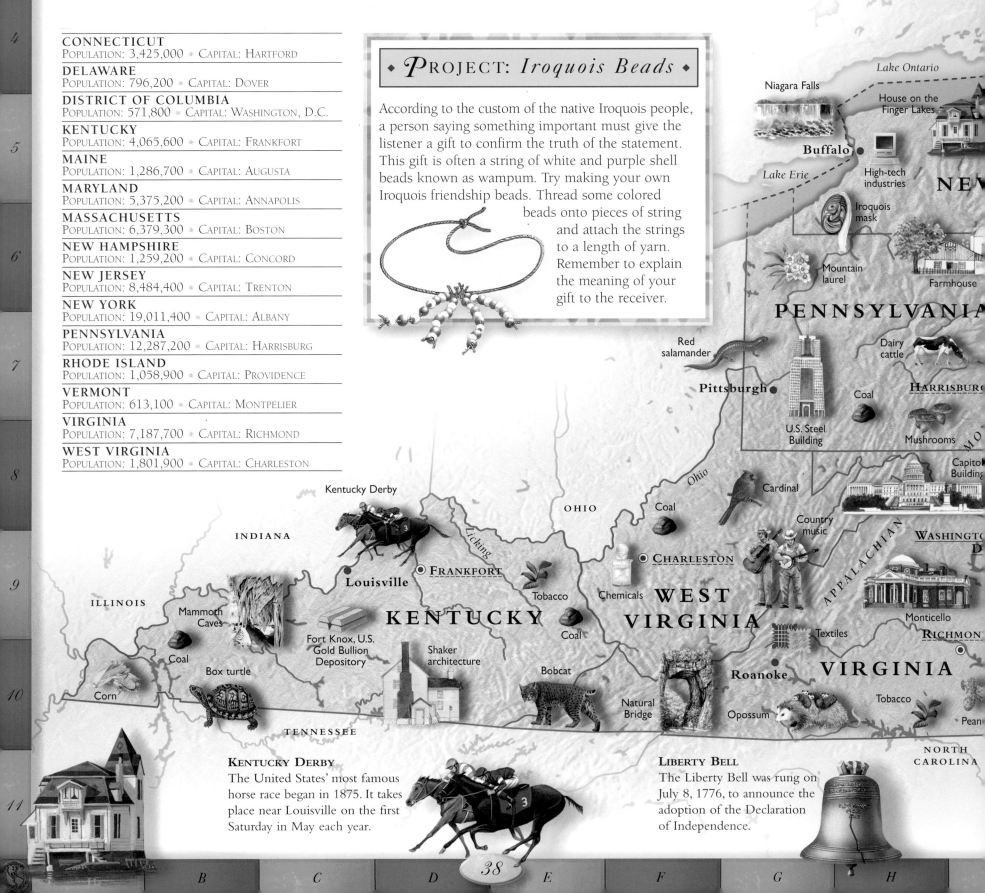

KENTUCKY DERBY
The United States' most famous horse race began in 1875. It takes place near Louisville on the first Saturday in May each year.

LIBERTY BELL
The Liberty Bell was rung on July 8, 1776, to announce the adoption of the Declaration of Independence.

Fort
Kent

Potatoes

Chipmunk

Chickadee

Timber

Blueberries

MAINE

Mt. Washington
Cog Railway

CANADA

Paper

Lighthouse

VERMONT

Zinc   Apples

MONTPELIER

Skiing

AUGUSTA

Poultry

Dairy cattle

Bluebird

Fort
Ticonderoga

Maple
syrup

**NEW
HAMPSHIRE**

Portland

CONCORD

Manchester

Salmon

ORK

Baseball Hall
of Fame

Albany

Basketball
Hall of Fame

Timber

MASSACHUSETTS

High-tech
industries

BOSTON

Cranberries

Amish
people

Chrysler
Building

CONNECTICUT

HARTFORD

PROVIDENCE

Mayflower

Chocolate

**RHODE
ISLAND**

Rhode
Island Red

New York

**NEW
JERSEY**

Statue of
Liberty

Tourism

Minke whale

Liberty
Bell

TRENTON

Philadelphia

Aircraft carrier

Poultry

Tourism

altimore

DOVER

Atlantic City

NNAPOLIS

DELAWARE

Blue marlin

MARYLAND

Crab

Norfolk

ATLANTIC OCEAN

◆ AMAZING FACT ◆

The Statue of Liberty was a gift from the people of France to the people of the United States. It was designed by Frédéric-Auguste Bartholdi and engineered by Alexandre Gustave Eiffel, who built the Eiffel Tower in Paris, France. The statue took nine years to build and was unveiled in 1886. It is made up of 300 copper sheets and stands 151 feet (46 m) tall on a base 154 feet (47 m) high.

LOCATION

N
W   E
S

SCALE

MILES

0   25   50   75   100   125

0   50   100   150   200

KILOMETERS

CHRYSLER BUILDING

This skyscraper was built by Walter Chrysler, founder of the Chrysler car empire. The steel arches at the top are modeled on car hubcaps.

MAYFLOWER

In 1620 the Mayflower carried the Pilgrims from England to America to establish one of the first permanent colonies.

Southern United States

THE SOUTHERN UNITED STATES is a warm, humid region of plains, rivers, swamps and coastal lagoons. From southern Texas, a broad belt of lowland stretches around the Gulf of Mexico, across Florida and along the shores of the Atlantic Ocean. In the north and west, the coastal plains rise to plateaus and mountain ranges, including the Appalachian Mountains, which formed about 400 million years ago and are North America's oldest mountains. Mixed crop and livestock farms cover the fertile eastern and southern plains. In the west, on the dry Texas grasslands, ranch hands tend huge herds of cattle. Texas is the second-biggest American state after Alaska, and its beef industry and large oil reserves have made it one of the richest parts of the country. Numerous rivers cross the southern United States, including the Mississippi, one of North America's longest rivers and busiest inland waterways. Along the Gulf Coast and in northern Florida, these rivers have formed shallow lakes, muddy deltas and steamy swamps that are home to snakes, turtles and alligators. Florida's sunny climate and sandy beaches make it a popular vacation spot. The Walt Disney World theme park near Orlando is the world's number one tourist attraction, with more than 25 million visitors each year.

Many of the first Europeans to settle in this region came from France and Spain in the 17th century, and their descendants are called Creoles. Other French-speakers known as Cajuns arrived soon afterward from Canada. Florida's large Spanish-speaking population includes immigrants from the island of Cuba, which lies just 135 miles (217 km) south of Key West, the southernmost tip of Florida and the United States.

ALABAMA
POPULATION: 4,464,400 • CAPITAL: MONTGOMERY

ARKANSAS
POPULATION: 2,692,100 • CAPITAL: LITTLE ROCK

FLORIDA
POPULATION: 16,396,500 • CAPITAL: TALLAHASSEE

GEORGIA
POPULATION: 8,383,900 • CAPITAL: ATLANTA

LOUISIANA
POPULATION: 4,465,400 • CAPITAL: BATON ROUGE

MISSISSIPPI
POPULATION: 2,858,000 • CAPITAL: JACKSON

NORTH CAROLINA
POPULATION: 8,186,300 • CAPITAL: RALEIGH

OKLAHOMA
POPULATION: 3,460,100 • CAPITAL: OKLAHOMA CITY

SOUTH CAROLINA
POPULATION: 4,063,000 • CAPITAL: COLUMBIA

TENNESSEE
POPULATION: 5,740,000 • CAPITAL: NASHVILLE

TEXAS
POPULATION: 21,325,000 • CAPITAL: AUSTIN

RODEO
Rodeo events test the riding and roping skills of both men and women. In the bull-riding event, riders have to stay on the bucking bull for eight seconds.

PADDLE STEAMER
In the 19th century, more than 400 of these elegant steamers provided transportation for people and goods along the Mississippi River.

♦ AMAZING FACT ♦

The Everglades, the vast wetland that covers southern Florida, is actually an enormous, slow-moving river 50 miles (80 km) wide, 100 miles (160 km) long and, on average, only six inches (15 cm) deep. The water comes from Lake Okeechobee, which overflows during the summer wet season.

♦ LOOK AGAIN ♦

- What kind of grain is grown in Arkansas?
- In which state is the space shuttle launch site found?
- Which river forms part of the border between the United States and Mexico?

2

3

VIRGINIA

KENTUCKY

SSOURI

CLARK PLATEAU

Tennessee walking horse

Mockingbird

Country music

Zinc

NASHVILLE

Tobacco

Gray squirrel

Black bear

RALEIGH

NORTH CAROLINA

ARKANSAS

Wild turkey

Soybeans

Memphis

Poultry

Tennessee

Mt. Mitchell 6,684 ft (2,037 m)

Charlotte

SOUTH CAROLINA

Venus flytrap

Wilmington

4

LITTLE ROCK

Rice

Harvesting cotton

Birmingham

Stone Mountain Memorial Carving

ATLANTA

Sewing a quilt

Pecans

Carolina wren

COLUMBIA

Charleston

Blue marlin

5

ldle mer

MISSISSIPPI

ALABAMA

Peanuts

Macon

Columbus

Cotton

Savannah

Savannah

6

OUISIANA

JACKSON

Raccoon

Cotton

MONTGOMERY

Shorter Mansion

GEORGIA

Albany

Tobacco

Flying squirrel

Shrimp

7

Oil

Jambalaya

Mississippi

Alabama

Jackson Square

Mobile

Purple gallinule

TALLAHASSEE

Avocadoes

Jacksonville

FLORIDA

Kennedy Space Center, Cape Canaveral

ATLANTIC OCEAN

LOCATION

BATON ROUGE

Lake Charles

Jazz

New Orleans

Lobster

Epcot Center and Walt Disney World

Orlando

8

Oil rig

Tampa

Oranges

Alligator

Lake Okeechobee

9

Gulf of Mexico

Great blue heron

Airboat in the Everglades

Miami

THE BAHAMAS

Tourism

Scuba diving

FLORIDA KEYS

Straits of Florida

10

N

W   E

S

Key West

SCALE

MILES

0   50   100   150   200

0   100   200   300

KILOMETERS

COUNTRY MUSIC

Nashville, Tennessee, is known as the home of country music. The city has about 180 record companies, 25 recording studios and 450 music publishers.

Central United States

THE CENTRAL UNITED STATES consists of a vast area of lowland known as the Midwest or prairies. In the northeastern part of this region lie the Great Lakes, the largest group of freshwater lakes in the world. Rivers and canals connect the lakes to the Atlantic Ocean and the Gulf of Mexico, forming a major transportation network. This network and the area's many natural resources (including coal and iron ore) have helped turn the Great Lakes region into the industrial heart of the United States. Factories now line the southern shores of Lake Michigan and Lake Erie, and supply most of the country's iron, steel and cars. Unfortunately, these industries create a great deal of waste, and the Great Lakes are now badly polluted. The area south and west of the lakes was once an enormous natural grassland, roamed by millions of bison and deer, and home to Native American tribes such as the Sioux and the Comanche. Now it is one of the world's most important farming regions. Iowa lies at the center of an area known as the Corn Belt because it produces half of the world's corn. Almost all of this corn is used to fatten the region's pigs and cattle, which provide most of the United States' meat. Farther west, on the Great Plains, is a "wheat belt." Here, immense fields of wheat stretch as far as the eye can see.

ILLINOIS
POPULATION: 12,482,300 ⋆ CAPITAL: SPRINGFIELD

INDIANA
POPULATION: 6,114,700 ⋆ CAPITAL: INDIANAPOLIS

IOWA
POPULATION: 2,923,200 ⋆ CAPITAL: DES MOINES

KANSAS
POPULATION: 2,694,600 ⋆ CAPITAL: TOPEKA

MICHIGAN
POPULATION: 9,990,800 ⋆ CAPITAL: LANSING

MINNESOTA
POPULATION: 4,972,300 ⋆ CAPITAL: ST. PAUL

MISSOURI
POPULATION: 5,629,700 ⋆ CAPITAL: JEFFERSON CITY

NEBRASKA
POPULATION: 1,713,200 ⋆ CAPITAL: LINCOLN

NORTH DAKOTA
POPULATION: 634,400 ⋆ CAPITAL: BISMARCK

OHIO
POPULATION: 11,373,500 ⋆ CAPITAL: COLUMBUS

SOUTH DAKOTA
POPULATION: 756,600 ⋆ CAPITAL: PIERRE

WISCONSIN
POPULATION: 5,401,900 ⋆ CAPITAL: MADISON

CANADA

Lake the Wo

MONTANA

Oil

Mallard duck

Hay

Hiking

Red

Sugar beets

Minot

Grand Forks

NORTH DAKOTA

Bald eagle

Red foxes

Coal

BISMARCK

Missouri

Food processing

Fargo

Moorhead

MI

Wheat

White-tailed deer

Dairy cattl

Corn

Prairie dogs

James

Hay

Minne

Gold

SOUTH DAKOTA

Rapid City

PIERRE

G R E A T

Sioux headdress

Food processing

Sioux Falls

Mount Rushmore

Badlands National Park

Missouri

Beef cattle

Sioux City

Windmill

P L A I N S

Lassoing cattle

WYOMING

Chimney Rock

Bison

North Platte

Food processing

Omaha

NEBRASKA

Platte

Grand Island

LINCOLN

Council Bluffs

Buffalo Bill's ranch house

Turkeys

Corn

COLORADO

Oil

Sunflowers

Ka

KANSAS

Harvesting wheat

Salina

Beef cattle

Wheat

Arkansas

Monument Rocks

Dodge City

Natural gas

Aircraft manufacturing

Wichita

OKLAHOMA

BISON
Before European settlers arrived, 25 million bison lived on the Plains. Hunters wiped out most of them, and now only 30,000 remain.

SIOUX HEADDRESS
The northern Great Plains is the traditional homeland of the Sioux people. Headdresses like this are still worn by their chiefs.

◆ AMAZING FACT ◆

At Mount Rushmore in South Dakota, sculptor Gutzon Borglum carved the faces of four great U.S. presidents—Washington, Jefferson, Theodore Roosevelt and Lincoln. Each face is more than 60 feet (18 m) high!

LOCATION

N E S W (compass)

SCALE

MILES
0   50   100   150

KILOMETERS
0   50   100   150   200   250

MARK TWAIN'S HOUSE
In 1835, author Mark Twain was born in this tiny cabin, which is now part of the Mark Twain Museum in Hannibal, Missouri.

AMERICAN FOOTBALL
Following the growth of this sport in the 19th century, the first American professional football association was founded in Canton, Ohio, in 1920.

Western United States

THE COLOSSAL ROCKY MOUNTAINS separate the western United States from the plains of the Midwest. Among the valleys and peaks of this spectacular range, mountain goats bound up steep rock faces and elk feed beside fast-flowing streams. There is little agriculture here, but herds of cattle graze the mountain meadows. West of the Rockies lies a series of dry plateaus, valleys and ranges. The Colorado Plateau has some of the continent's most spectacular scenery, including the world's largest gorge, the Grand Canyon. The states of Washington, Oregon and Idaho are known as the Pacific Northwest. The wet, densely forested western part of this area provides 40 percent of the United States' timber. The largest state in the region, California, is home to more people than any other American state. Most of the population lives in or near the coastal cities of Los Angeles and San Francisco. Inland, between the mountains of the Coast Ranges and the Sierra Nevada, farms form a patchwork of fields across the fertile, irrigated Central Valley. The most westerly state, Hawaii, lies 2,500 miles (4,000 km) off the coast, in the middle of the Pacific Ocean. Hawaii consists of 132 islands, which were formed by undersea volcanoes. Several Hawaiian volcanoes still erupt, including Mauna Loa, the largest active volcano in the world.

HAWAII (U.S.A.)

Pineapple
Kauai
Lihue
Niihau
Hula dancer
Oahu
Surfing
HONOLULU
Molokai
Lahaina
Lanai
Kahoolawe
Maui
Hawaii
Mauna Kea 13,796 ft (4,205 m)
Hilo
Ancient Hawaiian totem pole
Mauna Loa 13,680 ft (4,170 m)
PACIFIC OCEAN

MILES 0 50 100
KILOMETERS 0 100 200

CANADA

Aircraft manufacturing
Seattle skyline
Tacoma
Seattle
Spokane
Coeur d'Alene Mission
OLYMPIA
WASHINGTON
Missou
Mt. Rainier 14,410 ft (4,392 m)
Apples
Beef cattle
Rock climbing
Timber
Columbia
Mint
Portland
Timber
SALEM
Beef cattle
Hell's Canyon
Roses
OREGON
IDAH
Snake
Eugene
BOISE
Silver City ghost town
Pacific giant salamander
Pronghorn
Crater Lake
Twin Falls
California quail
Winnemucca
Gold
Eureka
Redwood tree
Skiing
Humboldt
Jackrabbit
Sacramento
NEVADA
Wine
SIERRA
Reno
CARSON CITY
Lake Tahoe
TransAmerica Building
SACRAMENTO
Mountain lion
Bristlecone pine
GREAT BASIN
Oakland
NEVADA
San Francisco
High-tech industries
Casino
Golden Gate Bridge
COAST
Oranges
Fresno
General Sherman tree
Mt. Whitney 14,495 ft (4,418 m)
DEATH VALLEY
Las Vegas
Lake Mead
In-line skating
RANGES
Rattlesnake
CALIFORNIA
Disneyland
Santa Barbara
Los Angeles
HOLLYWOOD
Desert tortoise
Hollywood sign
San Diego
PACIFIC OCEAN
MEXICO
Colorado

ARIZONA POPULATION: 5,307,300 ✳ CAPITAL: PHOENIX	**NEVADA** POPULATION: 2,106,100 ✳ CAPITAL: CARSON CITY
CALIFORNIA POPULATION: 34,501,100 ✳ CAPITAL: SACRAMENTO	**NEW MEXICO** POPULATION: 1,829,100 ✳ CAPITAL: SANTA FE
COLORADO POPULATION: 4,417,700 ✳ CAPITAL: DENVER	**OREGON** POPULATION: 3,472,900 ✳ CAPITAL: SALEM
HAWAII POPULATION: 1,224,400 ✳ CAPITAL: HONOLULU	**UTAH** POPULATION: 2,269,800 ✳ CAPITAL: SALT LAKE CITY
IDAHO POPULATION: 1,321,000 ✳ CAPITAL: BOISE	**WASHINGTON** POPULATION: 5,988,000 ✳ CAPITAL: OLYMPIA
MONTANA POPULATION: 904,400 ✳ CAPITAL: HELENA	**WYOMING** POPULATION: 494,400 ✳ CAPITAL: CHEYENNE

GENERAL SHERMAN TREE
This giant sequoia is the world's largest living thing. It is as tall as a 23-story building and is at least 2,300 years old.

**Map labels:**

Whitewater rafting
Wheat
Oil
Natural gas
NORTH DAKOTA
Missouri
Great Falls
MONTANA
HELENA
Yellowstone
Billings
Bighorn sheep
Grizzly bear
Bighorn Canyon
Coal
Devil's Tower
SOUTH DAKOTA
Old Faithful geyser
WYOMING
Beef cattle
Idaho Falls
Uranium
Casper
Potatoes
American kestrel
Great Salt Lake
Coyote
CHEYENNE
NEBRASKA
Rock Springs
Ogden
SALT LAKE CITY
Mormon Temple
Provo
Skiing
Boulder
Stegosaur skeleton
KANSAS
DENVER
Arches National Park
COLORADO
UTAH
Grand Junction
Colorado Springs
Pueblo
COLORADO PLATEAU
Cedar City
Lake Powell
Green
Monument Valley
Arkansas
Mountain goat
Cumbres and Toltec Scenic Railroad
Plains Indian dancer
Natural gas
Taos Pueblo (native village)
Appaloosa horses
Grand Canyon
Flagstaff
Navajo woman weaving
SANTA FE
Uranium
Albuquerque
Pueblo pottery
Zuni jewelry
NEW MEXICO
TEXAS
ARIZONA
Saguaro cactus
Rio Grande
Roswell
PHOENIX
Gila
High-tech industries
Copper
National Astronomy Observatory
Oil
Tucson
TEXAS
San Xavier de Bac Mission

◆ PROJECT: *Sand-Art Jars* ◆

The Navajo and Pueblo people of the southwestern United States make ceremonial paintings with colored sand. After the ceremony, the paintings are erased. You can make your own colored-sand painting in a jar.

❶ First sift the sand to make sure it is clean and fine. Divide the sand into small piles, adding a few drops of food coloring to each to make different-colored sands. Stir the sand every few hours to dry it.

❷ When the sand is dry, slowly pour some into a clean glass jar. Then pour a layer of another color. Keep pouring layers of different colors until the jar is full.

❸ Now make patterns by pushing a length of wire, or the end of a thin paintbrush, down the inside of the glass, between the sand and the jar. Be careful not to stir the sand! As the wire goes up and down, different colors will slide into the spaces and create designs.

❹ Finally, top off the jar with more of the colored sand and put on the lid.

◆ AMAZING FACT ◆

Carved out by the Colorado River, the Grand Canyon is 220 miles (350 km) long and about one mile (1.6 km) deep. The rocks at the bottom of the canyon are more than two billion years old!

N
W **E**
S

SCALE
MILES
0   50   100   150   200
0   100   200   300
KILOMETERS

ROADRUNNER
Roadrunners seldom fly, preferring to race along on their powerful legs. They can reach speeds of 20 miles per hour (32 kph).

PLAINS INDIAN DANCER
By dressing as buffalo (bison), dancers appeal to the sacred spirits of these animals to bring them health and good fortune.

Mexico, Central America and the Caribbean

MEXICO AND CENTRAL AMERICA form a land bridge between the United States and South America. At its narrowest point, this strip of land is only 50 miles (80 km) wide and is split by the Panama Canal, an artificial waterway that links the Atlantic and Pacific oceans. Mexico is more than twice the size of the seven Central American countries combined. It is dominated by a large dry plateau, and only 18 percent of the land can be farmed. The narrow plains on the east coast are warm and humid, and contain large oil reserves. Three-quarters of Mexicans live in cities and towns, and Mexico City is one of the largest and fastest-growing cities in the world. Most of Central America is mountainous, and much of the land is covered in rain forests where colorful parrots shriek from the treetops and chattering monkeys swing among branches. Although only a small proportion of Central America can be farmed, about half of the people live in rural areas and many grow their own food on small plots of land. To the east lie the Caribbean Islands, which are surrounded by sandy beaches, and are among the most heavily populated places on Earth. Spain ruled much of Mexico, Central America and the Caribbean for centuries, and today most of the people speak Spanish. Their ancestors may be settlers from Europe, Native American peoples or Africans who were first brought to the region as slaves.

ANTIGUA AND BARBUDA
POPULATION: 67,448 ✴ CAPITAL: ST. JOHN'S

THE BAHAMAS
POPULATION: 300,529 ✴ CAPITAL: NASSAU

BARBADOS
POPULATION: 276,607 ✴ CAPITAL: BRIDGETOWN

BELIZE
POPULATION: 262,999 ✴ CAPITAL: BELMOPAN

COSTA RICA
POPULATION: 3,834,934 ✴ CAPITAL: SAN JOSÉ

CUBA
POPULATION: 11,224,321 ✴ CAPITAL: HAVANA

DOMINICA
POPULATION: 70,158 ✴ CAPITAL: ROSEAU

DOMINICAN REPUBLIC
POPULATION: 8,721,594 ✴ CAPITAL: SANTO DOMINGO

EL SALVADOR
POPULATION: 6,353,681 ✴ CAPITAL: SAN SALVADOR

GRENADA
POPULATION: 89,211 ✴ CAPITAL: ST. GEORGE'S

GUATEMALA
POPULATION: 13,314,079 ✴ CAPITAL: GUATEMALA

HAITI
POPULATION: 7,063,722 ✴ CAPITAL: PORT-AU-PRINCE

HONDURAS
POPULATION: 6,560,608 ✴ CAPITAL: TEGUCIGALPA

JAMAICA
POPULATION: 2,680,029 ✴ CAPITAL: KINGSTON

MEXICO
POPULATION: 103,400,165 ✴ CAPITAL: MEXICO CITY

NICARAGUA
POPULATION: 5,023,818 ✴ CAPITAL: MANAGUA

PANAMA
POPULATION: 2,882,329 ✴ CAPITAL: PANAMA

ST. KITTS–NEVIS
POPULATION: 38,736 ✴ CAPITAL: BASSETERRE

ST. LUCIA
POPULATION: 160,145 ✴ CAPITAL: CASTRIES

ST. VINCENT AND THE GRENADINES
POPULATION: 116,394 ✴ CAPITAL: KINGSTOWN

TRINIDAD AND TOBAGO
POPULATION: 1,163,724 ✴ CAPITAL: PORT-OF-SPAIN

SINGING GRASSHOPPER MOUSE
This mouse is named for its habit of squeaking or "singing" to warn off rivals. Grasshoppers are its favorite food.

◆ PROJECT: *Make a Mexican Piñata* ◆

A piñata is a pot made from papier-mâché and filled with toys and candy, often shaped like a star or animal. It is a popular part of many celebrations and festivals in Mexico and Central America. Children hang the piñata from the ceiling or a tree branch and take turns trying to break it open. You can make a Mexican piñata for your next party.

❶ Cover a large balloon with strips of newspaper dipped in flour-and-water paste or white glue. Wait for this papier-mâché to dry and then repeat with at least two more layers of newspaper.

❷ When the papier-mâché is completely dry, cut a small hole in the top and fill the piñata with all sorts of goodies. Re-cover the hole with more papier-mâché.

❸ Make star points out of cardboard as shown. Tape them onto the ball using the tabs. Decorate the star with paint and colored tissue paper.

Step 3A
Step 3B

❹ Make two small holes next to each other at the top of the piñata. Thread curved wire through one hole and out the other. Hang up the piñata and have guests take turns hitting it with a stick to open it.

◆ AMAZING FACT ◆

The saguaro cactus is found only in the deserts of northwestern Mexico and the southwestern United States. It grows incredibly slowly, taking 25 years to reach a height of one foot (30 cm). But it can live for 200 years and grow as high as a four-story house. Like other cacti, the saguaro survives on water stored in its stem. A fully grown saguaro may contain enough water to fill 100 bathtubs!

Queen angelfish
Tourism
THE BAHAMAS
★ NASSAU
Traditional dancers
HAVANA
Cigars
CUBA
Ⓔ Cuban crocodile
TURKS AND CAICOS ISLANDS (U.K.)
Palm tree
Scuba diving
ANGUILLA (U.K.)
VIRGIN ISLANDS (U.S.A./U.K.)
ANTIGUA AND BARBUDA
SAN JUAN
ST. KITTS–NEVIS
GUADELOUPE (FRANCE)
MONTSERRAT (U.K.)
DOMINICA
Tourism
MARTINIQUE (FRANCE)
Bananas
SANTO DOMINGO ★
PUERTO RICO (U.S.A.)
Fort-de-France
PORT-AU-PRINCE ★
DOMINICAN REPUBLIC
ST. LUCIA
BARBADOS
Cricket
HAITI
CAYMAN ISLANDS (U.K.)
★ KINGSTON
ST. VINCENT AND THE GRENADINES
JAMAICA
Sailing
Sugarcane
Fishing boat
GRENADA
Steel band
NETHERLANDS ANTILLES (NETHERLANDS)
ARUBA (NETHERLANDS)
PORT-OF-SPAIN
TRINIDAD AND TOBAGO

ATLANTIC OCEAN

Caribbean Sea

LOCATION

HONDURAS
...as
Fishing boat
GUCIGALPA
Coffee
VENEZUELA
NICARAGUA
Panama Canal
Cuna Indian
COLOMBIA
...ANAGUA
Beef cattle
Bananas
SAN JOSÉ
★ PANAMA
PANAMA
Coffee
COSTA RICA
Sugarcane
Howler monkey

GREAT PLAZA, TIKAL
Tikal is an ancient city in Guatemala. It was built by the Maya between AD 75 and 900, and then mysteriously abandoned. It is now completely surrounded by jungle.

N
W · E
S

SCALE
MILES
0   100   200   300
0 100 200 300 400 500
KILOMETERS

South America

FROM ITS TROPICAL NORTHERN SHORE, South America stretches 4,500 miles (7,240 km) southward to the chilly, storm-battered peninsula of Cape Horn, just 600 miles (1,000 km) from Antarctica. The Andes run the entire length of the continent's west coast, forming the longest mountain chain in the world. In the north, the Amazon River (the world's second-longest river) snakes eastward from the Andes to the Atlantic Ocean, through vast rain forests that once covered more than one-third of the continent. To the south, the forests give way to the grasslands of the Gran Chaco and the Pampas. The southern tip of South America is a dry, windswept plateau known as Patagonia. South America's inhabitants include people of European, native Indian and African origin. Most people speak Spanish, but Portuguese is the official language in Brazil.

Major Mountains and Rivers

Aconcagua, Argentina 22,834 ft (6,960 m)
Cerro Ojos del Salado, Argentina-Chile 22,664 ft (6,908 m)
Bonete, Argentina 22,546 ft (6,872 m)
Huascarán, Peru 22,205 ft (6,768 m)
Mount Illimani, Bolivia 21,201 ft (6,462 m)
Chimborazo, Ecuador 20,702 ft (6,310 m)

Amazon 4,010 miles (6,450 km)
Paraná-Río de la Plata 2,800 miles (4,500 km)
Purus 2,080 miles (3,350 km)
São Francisco 1,800 miles (2,900 km)
Paraná 1,740 miles (2,800 km)
Orinoco 1,550 miles (2,500 km)

Political Map

VENEZUELA
GUYANA
SURINAME
FRENCH GUIANA (FRANCE)
COLOMBIA
GALÁPAGOS ISLANDS (ECUADOR)
ECUADOR
BRAZIL
PERU
BOLIVIA
MARTIN VAZ ISLANDS (BRAZIL)
PARAGUAY
EASTER ISLAND (CHILE)
CHILE
JUAN FERNANDEZ ISLANDS (CHILE)
URUGUAY
ARGENTINA
FALKLAND ISLANDS (U.K.)
SOUTH GEORGIA (U.K.)

Continent Facts

Regional land area: 6,877,943 sq. miles (17,818,505 sq. km)
Regional population: 354,885,240
Independent countries: Argentina, Bolivia, Brazil, Chile, Colombia, Ecuador, Guyana, Paraguay, Peru, Suriname, Uruguay, Venezuela

World Records

WORLD'S LONGEST MOUNTAIN CHAIN
ANDES, WESTERN SOUTH AMERICA 4,700 MILES (7,600 KM)

WORLD'S DRIEST PLACE
ATACAMA DESERT, CHILE, AVERAGE ANNUAL RAINFALL LESS THAN $1/250$ IN (0.1 MM)

WORLD'S HIGHEST WATERFALL
ANGEL FALLS, VENEZUELA, 3,212 FT (979 M)

WORLD'S HIGHEST CAPITAL CITY
LA PAZ, BOLIVIA, 11,913 FT (3,631 M)

WORLD'S HIGHEST NAVIGABLE LAKE
LAKE TITICACA, PERU-BOLIVIA, 12,500 FT (3,810 M)

WORLD'S LARGEST RIVER BY VOLUME
AMAZON, PERU-BRAZIL, DISCHARGES 7,100,000 CUBIC FEET (200,000 CUBIC M) PER SECOND INTO ATLANTIC OCEAN

WORLD'S LARGEST RIVER BASIN
AMAZON BASIN, NORTHERN SOUTH AMERICA, 2,720,000 SQ. MILES (7,045,000 SQ. KM)

WORLD'S LARGEST LAGOON
LAGOA DOS PATOS, BRAZIL, 3,803 SQ. MILES (9,850 SQ. KM)

Continent Records

HIGHEST MOUNTAIN
ACONCAGUA, ARGENTINA, 22,834 FT (6,960 M)

LOWEST POINT
VALDÉS PENINSULA, ARGENTINA, 131 FT (40 M) BELOW SEA LEVEL

LARGEST LAKE
LAKE TITICACA, PERU-BOLIVIA, 3,200 SQ. MILES (8,288 SQ. KM)

LONGEST RIVER
AMAZON RIVER, PERU-BRAZIL, 4,010 MILES (6,450 M)

LARGEST COUNTRY BY AREA
BRAZIL, 3,286,470 SQ. MILES (8,511,965 SQ. KM)

LARGEST COUNTRY BY POPULATION
BRAZIL, POPULATION 176,029,560

LARGEST CITY BY POPULATION
SÃO PAULO, BRAZIL, POPULATION 18,119,000

◆ AMAZING FACT ◆

The Atacama Desert in northern Chile is the driest place in the world. Rain showers occur only once or twice a century, and in some parts of the desert rain has never been recorded!

PHYSICAL MAP

NORTH AMERICA

Tropic of Cancer

Caribbean Sea

AFRICA

Lake Maracaibo

Orinoco

GUIANA HIGHLANDS

Amazon Delta

Gulf of Panama

LLANOS

Rio Negro

Rio Branco

Amazon

ATLANTIC OCEAN

GALÁPAGOS ISLANDS

▲ Chimborazo

Marañon

AMAZON BASIN

Gulf of Guayaquil

Equator

PACIFIC OCEAN

SELVAS

Purus

Madeira

Tapajos

Xingu

Tocantins

Sao Francisco

▲ Huascarán

A N D E S

Lake Titicaca

▲ Mt. Illimani

MATO GROSSO PLATEAU

BRAZILIAN HIGHLANDS

Lake Poopo

GRAN CHACO

Paraná

Tropic of Capricorn

ATACAMA DESERT

SERRA DO MAR

▲ Cerro Ojos del Salado

Paraguay

A N D E S

▲ Bonete

Uruguay

Lagoa dos Patos

Easter Island

▲ Aconcagua

Colorado

PAMPAS

Rio de la Plata

Blanca Bay

San Matias Gulf

VALDES PENINSULA

San Jorge Gulf

PATAGONIA

FALKLAND ISLANDS

Tierra del Fuego

South Georgia

CAPE HORN

Drake Passage

Antarctic Circle

ANTARCTICA

Northern South America

MOST OF NORTHERN SOUTH AMERICA is drained by the world's second-longest river, the Amazon, and its more than 200 tributaries. These waterways flow through lush tropical rain forests that are home to up to one third of all the plants and animals on Earth. Sadly, the rain forests are rapidly disappearing as a growing population clears the land for farming. More than one fifth of the rain forest, an area the size of France, has been cut down in the last twenty years. More than a quarter of the world's rain forests lie within Brazil, the largest country in South America. Brazil has many resources, including iron ore, oil and gold. It is the continent's most industrialized country and the world's leading producer of coffee, bananas and sugarcane. Northwest of Brazil lies Venezuela, a tropical country that is South America's top oil producer. From Venezuela, the Andes curve southward through Colombia, Ecuador and Peru. At the northern end of this mountain range, the climate is wet, and large coffee and banana plantations cover the hillsides. Farther south, little rain falls and crops can only be grown by using water from mountain streams. On the upper slopes of the Peruvian Andes, farmers grow potatoes and wheat and raise animals, including llamas and alpacas. Six hundred miles (1,000 km) off the coast of Ecuador lie the Galápagos Islands, which are famous for their unusual wildlife, which includes marine iguanas and giant tortoises.

BRAZIL
POPULATION: 176,029,560 • CAPITAL: BRASÍLIA

COLOMBIA
POPULATION: 41,008,227 • CAPITAL: BOGOTÁ

ECUADOR
POPULATION: 13,447,494 • CAPITAL: QUITO

GUYANA
POPULATION: 698,209 • CAPITAL: GEORGETOWN

PERU
POPULATION: 27,949,639 • CAPITAL: LIMA

SURINAME
POPULATION: 436,494 • CAPITAL: PARAMARIBO

VENEZUELA
POPULATION: 24,287,670 • CAPITAL: CARACAS

Barranquilla
Cartagena
Open-sided bus
Stilt house
Oil
Lake Maracaibo
CARAC
PANAMA
VENEZUEL
Bucaramanga
Medellín
Emeralds
Coffee
BOGOTÁ
Cali
Gold mask
Bogotá Cathedral
COLOMBIA
Valley of the Statues
Sugarcane
Jaguar
Bananas
QUITO
Guayaquil
Chimborazo
20,702 ft (6,310 m)
Oil
Putumayo
ECUADOR
Coffee
Beef cattle
Leticia
Strawberry poison dart fro
Silver
Marañón
Iquitos
AMAZO
Andean condor
Spider monkeys
Sardines
Trujillo
Quechua man
Huascarán
22,205 ft (6,768 m)
PERU
Indian panpipes
Scar ma
Machu Picchu
LIMA
Cuzco
Tin and lead
Alpaca
Arequipa
Reed b on La Titica
Chipaya sod homes

PACIFIC OCEAN

CHILE

GALÁPAGOS ISLANDS
(ECUADOR)

Pinta
Marchena
Genovesa
PACIFIC OCEAN
Giant tortoise
San Salvador
Isabela
Blue-footed booby
Fernandina
Santa Cruz
Puerto Ayora
San Cristóbal
Marine iguana
Puerto Baquerizo Moreno
Santa María
Española

MILES
0   20   40
0   25   50   75
KILOMETERS

STRAWBERRY POISON DART FROG
The skin of this colorful frog contains one of the strongest poisons on Earth. Native hunters use the poison on their arrow tips.

MACHU PICCHU
This ancient, mountaintop city in Peru was built by the Incas, a native people who ruled western South America between 1400 and 1532.

J K L M N O P Q

TRINIDAD AND
TOBAGO

Oil
Cacao

Ciudad Bolívar
inoco
Angel Falls
GEORGETOWN
Cock-of-
the-rock
PARAMARIBO
European Space
Agency Ariane rocket
Making
cassava
cakes
SURINAME
● Cayenne
GUYANA
FRENCH GUIANA
(FRANCE)
tle
Tapirs
Hummingbird
Black
caiman
Green
turtle

ATLANTIC OCEAN

Shrimp

omami
nter

Manaus Opera
House
Piranha

Amazon
Delta

Negro

Amazon

● Belém

São Luís

Thresher shark

Fortaleza

ASIN
Clearing
trees
Amazon
River dolphin

Madeira

Tapajós

Passenger boat

Amazon river and
rain forest

Xingu

Bananas

Brazil
nuts

Cotton

Fishing boat

● Manaus

Iron ore

Toucan

Conga
drum

Tarantula

Sloth

Kayapó
man

Gold

Harvesting
sugarcane

Recife

Tin

Guapore

Giant armadillo

Txukahamai
hunters with anaconda

BRAZIL

Tocantins

Topaz

Beef cattle

Oil

Lobster

Tourism

BOLIVIA

**MATO GROSSO
PLATEAU**

**BRAZILIAN
HIGHLANDS**

São Francisco

● Salvador

Church of Nosso
Senhor de Bomfim

Purple
gallinule

Diamonds

BRASÍLIA

Brasília Cathedral

Cacao

Oranges

PARAGUAY

Soccer

Rio de Janeiro
carnival dancer

Statue of
Christ

Belo Horizonte

Beef cattle

Coffee

Car
manufacturing

Rio de Janeiro

Parana

São Paulo

Sugarloaf Mountain

Shrimp

ARGENTINA

Uruguay

Iguazú Falls

Soybeans

**Pôrto
Alegre**

Sheep

Lagoa
dos Patos

URUGUAY

◆ AMAZING FACT ◆

The Amazon Basin is home to more wildlife than any other part of our planet. At least 1,000 species of birds live in the forests, and more than 3,000 species of fish swim in the rivers. A single tree may be home to as many as 400 animals!

LOCATION

SCALE

MILES

0   100   200   300   400

0 100 200 300 400 500 600

KILOMETERS

KAYAPÓ MAN
The Kayapó people of northeastern Brazil are known for their elaborate headdresses made from the tail feathers of macaws.

Southern South America

SOUTHERN SOUTH AMERICA IS SHAPED like a long, narrow triangle that tapers to a point on the southern island of Tierra del Fuego. The Andes run down the western side of the region, separating the country of Chile from its neighbors. Twenty times as long as it is wide, Chile has a variety of climates and landscapes. In the cold, wet, sparsely populated south, mountains rise steeply from the ocean, and glaciers snake through valleys. Central Chile has milder weather and many farms, vineyards and orchards. The north is very arid and includes the driest place in the world, the Atacama Desert. East of the Atacama, the Andes spread into Bolivia, one of the poorest countries in South America. From eastern Bolivia, wide plains stretch southward through Paraguay, Uruguay and northern Argentina. Enormous herds of cattle and sheep roam the eastern and southern parts of these plains, tended by ranch hands called gauchos. Argentina has more than 50 million cattle, and beef production is one of its most important industries. The country's most fertile grasslands, the Pampas, surround the capital, Buenos Aires. This city is home to one-third of the Argentinian population. Few people live in southern Argentina, a cold, barren plateau known as Patagonia, but the area is rich in minerals. The seas around Tierra del Fuego in the far south are often stormy. Hundreds of ships have been wrecked attempting to round Cape Horn or navigate the Strait of Magellan.

◆ PROJECT: *Easter Island Moai* ◆

Easter Island is covered with huge statues called "moai." Some are more than 30 ft (9 m) high! The early inhabitants of Easter Island may have built the statues to honor their ancestors. You can make an Easter Island statue, too.

① Mix equal parts of plaster and vermiculite (both available at hardware stores). Stir as you add enough water to make a thick plaster. Pour the mixture into an old shoe box.

② When the mixture hardens, tear away the cardboard. Carve the stone using tools such as a plastic knife or an ice pop stick.

③ Alternatively, make your carving out of a block of modeling clay, plaster of Paris or any other modeling material.

LLAMA
A common domestic animal in South America, the llama is a relative of the camel. It is kept for its wool and is also used for carrying goods through mountainous terrain.

Map labels

Hydroelectricity
Streetcar
PARAGUAY
Presidential palace
ASUNCIÓN
Maté (tea)
Polo
Corrientes
Chacoan peccary
GRAN CHACO
Beef cattle
Cotton
Natural gas
Corn
Maned wolf
San Miguel de Tucumán
Sugarcane
Oil
Greater rhea
Village musicians
Giant bromelia
Llamas
A N D E S
Cerro Ojos del Salado 22,664 ft (6,908 m)
Bonete 22,546 ft (6,872 m)
Motmot
Timber
Trinidad
BOLIVIA
Bolivian folk costume
Santa Cruz
SUCRE
Cochabamba
Tin
Zinc
Andean condor
Silver
ATACAMA DESERT
Copper
Copiapó
Iron
Guaporé
Mamoré
Giant anteater
Spectacled bear
Gold
La Paz
Mt. Illimani 21,201 ft (6,462 m)
Lake Titicaca
Lake Poopó
PERU
Arica
Iquique
Antofagasta
BRAZIL
Pilcomayo
Río Salado

ARGENTINA
POPULATION: 37,812,817 • CAPITAL: BUENOS AIRES
BOLIVIA
POPULATION: 8,445,134 • CAPITALS: LA PAZ, SUCRE
CHILE
POPULATION: 15,498,930 • CAPITAL: SANTIAGO
PARAGUAY
POPULATION: 5,884,491 • CAPITAL: ASUNCIÓN
URUGUAY
POPULATION: 3,386,575 • CAPITAL: MONTEVIDEO

LOCATION

TANGO DANCERS
The tango is both a style of music, and a dance that involves a series of long, gliding steps and sudden stops. It began in Argentina and is now popular around the world.

SCALE
MILES
KILOMETERS

BOLIVIAN COSTUME
Native people make up half of Bolivia's population. Many still wear traditional dress including striped ponchos, shawls and bowler hats.

♦ AMAZING FACT ♦
Found only on the slopes of the Bolivian Andes, the giant bromelia is the world's largest herb, and the slowest-flowering plant on Earth. Its single stem can grow to a height of 35 feet (11 m), but the plant doesn't usually bloom until it is between 80 and 150 years old. Each plant may have up to 8,000 white flowers.

EASTER ISLAND (CHILE)
Moai statues
Magnificent frigate bird
Mataveri
PACIFIC OCEAN
MILES
KILOMETERS

URUGUAY
Branding cattle
Tourism
Sheep
MONTEVIDEO
Bronze whaler shark
Wheat
Río de la Plata
La Plata
Mar del Plata
Soccer
Rosario
BUENOS AIRES
Tourism
Córdoba
Jesuit church
PAMPAS
Corn
Beef cattle
Tango dancers
Viscacha
Bahía Blanca
ARGENTINA
Mendoza
San Juan
Aconcagua 22,834 ft (6,960 m)
Pampas cat
Herding cattle
Iron ore
Crested caracara
VALDÉS PENINSULA
Oil
Oil
Colorado
Negro
Skiing
Eoraptor dinosaur fossils
Mara
Sheep
Guanacos
Natural gas
PATAGONIA
Comodoro Rivadavia
Sea lion
Puerto Deseado
Oil
Magellan penguin
Sheep
Río Gallegos
Strait of Magellan
Moreno Glacier
Oil
Fur seal
Punta Arenas
Tierra del Fuego
Ushuaia
CAPE HORN
CHILE
Valparaíso
SANTIAGO
Wine
Presidential palace
Concepción
Villarica volcano
Herding cattle
Puerto Montt
Timber
ANDES
Mackerel
Pygmy sperm whale
PACIFIC OCEAN
ATLANTIC OCEAN
Southern right whale
FALKLAND ISLANDS (U.K.)
Stanley
Albatross chick
Rockhopper penguin
Uruguay

N E S W

Europe

EUROPE IS A SMALL, DENSELY POPULATED CONTINENT made up of many countries, each of which has its own culture and, in most cases, its own language. It is bounded by the Arctic and Atlantic oceans in the north and west, and the Mediterranean Sea in the south. In the east, Russia's Ural Mountains separate Europe from Asia. A series of mountain ranges, including the Pyrenees, the Alps and the Carpathian Mountains, crosses Europe from east to west. South of these ranges, the land is rugged and the climate is warm and dry in summer and mild and wet in winter. To the north, a broad band of flat land known as the European Plain extends from the Atlantic coast to western Russia. Northwestern Europe has a mild, wet climate, but in the east and far north winters can be bitterly cold. At one time, most of Europe was covered in forest, but the trees were gradually cleared to make way for cities, farms and industries.

CONTINENT FACTS

Regional land area: 3,997,929 sq. miles (10,354,636 sq. km) (including European Russia)
Regional population: 695,812,202 (including European Russia)
Independent countries: Albania, Andorra, Austria, Belarus, Belgium, Bosnia and Herzegovina, Bulgaria, Croatia, Czech Republic, Denmark, Estonia, Finland, France, Germany, Greece, Hungary, Iceland, Ireland, Italy, Latvia, Liechtenstein, Lithuania, Luxembourg, Macedonia, Malta, Moldova, Monaco, The Netherlands, Norway, Poland, Portugal, Romania, Russia, San Marino, Slovakia, Slovenia, Spain, Sweden, Switzerland, Ukraine, United Kingdom, Vatican City, Yugoslavia

WORLD RECORDS

WORLD'S SMALLEST COUNTRY
VATICAN CITY, 0.17 SQ. MILES (0.44 SQ. KM)

WORLD'S TALLEST STALAGMITE
KRÁSNOHORSKÁ CAVE, SLOVAKIA, 105 FT (32 M)

CONTINENT RECORDS

HIGHEST MOUNTAIN
MOUNT ELBRUS, RUSSIA, 18,510 FT (5,642 M)

LOWEST POINT
VOLGA RIVER DELTA, 92 FT (28 M) BELOW SEA LEVEL

LARGEST LAKE
LAKE LADOGA, RUSSIA, 6,835 SQ. MILES (17,703 SQ. KM)

LONGEST RIVER
VOLGA RIVER, RUSSIA, 2,300 MILES (3,700 KM)

LARGEST COUNTRY BY AREA
EUROPEAN RUSSIA, 233,089 SQ. MILES (603,701 SQ. KM)

LARGEST COUNTRY BY POPULATION
EUROPEAN RUSSIA, POPULATION 113,083,287

LARGEST CITY BY POPULATION
PARIS, FRANCE, POPULATION 11,174,743

Major Mountains and Rivers

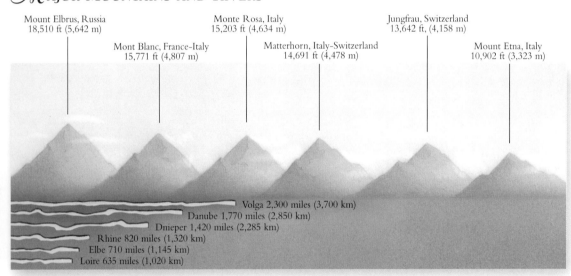

Mount Elbrus, Russia 18,510 ft (5,642 m)
Mont Blanc, France-Italy 15,771 ft (4,807 m)
Monte Rosa, Italy 15,203 ft (4,634 m)
Matterhorn, Italy-Switzerland 14,691 ft (4,478 m)
Jungfrau, Switzerland 13,642 ft, (4,158 m)
Mount Etna, Italy 10,902 ft (3,323 m)

Volga 2,300 miles (3,700 km)
Danube 1,770 miles (2,850 km)
Dnieper 1,420 miles (2,285 km)
Rhine 820 miles (1,320 km)
Elbe 710 miles (1,145 km)
Loire 635 miles (1,020 km)

Political Map

ICELAND

FAEROE ISLANDS (DENMARK)

SWEDEN

FINLAND

NORWAY

ESTONIA

UNITED KINGDOM

DENMARK

KALININGRAD OBLAST (RUSSIA)

LATVIA

LITHUANIA

RUSSIA

IRELAND

THE NETHERLANDS

BELARUS

BELGIUM

GERMANY

POLAND

LUXEMBOURG

CZECH REPUBLIC

SLOVAKIA

UKRAINE

FRANCE

1 AUSTRIA

SWITZERLAND

HUNGARY

MOLDOVA

SLOVENIA

ROMANIA

CROATIA

3

2

SPAIN

4 BOSNIA and HERZEGOVINA

YUGOSLAVIA

5 BULGARIA

ALBANIA MACEDONIA

PORTUGAL

ITALY

GREECE

MALTA

KEY TO NUMBERED COUNTRIES

■ 1 LIECHTENSTEIN
■ 2 ANDORRA
■ 3 MONACO
■ 4 SAN MARINO
■ 5 VATICAN CITY

PHYSICAL MAP

J K L M N O P Q

1
2
3
4
5
6
7
8
9
10

ARCTIC OCEAN

× NORTH POLE

NORTH AMERICA

Greenland

ATLANTIC OCEAN

Iceland

Norwegian Sea

Barents Sea

FAEROE ISLANDS

Arctic Circle

SCANDINAVIA

Lake Vänern

Gulf of Bothnia

Lake Onega

Lake Ladoga

URAL MOUNTAINS

ASIA

Ireland

North Sea

Baltic Sea

Volga

Great Britain

English Channel

EUROPEAN PLAIN

Elbe

Dnieper

Don

Bay of Biscay

Loire

Seine

Rhine

Caspian Sea

Jungfrau

Matterhorn

Mont Blanc

A L P S

Monte Rosa

CARPATHIAN MTS.

Mt. Elbrus

CAUCASUS MTS.

PYRENEES

Danube

Black Sea

IBERIAN PENINSULA

Corsica

Adriatic Sea

BALKAN PENINSULA

BALEARIC IS.

APENNINES

Sardinia

Mediterranean Sea

Sicily

Ionian Sea

Aegean Sea

Strait of Gibraltar

Mt. Etna

Crete

Tropic of Cancer

AFRICA

Equator

The United Kingdom and the Republic of Ireland

THE UNITED KINGDOM AND THE REPUBLIC OF IRELAND occupy islands known as the British Isles. The United Kingdom is made up of the countries of England, Wales, Scotland and Northern Ireland, which are ruled by one government based in London but have their own cultures. Scotland and Wales also have their own parliaments, and Scotland has its own legal and educational systems, churches and bank notes. England is a crowded country with many large cities. Almost eight million people live in London, the capital city. London is one of the world's most important centers of trade and finance and is famous for its many historic buildings. Southeastern England is flat and fertile and its farms provide most of the United Kingdom's crops. The country's most important industries are located in central England, an area known as the Midlands, and around the coalfields of the Pennine hills. To the west and north, the countryside is wet and mountainous and is used mainly for grazing animals. In the rugged, sparsely populated Scottish Highlands, red deer and sheep roam the hills and eagles soar overhead.

The Republic of Ireland occupies about 85 percent of the island of Ireland. It is a land of green plains surrounded by coastal mountains. Most of the country's industries are located in the capital, Dublin, and the southern city of Cork.

IRELAND
POPULATION: 3,883,159 ◆ CAPITAL: DUBLIN

UNITED KINGDOM
POPULATION: 58,836,700 ◆ CAPITAL: LONDON

ENGLAND
POPULATION: 49,181,300 ◆ CAPITAL: LONDON

NORTHERN IRELAND
POPULATION: 1,689,300 ◆ CAPITAL: BELFAST

SCOTLAND
POPULATION: 5,064,200 ◆ CAPITAL: EDINBURGH

WALES
POPULATION: 2,903,200 ◆ CAPITAL: CARDIFF

◆ AMAZING FACT ◆

In the 19th century, as a hoax, the name of the Welsh village Llanfairpwllgwyngyll was lengthened to the tongue-twisting Llanfairpwllgwyngyllgogerychwyrndrobwllllantysiliogogogoch. The name means "St. Mary's church by the pool of white hazel trees, near the rapid whirlpool, by the red cave of the Church of St. Tysilio." In 1988 the village officially returned to using the shorter name. However, the railway station is still called by the 58-letter version.

LLANFAIRPWLLGWYNGYLLGOGERYCHWYRNDROBWLLLLANTYSILIOGOGOGOCH

◆ LOOK AGAIN ◆

- Which famous railway bridge is located near the capital of Scotland?
- Name a sport that is played in Ireland.
- What is the name of the group of islands near Land's End?

Shetland pony

Lerwick

SHETLAND ISLANDS

Cod

ORKNEY ISLANDS

Kirkwall

John o'Groats

Thurso

Red deer

Highland piper

Salmon

Otter

Inverness

Urquhart Castle and Loch Ness

Capercaillie

Ben Nevis 4,406 ft (1,343 m)

Oban

Mull

Skye

Sheep

Lewis with Harris

Textiles

Stornoway

North Uist

South Uist

SOUTH HEBRIDES

Iona Abbey

Islay

Arran

Giant's Causeway rock formation

Hammer throwing, Highland Games

Highland cattle

Aberdeen

SCOTLAND

GRAMPIAN MTS.

Dee

Tay

Glamis Castle

Dundee

Golf

Forth

Clyde

EDINBURGH

Coal

Glasgow

Beef cattle

Tweed

Forth railway bridge

Hadrian's Wall

Coal

Oil rig

Haddock

Nort

N o r t

Fishing trawler

Thatched cottage
Norwich
Sugar beets
Poultry
Ipswich
Big Ben and the Houses of Parliament
Brighton Pavilion
Canal barge
Tennis
LONDON
Thames
Hovercraft
Brighton
FRANCE

Newcastle
Iron and steel
Castle Howard
Middlesbrough
Tyne
Hull
York
Iron and steel
Trent
Hedgehog
ENGLAND
Leeds
Textiles
Sheffield
Nottingham
Leicester
Coventry
Cambridge
Coldstream Guard
Oxford
Car manufacturing
Southampton
Isle of Wight
Hovercraft

Black pudding
Carlisle
Red squirrel
PENNINES
Cricket
Manchester
Tourism
Blackpool
Blackpool rock candy
Liverpool
Chatsworth House garden maze
Tudor architecture
Birmingham
Wheat
High-tech industries
Reading
Stonehenge
Bath
Dairy cattle
Bristol

Soccer
Stranraer
Motorcycle racing
Isle of Man
Irish Sea
Anglesey
Llanfairpwllgwyngyll
LLANFAIR...
Caernarfon Castle
Mt. Snowdon
3,561 ft (1,085 m)
Severn
WALES
Wye
Coal mining
Aberystwyth
Rugby
Swansea
Milford Haven
Puffins
Morris dancing
Exeter
Tourism
Plymouth
Pollock

CHANNEL ISLANDS
(U.K.)
Guernsey
Jersey

English Channel

Bangor
Stormont Castle
NORTHERN IRELAND
BELFAST
Beer
DUBLIN
Irish harp
St. George's Channel
Royal Navy rescue helicopter
Historic tin mine
LAND'S END
ISLES OF SCILLY

Potatoes
Hurling
Beef cattle
Dundalk
Newgrange prehistoric burial mound
Liffey
IRELAND
Kingfisher
Carlow
Waterford crystal
Waterford
Sailing
Mackerel

Sligo
Potatoes
Cross of Muireadach
Shannon
Limerick
Tipperary
Blarney Castle
Cork

Peat
Donkey
Galway
Crofter's cottage
Sugar beets
Carrantuohill
3,414 ft (1,041 m)
Sheep
Bantry
Gallarus Oratory
Lobster

Celtic Sea

N
W E
S

SCALE
MILES
0   50   100   150
KILOMETERS
0 50 100 150 200 250

STONEHENGE
This prehistoric stone monument, or megalith, was a religious and ceremonial site for thousands of years.

BLARNEY CASTLE
It is said that if you kiss the Blarney Stone in the tower of this castle you will become a clever and persuasive talker.

LOCATION

Sea

57

Spain and Portugal

SPAIN AND PORTUGAL OCCUPY the Iberian Peninsula, a wide, square-shaped piece of land in southwestern Europe. This peninsula is separated from the rest of the continent by the Pyrenees, a mountain range that contains the tiny country of Andorra. Most of the Iberian Peninsula consists of a huge plateau known as the Meseta, which is covered with dry grasslands, olive groves and forested hills. At the center of the Meseta, 2,120 feet (646 m) above sea level, lies Madrid—the largest city in Spain and the highest capital city in Europe. Spain's second-largest city, Barcelona, lies on the narrow plains of the east coast. This coastline and the nearby Balearic Islands are warm and sunny for much of the year, and in summer, crowds of vacationers from all over Europe sunbathe on the sandy beaches. The southern tip of Spain lies only nine miles (15 km) from Africa. Between AD 711 and the 12th century, most of Spain was ruled by the Moors, an Arabic people from North Africa, and towns such as Granada and Seville have many ornate Moorish buildings. West of Spain lies Portugal. Once the heart of a vast, worldwide empire, Portugal is now one of the poorest countries in western Europe. Olive groves and cork oak forests cover the dry, southern plains. In the many river valleys that cross the country, farmers grow grapes for winemaking. Among the best-known Portuguese wines is port, which is named after the country's second-largest city, Porto.

ANDORRA
POPULATION: 68,403 • CAPITAL: ANDORRA

PORTUGAL
POPULATION: 10,084,245 • CAPITAL: LISBON

SPAIN
POPULATION: 40,077,100 • CAPITAL: MADRID

AZORES (PORTUGAL)

Corvo

Flores

Wine — Graciosa
Terceira
Windmill

Faial
São Jorge
Pico

São Miguel

Santa Maria

MILES
0   50   100
0 50 100 150
KILOMETERS

MADEIRA (PORTUGAL)

Wine

Tourism

Funchal

MILES
0   25   50
0   25 50 75
KILOMETERS

CANARY ISLANDS (SPAIN)

La Palma

Cigars

Tenerife
Santa Cruz
de Tenerife
Tourism

Gomera

Camel

Lanzarote

Goat

Fuerteventura

Bananas
Las
Palmas

Hierro
Pineapples

Grand
Canary

MILES
0   25   50   75
0   50   100   150
KILOMETERS

AZORES
MADEIRA
CANARY ISLANDS

FLAMENCO DANCER
Flamenco is a style of music and dance created by the gypsies of southern Spain. Dancers in colorful costumes are accompanied by guitarists and singers.

FRANCE

Bay of Biscay

Gijón
Oviedo
Santander
MOUNTAINS
Brown bear
Altamira cave paintings
Bilbao
Iron and steel
Basque folk dancer
Donostia-San Sebastián
Running of the bulls
Pamplona
PYRENEES
Bearded vulture
Pico de Aneto 11,168 ft (3,404 m)
ANDORRA
ANDORRA
Vacationer
COSTA BRAVA

Wheat
Potatoes
Valladolid
Douro
Wild boars
Saragossa
Torre de Aragón
Beef cattle
Barley
Ebro
Wine
Textiles
Sagrada Familia church
Barcelona

Holy Week procession
Segovia
Alcazar
Salamanca
Wheat
El Escorial
High-tech industries
Statue of Don Quixote and Sancho Panza
Spanish guitarist
Olives
Oranges
Paella
Sardines
Oil
BALEARIC ISLANDS
Minorca
Jara Gate
Palma
Olives
Mahón
Majorca

MADRID
Toledo
MESETA
SPAIN
Tagus
Bullfighting
Guadiana
Car manufacturing
Farmhouse
Valencia
Tourism
Ibiza
Ibiza
Tourism

Mezquita Mosqué
Wine
Sunflowers
Windmills of La Mancha
Collecting saffron
Alicante
SIERRA MORENA
Guadalquivir
Córdoba
Olives
Alhambra Palace
Flamenco dancer
Citrus fruit
Murcia
Fishing boat
Mediterranean Sea

Seville
Granada
Mulhacén 11,407 ft (3,477 m)
Almería
Cartagena
Andalucian ranch hand
Tajo Bridge
Málaga
Tourism
COSTA DEL SOL
Sailing

GIBRALTAR (U.K.)
Algeciras
Ceuta (SPAIN)
Sardines

MOROCCO
Melilla (SPAIN)
ALGERIA

LOCATION

◆ AMAZING FACT ◆

Two-thirds of the world's cork is produced in Spain and Portugal. Cork is obtained from the thick bark of the cork oak tree and is used to make bottle stoppers, shoes, floor coverings and bulletin boards.

SAGRADA FAMILIA CHURCH
The spires of this Barcelona church are covered with shells and ceramics, and stand 350 foot (110 m) high. The building was begun in 1884. More than 100 years later, it is still being built.

SCALE
MILES
0   25   50   75   100
0   50   100   150
KILOMETERS

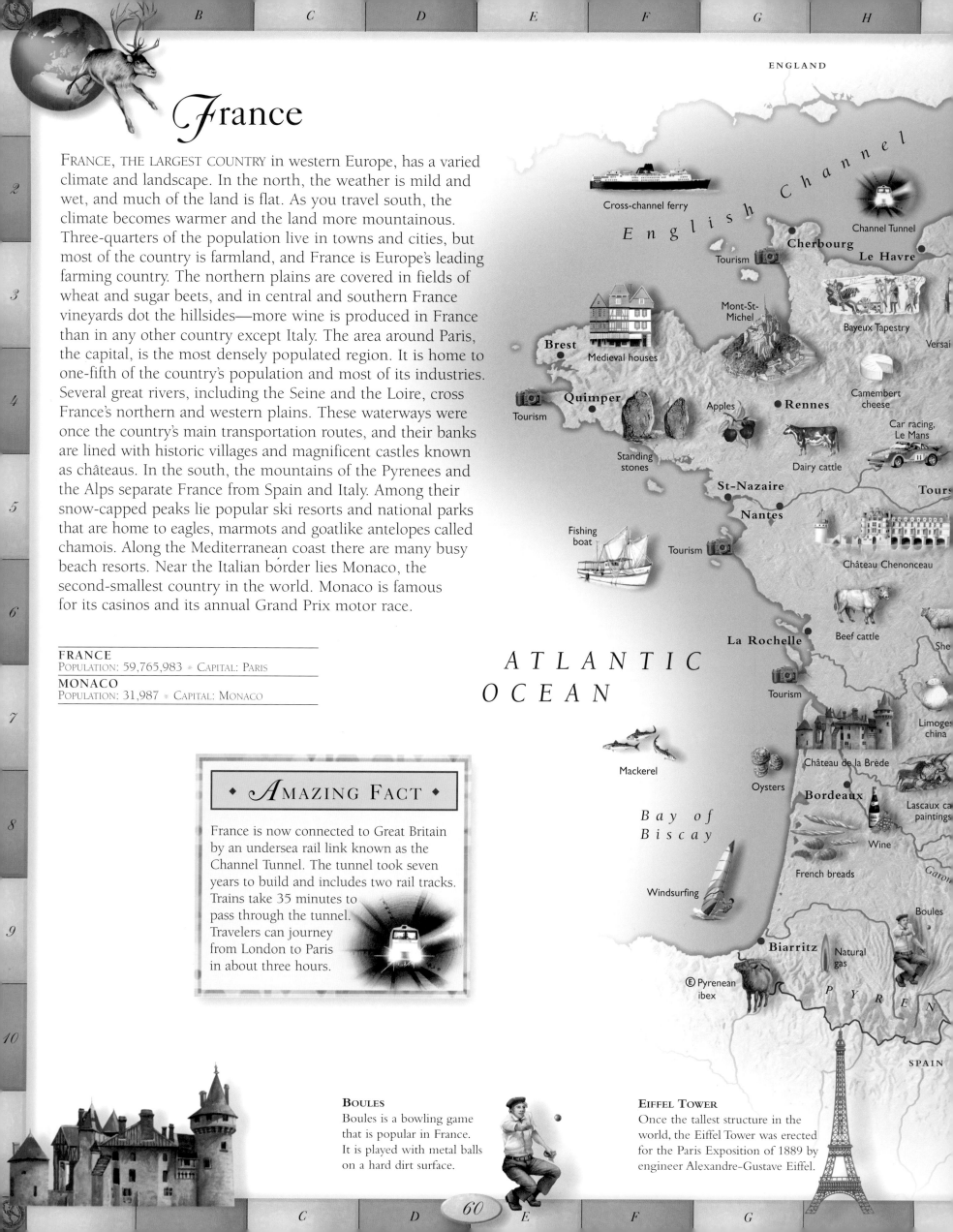

France

FRANCE, THE LARGEST COUNTRY in western Europe, has a varied climate and landscape. In the north, the weather is mild and wet, and much of the land is flat. As you travel south, the climate becomes warmer and the land more mountainous. Three-quarters of the population live in towns and cities, but most of the country is farmland, and France is Europe's leading farming country. The northern plains are covered in fields of wheat and sugar beets, and in central and southern France vineyards dot the hillsides—more wine is produced in France than in any other country except Italy. The area around Paris, the capital, is the most densely populated region. It is home to one-fifth of the country's population and most of its industries. Several great rivers, including the Seine and the Loire, cross France's northern and western plains. These waterways were once the country's main transportation routes, and their banks are lined with historic villages and magnificent castles known as châteaus. In the south, the mountains of the Pyrenees and the Alps separate France from Spain and Italy. Among their snow-capped peaks lie popular ski resorts and national parks that are home to eagles, marmots and goatlike antelopes called chamois. Along the Mediterranean coast there are many busy beach resorts. Near the Italian border lies Monaco, the second-smallest country in the world. Monaco is famous for its casinos and its annual Grand Prix motor race.

FRANCE
POPULATION: 59,765,983 ∗ CAPITAL: PARIS
MONACO
POPULATION: 31,987 ∗ CAPITAL: MONACO

♦ AMAZING FACT ♦

France is now connected to Great Britain by an undersea rail link known as the Channel Tunnel. The tunnel took seven years to build and includes two rail tracks. Trains take 35 minutes to pass through the tunnel. Travelers can journey from London to Paris in about three hours.

**Map labels:**

ENGLAND

English Channel

Cross-channel ferry
Channel Tunnel
Tourism
Cherbourg
Le Havre
Bayeux Tapestry
Versai
Mont-St-Michel
Medieval houses
Brest
Camembert cheese
Quimper
Apples
Rennes
Tourism
Standing stones
Dairy cattle
Car racing, Le Mans
St-Nazaire
Tours
Nantes
Château Chenonceau
Fishing boat
Tourism
Beef cattle
La Rochelle
She
ATLANTIC OCEAN
Tourism
Limoges china
Mackerel
Château de la Brède
Oysters
Bordeaux
Bay of Biscay
Lascaux ca paintings
Wine
French breads
Garon
Windsurfing
Boules
Biarritz
Natural gas
Ⓔ Pyrenean ibex
P Y R E N
SPAIN

BOULES
Boules is a bowling game that is popular in France. It is played with metal balls on a hard dirt surface.

EIFFEL TOWER
Once the tallest structure in the world, the Eiffel Tower was erected for the Paris Exposition of 1889 by engineer Alexandre-Gustave Eiffel.

FRANCE *See World Fact File page 107*

Dunkerque
Calais
Boulogne
Lille
ssels
Nuclear energy
Potatoes
Sugar beets

BELGIUM

LUXEMBOURG

Dieppe
Amiens
Wheat

Rouen

Car manufacturing

PARIS
Fashion

Chartres Cathedral
Eiffel Tower

FRANCE

Cafe

Reims
Metz
Champagne
Iron ore
Iron and steel

GERMANY

Nuclear energy
Coal

Nancy
Wine

Strasbourg

Folk costume

Troyes

Gaul fort

Chapel of Notre Dame du Haut

Château de Chambord
Bourges

Dijon
Mustard

Besançon
Mountain climbing

T.G.V. high-speed train

Doubs

Dairy cattle

SWITZERLAND

Snail

Farmer with goats
Coal

Tungsten

Playing the cabrette

Textiles

Marmot

Lyon

Chapel of St-Michel D'Aiguilhe

French breads

Wine

St-Étienne

Mont Blanc
15,771 ft (4,807 m)

Chamois

Grenoble

Skiing

ITALY

Hunting for truffles

Geese

Nuclear energy

Avignon
Harvesting lavender

Perfume

Casino, Monte Carlo

MONACO

Mackerel

Nice
Cannes

Aircraft manufacturing

Toulouse
Montpellier

Walled town of Carcassonne

Cannes Film Festival

Marseille
Tourism

Pont du Gard

Sailing
Flamingo

Waterskiing

Perpignan

ORRA

Solar furnace

Mediterranean Sea

Osprey

Corsica
Tourism

Ajaccio

Statue of Napoleon

TOUR DE FRANCE
France's most famous sporting event, this cycle race around the entire country covers about 2,500 miles (4,000 km).

• PROJECT: *Cave Painting* •

The cave paintings at Lascaux were created about 15,000 years ago. Here's how you can create your own painting that will look thousands of years old.

❶ Stuff a strong paper bag with crumpled newspaper and then staple the bag closed.

❷ Mix some glue and sand and use this to paint the whole bag. When it dries it will look like a rock.

❸ Collect three or four different-colored soils. Sift out the lumps and then mix each color with glue to make earth paints (add water if the paints are too thick). Now you are ready to paint. Like the artists who created the Lascaux cave paintings, you can paint animals living in your area.

• LOOK AGAIN •

● Which cathedral lies southwest of Paris?

● Name a horned animal found in the Pyrenees.

● What kind of food is produced in Dijon?

● Which small country is located east of Nice?

LOCATION

N
W   E
S

SCALE
MILES
0   25   50   75   100
0   50   100   150
KILOMETERS

The Low Countries

THE DENSELY POPULATED COUNTRIES of the Netherlands (also called Holland), Belgium and Luxembourg are known as the Low Countries because they have no high mountains and few hills. Much of the land, including one-third of the Netherlands, actually lies below sea level. Over the centuries, local people have built large barriers known as dikes to keep the sea out, pumped water out of the marshes behind the dikes to create areas of new land called polders, and constructed thousands of miles of canals. Throughout the region, barges chug along these waterways, past windmills, dairy farms and colorful fields of tulips—both Belgium and the Netherlands export flowers and bulbs all over the world. The capital of the Netherlands, Amsterdam, has more than 150 canals, many of which are lined with tall, narrow, 17th-century buildings. In Belgium, canals link the country's ports to the historic cities of Bruges and Ghent, and to Brussels, the capital. Brussels is often referred to as the capital of Europe because it is the headquarters of the European Union (EU). Southeast of Brussels lies the only high part of the Low Countries, the Ardennes. This range of forest-covered hills spreads across the northern half of Luxembourg, one of Europe's smallest countries but also one of its most important financial centers.

BELGIUM
POPULATION: 10,274,595 • CAPITAL: BRUSSELS

LUXEMBOURG
POPULATION: 448,569 • CAPITAL: LUXEMBOURG

THE NETHERLANDS
POPULATION: 16,067,754 • CAPITALS: AMSTERDAM, THE HAGUE

THE ATOMIUM
The Atomium represents an iron molecule and is one of the rare remains of the World Exhibition held in Brussels in 1958.

◆ AMAZING FACT ◆

The Low Countries have more than 5,000 miles (8,000 km) of canals, which are used for transportation and for draining the land. Because much of the region lies below sea level, water has to be pumped into canals built high above ground level. You could be standing in a field in the Low Countries and see a ship pass by above your head!

THE NETHERLANDS

Wheat
Natural gas
Groningen
Prehistoric hunebed (burial tomb)
Sheep
Dairy cattle
Cycling
Clogs
Beef cattle
Pigs
Folk dancers
Leeuwarden
Tourism
Potatos
Windmill
Dairy cattle
Zuider Zee folk costume
Poultry
Beef cattle
Apeldoorn
Eurasian spoonbill
Arnhem
Rhine
Soccer
Dom Cathedral tower
Utrecht
Amsterdam
AMSTERDAM
Lek
Fruit
Delft
Flowers
Diamond cutting
Tulips
Alkmaar
Iron and steel
Alkmaar cheese market
Haarlem
Herring
Mackerel
Peace Palace
THE HAGUE
Rotterdam
Container ship
Ijsselmeer
Waddenzee
WEST FRISIAN ISLANDS
Terschelling
Ameland
Harbor seals
Vlieland
Texel

LOCATION

CLOGS
Worn by Dutch farmers, these traditional wooden shoes help keep feet warm and dry in damp fields. They are known locally as *klompen*.

LUXEMBOURG
Wine
National Savings Bank
★ LUXEMBOURG
Iron and steel
Esch-sur-Alzette

Red squirrel

ALKMAAR CHEESE MARKET
Every Friday during summer in the Dutch town of Alkmaar, round balls of cheese are carried to the market on traditional wooden "sledges."

GERMANY

Maas

Rye
Vegetables
Eindhoven
High-tech industries
Dairy cattle
Wheat
Bicycle racing
Crystal
Liège
Iron and steel
Meuse
Red deer
A R D E N N E S
Ardennes
Wild boars

's Hertogenbosch Cathedral
Tilburg
Breda
BAARLE-HERTOG (BELGIUM)
Vegetables
Sugar beets
Antwerp
Chemicals
Diamond cutting
Atomium building
✪ **BRUSSELS**
Beer
Louvain Town Hall
Sugar beets
Chocolate
Beef cattle
Fortress and town of Dinant
Sambre

BELGIUM

Delta Dam
Mussels
Oysters
Wheat
Dockside cranes, Antwerp port
Iron and steel
Ghent
High-tech industries
Brugge
Vegetables
Ghent
Textiles
Dairy cattle
Wheat
F L A N D E R S
FRANCE
Barley
Ostende
Tourism
Damme Canal
Pigs
Sugar beets

N o r t h   S e a

N E S W

SCALE
MILES
0 10 20 30
0 10 20 30 40 50
KILOMETERS

◆ PROJECT: *Make a Paper Windmill* ◆

At one time, much of the land in the western part of the Netherlands lay under water. Windmills were used to pump and drain water from land as well as to grind grain. Windmills harness the force of the wind to produce energy. The wind turns the sails of the windmill, which are connected to a pillar. This pillar transmits the energy through a system of gears to a vertical shaft that carries the power to a water pump or mill. You can make a paper windmill and power it by blowing on it.

❶ Cut a 7½- x 7½-inch (19- x 19-cm) piece of paper. Draw an X across the paper. Using a large coin or a compass, trace a circle in the center of the square.

❷ Cut along the four diagonal lines up to the edge of the circle. Without folding the paper, bend every other point in to the center of the circle.

❸ Stick a pushpin through the center of the circle and through all the bent-in points. Now stick the pushpin into the side of the eraser at the end of a pencil. Hold the windmill by the pencil tip and blow on it.

Western Central Europe

AFTER WORLD WAR II, GERMANY was divided into two countries: East Germany and West Germany. They were reunited in 1990 and Germany is now home to more than 80 million people, the largest population of any European country except Russia. Many of Germany's cities lie on rivers. The Rhine River connects the country's most important industrial region, the Ruhr Valley, to the ports of the Netherlands and the Swiss city of Basel. On its journey northward, the Rhine meanders past forests of spruce and fir, steep hillsides covered with vineyards, and cliffs crowned by medieval castles. From southern Germany, the spectacular Alps mountain range stretches across the countries of Switzerland and Austria, where it covers about two-thirds of the land. Throughout these mountains, roads and railways wind through narrow river valleys and cross steep passes. In summer, cows graze in the alpine meadows; in winter, skiers hurtle down the slopes. Switzerland is a peaceful country which hasn't been involved in a war since 1814. This has encouraged people from all over the world to deposit money in Swiss banks, and the country is now a leading financial center. In Austria, many farms and industries lie on the northeastern lowlands. This area is crossed by the Danube, Europe's second-longest river. The Danube passes through Austria's capital, Vienna—home to one-fifth of Austria's population and one of Europe's grandest cities.

AUSTRIA
POPULATION: 8,169,929 • CAPITAL: VIENNA

GERMANY
POPULATION: 83,251,851 • CAPITAL: BERLIN

LIECHTENSTEIN
POPULATION: 32,842 • CAPITAL: VADUZ

SWITZERLAND
POPULATION: 7,301,994 • CAPITAL: BERN

◆ PROJECT: *Swiss Chocolate Fondue* ◆

The Swiss eat a dish called fondue, which is often made from cheese. Pieces of bread are dipped in a mixture of hot melted cheese and white wine. This fondue is different—it's made with chocolate!

❶ Place 8 oz (250 g) semisweet chocolate pieces into a saucepan with 1 cup (8 oz/250 ml) whipping cream.

❷ Ask an adult to help you warm the ingredients gently until the chocolate has melted. Beat the mixture until it becomes glossy.

❸ Let the mixture cool a little. Then spear a piece of fruit (strawberries or grapes are good) on a fork, dip it in the fondue and have a taste. Yum!

◆ AMAZING FACT ◆

The country of Liechtenstein is home to only 32,842 people and is just four miles (6 km) wide. That means you could walk across it in less than two hours! The prince of Liechtenstein lives in this castle at Vaduz, the capital.

SCALE

ALPENHORN
For hundreds of years, the farmers of the Swiss Alps used these gigantic wooden horns to call in their cattle from high mountain pastures.

NEUSCHWANSTEIN CASTLE
This spectacular building was the model for the fairy-tale castles in Walt Disney theme parks. It was built in the late 19th century by King Ludwig II.

LIPIZZANER HORSE
Lipizzaners are trained to perform graceful steps and leaps at the Winter Riding School in Vienna. They are named after the town of Lipizza in Slovenia where they were first bred.

Italy

ITALY CONSISTS OF A LONG, boot-shaped peninsula, the large islands of Sicily and Sardinia, and about 70 smaller islands. Within Italy lie two other countries: San Marino in the east, and the Vatican City (the world's smallest country) in the city of Rome. The Vatican City is the home of the Pope, the head of the Roman Catholic Church. Most of mainland Italy is mountainous. The Alps form a great arc around the northern border, and the Apennines stretch almost the entire length of the peninsula. Between these two mountain ranges lies the Northern Plain, a flat, fertile region drained by the Po River. This plain has Italy's richest farmland and is home to the country's most important industries, including the car factories of Turin, and Milan's fashion and design houses.

Each year, more than 50 million tourists travel to Italy to visit its ancient ruins, historic cities and museums, and to enjoy the sunny summer weather. The country's mild climate allows farmers to grow large quantities of wheat, citrus fruit, olives and grapes—Italy is the world's leading producer of olive oil and wine. Parts of Italy are regularly rocked by earthquakes, and the country has the only active volcanoes on mainland Europe. On the island of Sicily, Mount Etna has erupted at least 260 times since the first recorded eruption in 70 BC. About 60 miles (95 km) south of Sicily lie the islands of Malta. At various times in its history, Malta was ruled by the Romans, Arabs, Turks, French and British. It is now an independent republic.

ITALY
POPULATION: 57,715,625 • CAPITAL: ROME

MALTA
POPULATION: 397,499 • CAPITAL: VALLETTA

SAN MARINO
POPULATION: 27,730 • CAPITAL: SAN MARINO

VATICAN CITY
POPULATION: 900 • CAPITAL: VATICAN CITY

◆ AMAZING FACT ◆

The Leaning Tower of Pisa was constructed as a bell tower between AD 1173 and 1370. Unfortunately, it was built on unstable ground, and it began to sink and tilt to one side after completion of the first three stories. Although the tower leans about 15 feet (4.5 m) out of line, it has recently been stabilized so that it will not fall over.

MOUNT VESUVIUS AND POMPEII
In AD 79, Mount Vesuvius erupted, burying the town of Pompeii under stone and ash. The ruins were not discovered until the 18th century.

COLOSSEUM
This Roman stadium was built in the first century AD and used for events such as gladiator contests. It was even flooded for mock sea battles.

SLOVENIA

CROATIA

Chamois

Rock climbing

Corn

Trieste

Gulf of Venice

Sole

AUSTRIA

Pinnacles of the Dolomites

Rialto Bridge

Venice

Church of San Vitale

Ravenna

Rimini

⭑**SAN MARINO**

SAN MARINO

Marmot

Bolzano

Dairy cattle

Verona

Padua

Wheat

Po

Rocca Tower, San Marino

Ancona

D O L O M I T E S

Skiing

Violin making

Lake Garda

Sugar beets

Rice

Ferrara

Bologna

Florence Cathedral

A P E N N I N

SWITZERLAND

Brescia

Parma Baptistry

Modena

Parma

Parmesan cheese

Florence Cathedral

Florence

Chianti wine

Arezzo

Siena

Lake Como

Car manufacturing

Rice

Milan Cathedral

Arno

Pisa

Livorno

Monte Rosa 15,203 ft (4,634 m)

Lake Maggiore

Fashion

Milan

Marble

La Spezia

Leaning Tower of Pisa

Matterhorn 14,691 ft (4,478 m)

Hydroelectricity

Car manufacturing

Turin

Walnuts

Genoa

Fishing boat

Ligurian Sea

Mont Blanc 15,771 ft (4,807 m)

FRANCE

A L P S

Skiing

Wine

Rice

Tourism

Olives

Squid

Elba

N

E

S

W

LOCATION

Strait of Otranto

Adriatic Sea

Ionian Sea

Winemaking

Trulli houses

Crabs

Brindisi

Bari

Oysters

Taranto

Gulf of Taranto

Appian Way (Roman road)

Vesuvius and the ruins of Pompeii Forum

Octopus

Potatoes

Foggia

Sea horse

Red mullet

Oil

Olives

Pescara

Wolf

Abbey of Monte Cassino

Soccer

Pizza maker

Naples

Mt. Vesuvius 4,190 ft (1,277m)

Salerno

Capri

Ischia

Wine

Goats

Olives

Wall lizard

Cosenza

Sheep

Reggio di Calabria

Great barracuda

Oranges

Anchovies

Garfish

LIPARI ISLANDS

Stromboli

Tourism

Citrus fruit

Mt. Etna 10,902 ft (3,323 m)

Messina

Tourism

Syracuse

Sicily

Temple of Concordia

Palermo

Wheat

Oil

SAN MARINO
The smallest republic in Europe and the oldest republic in the world, San Marino was founded around AD 300 by Christians fleeing religious persecution.

Ustica

Swordfish

Wine

Sardines

Mediterranean Sea

Tourism

MALTA ★ VALLETTA

Basilica, Vatican City

Tiber

ITALY

VATICAN CITY ★ ROME

Vatican guard

Colosseum

Container ship

Sunflowers

Giglio

Olives

Sardines

Iron ore

Goats

Sheep

Olives

Sassari

Sardinia

Woman in folk costume

Cagliari

Tourism

Tyrrhenian Sea

Scuba diving

Bluefin tuna

Sardines

CORSICA (FRANCE)

SCALE
MILES
0 25 50 75 150
KILOMETERS
0 50 100

◆ PROJECT: *Making a Mosaic* ◆

A mosaic is a design made by pressing small pieces of cut stone or colored glass into a soft plaster surface. In ancient Rome, the walls and floors of public places and private homes were decorated with mosaics. There are many colorful mosaics in the Church of San Vitale in Ravenna, which were made around AD 526–47. You can make your own mosaic using tiny pieces of colored paper instead of stone or glass.

❶ Cut ¼-inch (0.5-cm) squares out of several sheets of different-colored paper.

❷ On a surface of white or colored paper, draw the outline of a simple design for your mosaic. It could be a landscape, a flower, an animal or even a portrait of a friend.

❸ To create your mosaic, carefully glue the tiny pieces of paper close together within the outlines of your design.

Southeastern Europe

THIS REGION IS OFTEN REFERRED TO as the Balkans. It lies at the edge of Europe, close to Asia, and is home to many peoples from both continents. Throughout history, disputes between countries and ethnic groups have occurred here regularly. In 1991, the republics of Slovenia, Croatia, Bosnia and Herzegovina, and Macedonia declared their independence from Yugoslavia. This led to a war that destroyed cities, farms and industries, and left thousands of people homeless. Most of southeastern Europe is rugged and mountainous. Along the coast of Croatia, rocky slopes rise steeply from the water. Inland, forests and farms surround the peaks that spread eastward through Yugoslavia and into Romania and Bulgaria. In Bulgaria's Balkan

Mountains, an area known as the Valley of the Roses produces more than two-thirds of the world's rose oil, an essential ingredient in most perfumes. Southeastern Europe's best farmland lies along the Danube River, which connects many of the region's towns to the ports of the Black Sea. In Greece, overgrazing by sheep and goats has stripped some of the land of trees and shrubs, but the warm climate allows farmers to grow olives, grapes, citrus fruit and wheat. Greece's sunny weather and scenic attractions bring tourists from all over the world. In Athens, home to one-third of Greece's population, rush-hour traffic roars past 2,000-year-old temples. On the Greek islands, clusters of white buildings cling to cliffs, and fishing boats drift across clear turquoise bays.

ALBANIA
POPULATION: 3,544,841 ◆ CAPITAL: TIRANË

BOSNIA AND HERZEGOVINA
POPULATION: 3,964,388 ◆ CAPITAL: SARAJEVO

BULGARIA
POPULATION: 7,621,337 ◆ CAPITAL: SOFIA

CROATIA
POPULATION: 4,390,751 ◆ CAPITAL: ZAGREB

GREECE
POPULATION: 10,645,343 ◆ CAPITAL: ATHENS

MACEDONIA
POPULATION: 2,054,800 ◆ CAPITAL: SKOPJE

ROMANIA
POPULATION: 22,317,730 ◆ CAPITAL: BUCHAREST

SLOVENIA
POPULATION: 1,932,917 ◆ CAPITAL: LJUBLJANA

YUGOSLAVIA
POPULATION: 10,656,929 ◆ CAPITAL: BELGRADE

SCALE

MILES

KILOMETERS

LOCATION

Map labels

Black Sea

ITALY

Adriatic Sea

Shipka Memorial Church

SOFIA
Food processing
Plovdiv
Mt Musala 9,596 ft (2,925 m)
Tobacco
Wheat
RHODOPE MTS.
Skiing
Struma
TURKEY

Podgorica
Copper
Shkodër
Black kite
Durrës
Corn
Vlorë
Inspecting carpets
KOSOVO
Eastern Orthodox Church
SKOPJE
MACEDONIA
Bitola
Korçë
ALBANIA
TIRANË
Vardar
Iron and steel
Goats
Cotton
Bouzouki
Monastery, Meteora
Mt. Olympus 9,570 ft (2,917 m)

Greek Orthodox monk
Thessaloniki
Volos
NORTHERN SPORADES
GREECE
Wine
Ruins of Delphi
Levkás
Olives
Corfu
Tourism
IONIAN ISLANDS
Zákinthos
Cephalonia

Alexandroúpolis
TURKEY
Thásos
Samothráki
Lemnos
Sailing
Lesbos
Olives
Sardines
Skyros
Euboea
Khalkís
ATHENS
Piraeus
Parthenon
Evzones guards
Tripolis
Patras
PELOPONNESE
Kíthira
King Agamemnon's gold death mask
Ruins of Olympia

Aegean Sea
Chios
Mackerel
Lignite
Sámos
Tinos
Andros
Mykonos
Páros
Naxos
CYCLADES

DODECANESE
Rhodes
Kárpathos
Windmill
Traditional church
Thíra
Sea of Crete
Canea
Iráklion
Crete
Wine
Bull's head sculpture, Knossos

Mediterranean Sea
Ionian Sea
Cruise ship
Tourism

BLACK KITE
These birds of prey are found throughout southeastern Europe. At night, they roost in trees in huge flocks of as many as 100 birds.

CASTLE OF VLAD TEPES
Vlad Tepes, a 15th-century Romanian prince known as Vlad the Impaler, is said to have inspired the legend of Dracula the vampire.

EVZONES GUARDS
Wearing their traditional skirts and tasseled hats and shoes, the evzones stand guard outside the parliament in Athens.

◆ PROJECT: *Make a Cave* ◆

The Postojna Caves in Slovenia are famous for their stalactites and stalagmites. These formations took thousands of years to develop, but you can make your own cave with stalactites and stalagmites in just a few days.

❶ Draw a cave scene on the inside bottom of a shoe box. Line the outside and inside walls of the box with aluminum foil. Turn the box on its side so that the scene becomes the cave's back wall. Ask an adult to help you punch two holes close together at each end of the top of the box. Place a glass outside each end of the box.

❷ Thread a length of string in through one hole at one end and out through one hole at the other end. Repeat with the other two holes. Make sure the strings reach the bottom of each glass and hang down a little inside the cave.

❸ Fill the glasses with hot water and stir in washing soda until no more will dissolve. Make sure you wash your hands well after using the washing soda. Over the next few days, as the water soaks into the strings and then starts to evaporate, small salt formations will appear where the strings sag. At the same time, small mounds of salt will form where the water drips onto the cave floor. Gradually, these formations will grow into stalactites and stalagmites.

Eastern Europe

IN RECENT YEARS, MANY POLITICAL CHANGES have occurred within this vast region. During 1990 and 1991, the republics of Latvia, Estonia, Lithuania, Belarus, Moldova and the Ukraine, all formerly part of the Soviet Union, became independent countries. In 1993, Czechoslovakia divided into two countries, the Czech Republic and Slovakia. Mountains line the borders of the Czech Republic and cover most of Slovakia, but elsewhere eastern Europe is generally flat. Wide grasslands cover central Hungary and most of the Ukraine. In Poland, rivers that rise in the southern mountains meander northward across a wide plain of rich farmland toward coastal swamps and sand dunes. The Baltic States of Lithuania, Latvia and Estonia are covered with meadows, marshes and more than 9,000 lakes. Around the Baltic Sea, winters can be bitterly cold, and icebreaker ships often have to clear a path between the region's ports. About two-thirds of eastern Europe's people live in cities, and many work in heavy industries such as mining, steelmaking and shipbuilding. These industries have created serious pollution problems. Acid rain has destroyed forests in Poland and the Czech Republic, and people are no longer allowed to swim in some polluted lakes in Hungary. In the Ukraine and Belarus, large areas of land can no longer be farmed because they were contaminated by radioactivity after an accident at the Chernobyl nuclear power plant near Kiev in 1986. Despite this, the Ukraine remains one of the largest producers of wheat in the world.

◆ LOOK AGAIN ◆

- What kind of glassware is produced in the Czech Republic?
- Name a mineral that is mined in eastern Hungary.
- Ukrainians eat a soup called borscht. What is it made of?

BELARUS
POPULATION: 10,335,382 ◦ CAPITAL: MINSK

CZECH REPUBLIC
POPULATION: 10,256,760 ◦ CAPITAL: PRAGUE

ESTONIA
POPULATION: 1,415,681 ◦ CAPITAL: TALLINN

HUNGARY
POPULATION: 10,075,034 ◦ CAPITAL: BUDAPEST

LATVIA
POPULATION: 2,366,515 ◦ CAPITAL: RIGA

LITHUANIA
POPULATION: 3,601,138 ◦ CAPITAL: VILNIUS

MOLDOVA
POPULATION: 4,434,547 ◦ CAPITAL: CHIŞINĂU

POLAND
POPULATION: 38,625,478 ◦ CAPITAL: WARSAW

SLOVAKIA
POPULATION: 5,422,366 ◦ CAPITAL: BRATISLAVA

UKRAINE
POPULATION: 48,396,470 ◦ CAPITAL: KIEV

Black stork

Gulf

Riga

Pigs

Amber

Baltic Sea

Shipbuilding

Herring

KALININGRAD OBLAST (RUSSI

Gdańsk

Folk costumes

Timber

Camping

European bis

Szczecin

Chemicals

POLAND

Bydgoszcz

Horse-drawn sled

Royal Castle

GERMANY

Oder

Poznań

Food processing

Oleśnica Castle

★ **WARSAW**

Textiles

Church of Our Lady Before Tyn

Karkonosze Mountains

Łódź

Wheat

Pigs

Potatoes

SUDETEN MTS.

Wrocław

Iron and steel

Coal

Baroque houses

Brown bear

Plzeň

★ **Prague**

Car manufacturing

Bohemian crystal

CZECH REPUBLIC

Soccer

Katowice

Coal

Kraków

Vistula

B O H E M I A N   F O R E S T

Brno

SLOVAKIA

Stalagmites, Krásnohorská Cave

Bratislava Castle

Košice

AUSTRIA

BRATISLAVA

Hortobágy horseman

Bauxite (aluminum)

★ **BUDAPEST**

Debrec

SLOVENIA

Parliament Building

HUNGARY

Danube

Curing ham

CROATIA

Poultry

Corn

Pécs

YUGOSLAVIA

CHURCH OF OUR LADY BEFORE TYN
The towers of this 14th-century church are known as Adam and Eve towers because one (the right-hand tower) is larger than the other.

HORTOBÁGY HORSEMAN
The Hortobágy region of Hungary is a famous horse-breeding center. Locals pride themselves on their riding skills.

Map labels (left to right, top to bottom):

Gulf of Finland

Old Town, Tallinn

TALLINN
Tourism

ESTONIA

Lake Peipus

Beef cattle
Fallow deer

ga

LATVIA

RIGA
Food processing

Folk dancers

Daugava

HUANIA

Island Castle, Trakai

Timber

Vitsyebsk

Red foxes

Rye

Dnieper

RUSSIA

VILNIUS
Chemicals

Neman

Station Square

Flax

MINSK
High-tech industries

Mahilyow

Clocks and watches

BELARUS

Dairy cattle

Barley

Potatoes

Homyel´

Brest Fortress

Pripyat'

Folk costume

Cossack dancer

Osprey

Dairy cattle

Chernobyl nuclear reactor

St. Sophia's Cathedral

Tobacco

Kharkiv

Borscht (beet soup)

Natural gas

Wolf

Sugar beets

Porcelain manufacturing

KIEV
High-tech industries

Textiles

Hydroelectricity

Collecting corn

Manganese

Sugar beets

Wild boars

L´viv

Painted eggs

Car manufacturing

UKRAINE

Dnieper

Dnipropetrovs´k

Coal

Natural gas

Lynx

Geese

Wheat

Bug

Wheat

Iron and steel

Donets´k

CARPATHIAN MTS.

Wine

Dniester

Folk dancers

Hydroelectricity

Kakhovka Reservoir

Corn

Wildcat

Prut

RUSSIA

ROMANIA

MOLDOVA

Sunflowers

CHIŞINĂU

Odessa

Tourism

Swallow's Nest Castle

Caviar

E Sturgeon

Sea of Azov

Harvesting hay

Wheat

Fishing boat

Wine

Food processing

Sevastopol´

CRIMEAN MTS.

Black Sea

EUROPEAN BISON
Bison once roamed through the forests of Europe. They still live in their natural environment in parts of Poland.

◆ PROJECT: *Painted Eggs* ◆

Symbols of rebirth and a new beginning, decorated eggs are an Easter tradition in eastern Europe. It's easy to paint an egg—the tricky part is preparing the shell. Take the raw eggs out of the refrigerator a few hours before you start. If they are too cold, they will be hard to blow.

❶ Take an egg and gently prick the larger end of the shell with a pin. Chip the shell away until the hole is about ¼-inch (0.5 cm) across.

❷ Make a tiny hole in the smaller end. Put your fingers over both holes and gently shake the egg to break up the yolk. Hold the egg over a dish and blow through the small hole. The insides of the egg will slowly empty into the dish. Rinse the eggshell with water and let it dry.

❸ Now you are ready to paint. Carefully thread a piece of stiff wire through the holes in the shell. Hold the egg by the wire and paint your design on it.

❹ Lay the wire across a bowl so the painted egg can dry without being touched.

LOCATION

SCALE
MILES
0 50 100 150
0 50 100 150 200 250
KILOMETERS

Northern Europe

THE COUNTRIES OF NORTHERN EUROPE are known as the Nordic countries. They are sometimes called Scandinavia, but strictly speaking this name refers only to the wide peninsula occupied by Norway and Sweden. On the western side of this peninsula, fjords—spectacular, steep-sided bays formed by glaciers—and more than 150,000 islands create a maze of waterways. Inland, mountain peaks and high plateaus cover most of Norway. To the east, the marshy plains of Sweden and Finland are studded with thousands of lakes and cloaked in coniferous forests that are home to moose, brown bears and wolves. The northern half of this region has a cold climate, with long, dark, snowy winters. In the far south, the climate is more temperate and the land more fertile.

Only one-twentieth of Norway can be farmed, but more than three-quarters of Denmark is used for agriculture. There is little farmland on Iceland, a volcanic island which lies 600 miles (1,000 km) west of Norway. The island's barren interior consists mainly of volcanoes, hot springs and lava fields. Parts of Iceland are so like the surface of the moon that astronauts trained there for moon landings. Some upland areas are covered by huge sheets of ice. Vatnajökull, an ice sheet in the southeast, is larger than all the glaciers in Europe combined.

DENMARK
POPULATION: 5,368,854 • CAPITAL: COPENHAGEN
FINLAND
POPULATION: 5,183,545 • CAPITAL: HELSINKI
ICELAND
POPULATION: 279,384 • CAPITAL: REYKJAVÍK
NORWAY
POPULATION: 4,525,116 • CAPITAL: OSLO
SWEDEN
POPULATION: 8,876,744 • CAPITAL: STOCKHOLM

◆ PROJECT: Sami Tent ◆

Some of the nomadic Sami people of Northern Europe still live in tents made from reindeer skins stretched over poles. These tents are easily set up and taken down as the Sami follow their grazing herds of reindeer. Here's an easy way to make a model of a Sami home.

1 Use several straws for the poles. Loosely tie one end of the straws together with string. Spread out the other ends of the straws to form the base of the tent.

2 Now use parchment paper for the reindeer-skin covering. Roll the paper into a cone shape and tape it together. Leave a hole at the top of the cone (real Sami tents have a large smoke hole at the top). Slip the cone over the straws and cut an opening for the door.

3 You can also create a full-size Sami tent for backyard camping. Use bamboo poles about 4 to 5 feet (1.2 to 1.5 m) long, canvas and strong twine.

LITTLE MERMAID STATUE
At the edge of Copenhagen harbor sits this statue of the main character in Danish author Hans Christian Andersen's much-loved fairy tale, *The Little Mermaid*.

ST. ANDREW'S CHURCH
Built about AD 1150 in Norway, this wooden church stands more than four stories tall. Its gables are carved in the shape of dragons, important symbols in Viking mythology.

LOCATION

NORWAY
DENMARK
ESTONIA
LATVIA
POLAND.
GERMANY

JOTUNHEIM MOUNTAINS
Galdhøpiggen 8,100 ft (2,469 m)

ÅLAND ISLANDS

Gulf of Finland
Gulf of Bothnia
Baltic Sea
North Sea
Skagerrak
Nordfjord
Sognefjord
Osterdal
Indal
Lake Vänern
Lake Vättern
Gotland
Öland
Bornholm
Sjælland
Fyn
Lolland

Kuopio — Hydroelectricity
Joensuu
Jyväskylä — Paper
Trout
Lake Saimaa
Lahti
Helsinki Cathedral
HELSINKI
Kick-sledding
Timber
Ice pool
Vaasa
Pori
Tampere
Turku
Dairy cattle
Hydrofoil

Capercaillie
Hydroelectricity
Sundsvall
Traditional church and bell tower
Folk dancing
Cross-country skiing
Drottningholm Palace
Fiddle player in national dress
Uppsala
STOCKHOLM
Parliament building
Norrköping
Linköping
Örebro
Iron and steel
Karlstad
Borås
Göteborg
Jönköping
Orrefors glass
Kalmar Castle
Hälsingborg
Malmö
Pigs

Icebreaker ship

Trondheim
Traditional storehouse
Chemicals
Ski jumping
Skiing
Drammen
OSLO
Fredrikstad
Shipbuilding
Jarlsberg cheese
Hydroelectricity
St. Andrew's Church
Kristiansand
Ice fishing
Bergen
Bergen wharf
Stavanger
Natural gas
Oil rig
Fishing boat

Ålborg
Little Mermaid statue
COPENHAGEN
Odense
DENMARK
Århus
Esbjerg
Legoland
Egeskov Castle
Pigs
Cod
Folk costume
Car manufacturing

Asia

THE WORLD'S BIGGEST CONTINENT, Asia stretches almost halfway around the globe and covers one-third of Earth's landmass. It has the world's tallest mountains, the world's largest lake and the world's lowest point on land. It was the birthplace of many great religions and important civilizations, and is now home to 60 percent of the people on Earth. Most Asians live in the east and south, where the climate is warm and wet and there are large areas of forest, fertile plains and hundreds of tropical islands. Deserts and barren mountain ranges dominate the southwest and center of the continent. To the north, the grasslands, or steppes, of central Asia give way to the immense coniferous forests of Russia. A belt of freezing tundra extends along the continent's north coast. Russia is the world's largest country by area, but China has the world's largest population.

CONTINENT FACTS

Regional land area: 17,139,445 sq. miles (44,391,162 sq. km) (excluding European Russia)
Regional population: 3,806,418,195 (excluding European Russia)
Independent countries: Afghanistan, Armenia, Azerbaijan, Bahrain, Bangladesh, Bhutan, Brunei, Cambodia, China, Cyprus, East Timor, Georgia, India, Indonesia, Iran, Iraq, Israel, Japan, Jordan, Kazakstan, Kuwait, Kyrgyzstan, Laos, Lebanon, Malaysia, Maldives, Mongolia, Myanmar (Burma), Nepal, North Korea, Oman, Pakistan, Philippines, Qatar, Russia, Saudi Arabia, Singapore, South Korea, Sri Lanka, Syria, Taiwan, Tajikistan, Thailand, Turkey, Turkmenistan, United Arab Emirates, Uzbekistan, Vietnam, Yemen

MAJOR MOUNTAINS AND RIVERS

Mount Everest, China-Nepal 29,035 ft (8,850 m)
K2, China-Pakistan 28,250 ft (8,611 m)
Kanchenjunga, India-Nepal 28,169 ft (8,586 m)
Annapurna, Nepal 26,504 ft (8,078 m)
Kommunizma, Tajikistan 24,590 ft (7,495 m)
Mount Ararat, Turkey 16,945 ft (5,165 m)

Chang (Yangtze) 3,960 miles (6,380 km)
Yenisey-Angara 3,445 miles (5,550 km)
Huang (Yellow) 3,395 miles (5,464 km)
Ob'-Irtysh 3,360 miles (5,410 km)
Mekong 2,795 miles (4,500 km)
Lena 2,730 miles (4,400 km)

WORLD RECORDS

WORLD'S HIGHEST MOUNTAIN
MOUNT EVEREST, CHINA-NEPAL, 29,035 FT (8,850 M)

WORLD'S LOWEST POINT ON LAND
DEAD SEA, ISRAEL-JORDAN, 1,348 FT (411 M) BELOW SEA LEVEL

WORLD'S LARGEST LAKE BY AREA
CASPIAN SEA, WESTERN ASIA, 143,550 SQ. MILES (371,800 SQ. KM)

WORLD'S OLDEST, DEEPEST AND LARGEST (BY VOLUME) LAKE
LAKE BAIKAL, RUSSIA, 25 MILLION YEARS OLD; 5,371 FT (1,637 M) DEEP; 5,500 CUBIC MILES (23,000 CUBIC KM) OF WATER

WORLD'S LARGEST COUNTRY BY AREA
RUSSIA, 6,592,812 SQ. MILES (17,075,383 SQ. KM)

WORLD'S LARGEST COUNTRY BY POPULATION
CHINA, POPULATION 1,284,303,705

WORLD'S LARGEST CITY BY POPULATION
TOKYO, JAPAN, POPULATION 33,418,366

WORLD'S LONGEST WALL
GREAT WALL OF CHINA, 2,150 MILES (3,460 KM)

WORLD'S LONGEST RAILWAY LINE
TRANS-SIBERIAN, RUSSIA, 5,777 MILES (9,297 KM)

POLITICAL MAP

RUSSIA
KAZAKSTAN
MONGOLIA
GEORGIA
UZBEKISTAN KYRGYZSTAN
TURKEY
TURKMENISTAN
TAJIKISTAN
CYPRUS
SYRIA
IRAQ
JORDAN
IRAN
AFGHANISTAN
PAKISTAN
NEPAL
CHINA
NORTH KOREA
SOUTH KOREA
JAPAN
TAIWAN
INDIA
SAUDI ARABIA
OMAN
YEMEN
MYANMAR (BURMA)
LAOS
THAILAND
PHILIPPINES
CAMBODIA
VIETNAM
SRI LANKA
MALDIVES
MALAYSIA
INDONESIA
EAST TIMOR

CONTINENT RECORDS

LONGEST RIVER
CHANG (YANGTZE), 3,960 MILES (6,380 KM)

KEY TO NUMBERED COUNTRIES

1 ARMENIA	7 QATAR
2 AZERBAIJAN	8 UNITED ARAB EMIRATES
3 LEBANON	9 BHUTAN
4 ISRAEL	10 BANGLADESH
5 KUWAIT	■ 11 SINGAPORE
■ 6 BAHRAIN	12 BRUNEI

*P*HYSICAL MAP

ARCTIC OCEAN
× NORTH POLE

Barents Sea

Kara Sea

Laptev Sea

East Siberian Sea

Bering Sea

EUROPE

Arctic Circle

VERKHOYANSKI MTS.

KAMCHATKA PENINSULA

URAL MOUNTAINS

Ob

Yenisey

Angara

Lena

CENTRAL SIBERIAN PLATEAU

Sea of Okhotsk

Sakhalin

KURIL ISLANDS

WEST SIBERIAN PLAIN

Black Sea

▲ Mt. Elbrus

CAUCASUS MTS.

Mt. Ararat ▲

Caspian Sea

Irtysh

S I B E R I A

Amur

Lake Baikal

MANCHURIAN PLAIN

Sea of Japan (East Sea)

Hokkaidō

Honshū

SYRIAN DESERT

ZAGROS MTS.

Lake Balkhash

Aral Sea

ALTAY MTS.

GOBI DESERT

PLATEAU OF IRAN

TIEN MTS.

Kommunizma ▲

TAKLIMAKAN DESERT

▲ K2

Yellow Sea

Shikoku

Kyūshū

Persian Gulf

Red Sea

HINDU KUSH

Indus

HIMALAYAS

KUNLUN MTS.

PLATEAU OF TIBET

Huang (Yellow)

East China Sea

RYUKYU ISLANDS

Tropic of Cancer

ARABIAN PENINSULA

GREAT INDIAN DESERT

INDO-GANGETIC PLAIN

Ganges

Annapurna ▲
▲ Mt. Everest
▲ Kanchenjunga

Chang (Yangtze)

NAN MTS.

Gulf of Oman

Gulf of Aden

DECCAN

Bay of Bengal

Irrawaddy

Mekong

Taiwan

Hainan

Luzon

PHILIPPINE ISLANDS

Arabian Sea

ANDAMAN ISLANDS

Andaman Sea

South China Sea

Mindanao

MALDIVES

Sri Lanka

NICOBAR ISLANDS

MALAY PENINSULA

Gulf of Thailand

Equator

Borneo

MOLUCCAS

New Guinea

Sumatra

Sulawesi

GREATER SUNDA ISLANDS

Java Sea

Java

LESSER SUNDA ISLANDS

P A C I F I C   O C E A N

I N D I A N   O C E A N

A U S T R A L I A   A N D   O C E A N I A

Tropic of Capricorn

Russia

RUSSIA IS THE LARGEST country in the world. It covers two-thirds of Asia and one-third of Europe, and is so wide that it has eleven time zones. When the citizens of St. Petersburg are getting ready for bed, the miners and reindeer herders who live in the remote far east are already starting their next day's work. Most of Russia has a cold climate, with mild to cool summers and cold to freezing winters. In the far north, where most of the land is tundra, winter temperatures can drop to –94°F (–70°C). South of the tundra, a wide band of coniferous woodland stretches almost all the way across the country. The Ural Mountains divide Russia into two regions. West of the Urals is European Russia, which has only one-quarter of the land, but four-fifths of the population, the largest industries and the most fertile farmland. East of the Urals, in Asia, is Siberia, a vast wilderness region that is bigger than the United States and western Europe

combined. In the southern part of this region near Mongolia lies Lake Baikal, the world's deepest lake, which holds one-fifth of the world's fresh water. Siberia is also rich in minerals, such as coal and oil. The Chukchi Peninsula in eastern Siberia is the most easterly point in Asia. It lies only 50 miles (82 km) from North America. Before 1991, Russia was part of an even larger country—the Soviet Union—which also included 14 present-day countries in eastern Europe and central Eurasia.

RUSSIA
POPULATION: 144,978,573 ∙ CAPITAL: MOSCOW

ARCTIC

FRANZ JOSEF LAND

SEVERNAY ZEMLY

NOVAYA ZEMLYA

NORWAY

Icebreaker ship

Murmansk

Barents Sea

Kara Sea

Harp seals

Puffins

Haddock

Fishing through ice

Ptarmiga

Nickel and platinum

Natural gas

FINLAND

Iron ore and copper

KALININGRAD OBLAST (RUSSIA)

ESTONIA

LATVIA

LITHUANIA

Fabergé egg

St. Petersburg

Lake Ladoga

Lake Onega

Chess

Arkhangel'sk

Nenet woman

Coal

Troika

Dairy cattle

Demetrius Cathedral

URAL MOUNTAINS

Ob'

Khanty tribesmen

Oil

Woolly mammoth fossils

Yenisey

WEST SIBERIAN PLAIN

BELARUS

St. Basil's Cathedral

Ballet

Moscow

Yaroslavl'

Vyatka

Russian Orthodox priest

Rye

Iron ore

Steppe herder

Nizhniy Novgorod

Matreshka dolls

Church of the Nativity

Perm'

Kazan'

Bauxite (aluminum)

Geese

Ob'

Hay cart

Yenisey

Tim

The Kremlin

Gymnastics

Balalaika

Ufa

RU

Don

UKRAINE

Samara

Saratov

Corn

Capercaillie

Oats

Yekaterinburg

Chelyabinsk

Samovar

Omsk

Novosibirsk

Krasnoyars

Wild boars

Rostov-na-Donu

Volgograd

Volga

Wheat

Farm workers

KAZAKSTAN

Trans-Siberian Railroad

Black Sea

Krasnodar

Volga-Don Canal

CAUCASUS MTS.

Mt. Elbrus 18,510 ft (5,642 m)

Caviar

Grozny

Astrakhan

Fisherman with sturgeon

Wheat

Hydroelect

Sheep

GEORGIA

Caspian Sea

AZERBAIJAN

ST. BASIL'S CATHEDRAL
This colorful Moscow cathedral was built in the 16th century to celebrate Czar Ivan the Terrible's victory over his Tartar enemies.

ALASKA
(U.S.A.)

◆ AMAZING FACT ◆

Stretching almost one-quarter of the way around the globe, the Trans-Siberian Railroad is the longest railway in the world. The journey from Moscow to Vladivostok takes eight days and covers a distance of 5,777 miles (9,297 km).

◆ LOOK AGAIN ◆

- What kind of fossils have been discovered on the West Siberian Plain?
- On which peninsula is the Klyuchevskaya volcano located?
- Name a form of dance that is popular in Moscow.

Chukchi Sea *Bering Strait*

CHUKCHI
PENINSULA

Harbor seals

Chukchi hunter

East Siberian Sea

NEW
SIBERIAN
ISLANDS

OCEAN

Polar bears

Wolf

Bering Sea

Kittiwake

Laptev Sea

Arctic fox

Walrus

Reindeer

Furs

Timber

Lynx

Gold

KAMCHATKA PENINSULA

Snowy owl

Nordvik

Yakut woman and children

Klyuchevskaya volcano
15,580 ft (4,749 m)

Reindeer sled

Verkhoyansk

Natural gas

Petropavlovsk-
Kamchatskiy

Evenki woman and baby

CENTRAL SIBERIAN
PLATEAU

VERKHOYANSKI MTS.

Lena

Magadan

Brown bear

Okhotsk

Salmon

LOCATION

Elk (moose)

Timber

Yakutsk

Osprey

Sea of Okhotsk

Furs

Diamonds

Herring

Wolf

Gold

Oil

Natural gas

Sakhalin

KURIL
ISLANDS

Lena

STANOVOY MTS.

Coal

Coal

SIA

Hydroelectricity

Hydroelectricity

Ⓔ Siberian tiger

Bratsk

YABLANOVYY MTS.

Amur

Khabarovsk

Udegei dancers

JAPAN

Baroque architecture

Buryat archer

CHINA

Wheat

Coal

Irkutsk

Siberian house

Udegei building

Sea of Japan (East Sea)

SAYAN MTS.

Lake Baikal

Ulan-Ude

Vladivostok

MONGOLIA

MATRESHKA DOLLS
These traditional wooden dolls are shaped so that they fit inside one another. Some matreshka sets include more than 12 dolls.

SIBERIAN TIGER
Siberian tigers are the world's biggest tigers. They live in southeastern Siberia and hunt bears, deer and, occasionally, people!

SCALE
MILES
0 100 200 300 400 500

0 200 400 600 800
KILOMETERS

Central Eurasia

EURASIA IS THE LANDMASS that contains Europe and Asia. Central Eurasia extends from the southeastern corner of Europe into the dry heart of Asia. Turkey forms a bridge between the two continents, which are separated by the narrow Bosporus strait. Turkey's interior is hilly and barren, but its fertile coastal regions produce tea, tobacco, and the world's largest crops of hazelnuts and raisins. South of Turkey lies the island of Cyprus, which is home to people of Turkish and Greek descent. Beyond Turkey's eastern border, the countries of Georgia, Armenia and

Azerbaijan are flanked by the massive Caucasus mountains. These countries are rich in minerals: at one time, Baku, the capital of Azerbaijan, supplied half of the world's oil. Across the Caspian Sea, deserts cover most of Turkmenistan, Uzbekistan and Kazakstan. Ancient trade routes between China and Europe passed through these lands, linking cities such as Samarkand and Tashkent. In the north, the desert merges with the Steppe, a vast grassland; in the southeast, the Tien Mountains cover most of Kyrgyzstan and Tajikistan. Many of central Eurasia's rivers are diverted to irrigate crops. This has lowered the levels of some lakes. The Aral Sea, once the world's fourth-largest lake, has shrunk to less than half its former size, stranding fishing villages and boats over 20 miles (30 km) from the shore.

ARMENIA
POPULATION: 3,330,099 • CAPITAL: YEREVAN

AZERBAIJAN
POPULATION: 7,798,497 • CAPITAL: BAKU

CYPRUS
POPULATION: 767,314 • CAPITAL: NICOSIA

GEORGIA
POPULATION: 4,960,951 • CAPITAL: TBILISI

KAZAKSTAN
POPULATION: 16,741,519 • CAPITAL: ASTANA

KYRGYZSTAN
POPULATION: 4,822,166 • CAPITAL: BISHKEK

TAJIKISTAN
POPULATION: 6,719,567 • CAPITAL: DUSHANBE

TURKEY
POPULATION: 67,308,928 • CAPITAL: ANKARA

TURKMENISTAN
POPULATION: 4,688,963 • CAPITAL: ASHKHABAD

UZBEKISTAN
POPULATION: 25,563,441 • CAPITAL: TASHKENT

BLUE MOSQUE
Built for Sultan Ahmet I in the 17th century, this mosque in Istanbul, Turkey, is named for the more than 21,000 blue tiles that cover its interior.

◆ AMAZING FACT ◆

In Cappadocia in central Turkey, an eerie landscape of strange rock formations has been created by wind and water erosion. Early Christians made homes and churches inside caves cut into the rock. Some of these caves are still in use today.

◆ PROJECT: *Kilim Weaving* ◆

A kilim is a flat, woven rug traditionally made in Turkey. To make a simple kilim, you will first need to make a loom.

❶ Cut notches into the corners of a rectangular piece of cardboard. Tie a length of string to the left-hand notch and then wrap it around the cardboard, moving from left to right and leaving about ½ inch (1 cm) between strings. Tie the string off on the right-hand notch.

❷ Now weave by threading wool under and then over the strings. If you begin the first row weaving under, begin the second row weaving over, and so on. When you add a new piece of wool, tie it to the old piece. As you weave, push the rows tightly together.

❸ When the loom is full, turn it over so that it is face down and cut the two middle strings. Tie them together at the top and bottom edges of the weaving. Repeat with the rest of the strings.

❹ When all the strings have been cut and tied, remove the weaving from the loom. Trim the ends of the tied-off strings to make a fringe for your weaving.

Step 1 Step 2 Step 3

SNOW LEOPARD
Living high in the mountains, the snow leopard needs strong paws for rock climbing and long, thick fur to keep warm.

Qostanay Petropavl
Iron ore
Marmot
Wheat Ishim
Aktyubinsk
THE STEPPE
Sarsembek herder
Pavlodar
Barley
ASTANA
Irtysh
RUSSIA
heep
Bearded vulture
Yurts (nomad tents)
Gold
Stranded fishing boats, Aral Sea
Textiles
Semey Oskemen
Manganese
Copper
Qaraghandy
Hydroelectricity
Former coastline 1993
KAZAKSTAN
Aral Sea
Coal
Baking bread in traditional oven
Lake Zaysan
Baykonur Cosmodrome
Lake Balkhash
White-throated kingfisher
Cotton
Saiga antelope
Nukus Folk costume
Cotton
Spoonbill
Kirgiz farmer
LOCATION
UZBEKISTAN
Chemicals
Street vendor selling apples
CHINA
Registan Square
Shymkent
Almaty
Ⓔ Snow leopard
BISHKEK
SCALE
Bukhara
Samarkand
TASHKENT
Namangan
KYRGYZSTAN
MILES
0   100   200   300
menabat
Rice
Sheep
TIEN MTS.
0   100   200   300   400   500
Cotton
Osh
Cotton
Yak
KILOMETERS
DUSHANBE
Karakumskiy Canal
Amu Dar'ya
Sheep
Kommunizma 24,590 ft (7,495 m)
Musician playing longhorn
BAYKONUR COSMODROME
Formerly a Soviet Union space center, Baykonur is now leased from Kazakstan by Russia for use as its main space shuttle and rocket launching site.
TAJIKISTAN
Hissar fortress
AFGHANISTAN

The Middle East

The Middle East is a land of ancient cities and vast deserts. It is home to some of the world's oldest civilizations and was the birthplace of three of the most widespread religions—Islam, Christianity and Judaism. Though there are narrow strips of fertile land on the densely populated Mediterranean coast, along the Tigris and Euphrates rivers in Iraq, and in the highlands of northern Iran, most of this region is hot, dry and barren. Deserts extend southward from Syria, Jordan and Israel, covering most of the Arabian Peninsula. Parts of this peninsula receive no rain for up to 10 years! Deserts also cover two-thirds of Iran. The enormous Dasht-e Kavīr salt desert in eastern Iran has almost no vegetation. Among its few inhabitants are gazelles that survive on tiny amounts of salty water. Over the centuries, the people of the Middle East have made skillful use of their limited water supplies. For thousands of years, the Tigris and Euphrates rivers have been used to water crops. Today, desalination plants on the shores of the Persian Gulf turn sea water into fresh water. The Gulf region holds half the world's reserves of oil and gas, and this has made some countries very wealthy. On average, people in the United Arab Emirates earn twice as much as people in the United States. In contrast, Yemen, which has little oil, is one of the poorest countries in the world.

BAHRAIN
Population: 656,397 ∗ Capital: Manama

IRAN
Population: 66,622,704 ∗ Capital: Tehran

IRAQ
Population: 24,001,816 ∗ Capital: Baghdad

ISRAEL
Population: 6,029,529 ∗ Capital: Jerusalem

JORDAN
Population: 5,307,470 ∗ Capital: Amman

KUWAIT
Population: 2,111,561 ∗ Capital: Kuwait

LEBANON
Population: 3,677,780 ∗ Capital: Beirut

OMAN
Population: 2,713,462 ∗ Capital: Muscat

QATAR
Population: 793,341 ∗ Capital: Doha

SAUDI ARABIA
Population: 23,513,330 ∗ Capital: Riyadh

SYRIA
Population: 17,155,814 ∗ Capital: Damascus

UNITED ARAB EMIRATES
Population: 2,445,989 ∗ Capital: Abu Dhabi

YEMEN
Population: 18,701,257 ∗ Capital: Sanaa

∗ Amazing Fact ∗

The Rub' al-Khali Desert, or Empty Quarter, in southern Saudi Arabia is the biggest sand desert in the world. It is as large as France and has no towns or villages. Its only inhabitants are nomadic Bedouin people.

DOME OF THE ROCK
This Muslim temple in Jerusalem backs onto the Western Wall, a site sacred to Jews. Inside the temple is a rock that some say marks the center of the world.

VEILED WOMAN
Traditionally, Muslim women must keep their face and hair hidden from strangers. Many wear a long black cloak and a veil or eye-mask.

Map labels

ARMENIA AZERBAIJAN

Tobacco
Araks
Caspian Sea
TURKMENISTAN

Oil
Tabrīz
Barley
Rasht
Caviar
Ⓔ Sturgeon

Mosul

Cotton
TEHRAN
Winnowing grain
Mashhad
Turquoise

Friday Mosque, Samarra
Musician
DASHT-E KAVĪR (GREAT SALT DESERT)

Kurdish woman
Royal Mosque
PLATEAU OF IRAN
Ⓔ Leopard

BAGHDAD
Tigris
Eşfahān
Making rugs
AFGHANISTAN

Q
Bedouin shepherd
Oil
IRAN
Kermān

Ziggurat (temple), Ur
Al Basrah
Ābādān
Stone carvings, Persepolis
DASHT-E LŪT

KUWAIT
Oil
Shīrāz
Wine
PAKISTAN

KUWAIT
Camel race
Oil
Persian Gulf
Oil
Caracal
Walled city of Bam
Shepherd in traditional felt coat

BAHRAIN
Eurasian griffon
Goats

Ad Dammām
AL MANAMA
QATAR
Oil
Strait of Hormuz
Dubai **OMAN**
Gulf of Oman

Water tower
AD DAWHAH
Natural gas
ABU DHABI
MUSCAT

RIYADH
Zubara fort
UNITED ARAB EMIRATES
Date palm
Oil tanker

Bedouin with falcon
Arabian horse
(UNDEFINED BORDER)
Al Khuwair Mosque
Şūr

SAUDI ARABIA
Solar-powered telephone
Coconuts
Sardines

Great Mosque
Arabian Sea

Bedouin tent
RUB' AL-KHALI DESERT (EMPTY QUARTER)
Collecting frankincense

Baboon
OMAN

Sand cat
Woman at well
Ⓔ Arabian oryx
Tiger shark

Salālah

Wheat Apricots
YEMEN

SANAA
Men with narghile

Al Hajrah

Ta'izz
Coffee
Oil
Gulf of Aden
Socotra (Yemen)

Aden

BOUTI

Look Again box

⬧ LOOK AGAIN ⬧

- Which animals are raced in Saudi Arabia?
- Name a gemstone that is found in northeastern Iran.
- In which Middle Eastern country can you find the Dome of the Rock?

Location

LOCATION

Scale

N
W E
S

SCALE

MILES
0 50 100 150 200 250

0 100 200 300 400
KILOMETERS

Arabian Oryx

ARABIAN ORYX
This antelope may have been the origin of the myth of the unicorn. Viewed from the side, the oryx looks as though it has only one horn.

Southern Asia

SOUTHERN ASIA, OR THE Indian Subcontinent as it is also known, is separated from the rest of Asia by a series of massive mountain ranges. In the northeast, the mighty Himalayas, the highest mountains on Earth, tower over northern India and the two small kingdoms of Nepal and Bhutan. In the northwest, the dry, rugged Hindu Kush— the world's second-highest mountain range—spreads across central Afghanistan. South of these mountains, the land drops steeply to a wide, fertile plain that stretches from Pakistan to Bangladesh and covers most of northern India. Southern India consists of a large triangular plateau (the Deccan) fringed by narrow coastal plains. Just off the southeast coast lies the island of Sri Lanka.

Southern Asia has large areas of fertile land, valuable mineral reserves and expanding industries, but these resources barely support the region's huge population, and many people are very poor. One-fifth of the world's people live in southern Asia, and the population is growing rapidly. In India alone, almost 20 million babies are born each year. Four-fifths of southern Asians live in small villages, and most grow their own food. In India, Sri Lanka and Bangladesh, farmers rely on summer rains to water their crops. These rains are brought by winds known as monsoons. If too little rain falls, the crops fail. If too much rain falls, the crops, as well as buildings and people, can be washed away by devastating floods.

AFGHANISTAN
POPULATION: 27,755,775 • CAPITAL: KABUL
BANGLADESH
POPULATION: 133,376,684 • CAPITAL: DHAKA
BHUTAN
POPULATION: 2,094,176 • CAPITAL: THIMPHU
INDIA
POPULATION: 1,045,845,226 • CAPITAL: NEW DELHI
MALDIVES
POPULATION: 320,165 • CAPITAL: MALE
NEPAL
POPULATION: 25,873,917 • CAPITAL: KATHMANDU
PAKISTAN
POPULATION: 147,663,429 • CAPITAL: ISLAMABAD
SRI LANKA
POPULATION: 19,576,783 • CAPITAL: COLOMBO

◆ PROJECT: *Taj Mahal Tile* ◆

The Taj Mahal in India was built by Emperor Shah Jahan in memory of his beloved wife Mumtaz. Construction began in 1631, and it took 20,000 workers about 20 years to complete the building. It is covered in tiles of dazzling white marble. Each tile is carved with floral designs and inlaid with semi-precious stones. You can make your own paper Taj Mahal tile.

❶ Draw floral patterns on a square of white paper.
❷ Color the patterns and then use glitter, sequins, buttons or colored plastic wrap to "fashion" the jewels in the Taj Mahal's intricate designs.

LOCATION

Arabian Sea

Ahmadabad
Plowing with cattle
Pangolin
Sardines
Gateway to India
Palace guard
Painted elephant
Bhopal
Cobra and mongoose
INDIA
Coal
Langur monkeys
Great Stupa (shrine)
Nagpur
Ⓔ Tiger
Brahman
Spice seller
Snake charmer
Cray fisherman
Iron and steel
Washing in the Ganges
Kolkata (Calcutta)
Ⓔ Ganges dolphin **Chittagong**
DHAKA
Transporting jute
Ⓔ Garial
Bhubaneswar

Bay of Bengal

Mackerel
Weasel shark

ANDAMAN ISLANDS

NICOBAR ISLANDS

Mumbai (Bombay)
Zebu cow
Millet
Sitar
Cotton
DECCAN
Cotton
Gol Gumbaz Mosque
Panaji (Goa)
Hyderabad
Bharatnatyam temple dancer
High-tech industries
Bangalore
Planting rice
Cricket
Cotton
Chenai (Madras)
Meenakshi Temple
Tea
Tea
Fishermen on stilts
Jaffna
Cinnamon
SRI LANKA
Sloth bear
COLOMBO
Blue peacock
Ernakulam (Cochin)
Fishing boat
Thiruvananthapuram (Trivandrum)
Fishing boat

INDIAN OCEAN

N E S W
SCALE
MILES 0 100 200 300
KILOMETERS 0 100 200 300 400 500

◆ AMAZING FACT ◆

The Himalayas were once under the sea! About 40 million years ago the Indian landmass collided with Eurasia, pushing rocks up from the sea floor to form this vast mountain range. Fossilized seashells have been found on many Himalayan peaks.

MALDIVES

Coconut palm
MALE
Tourism
Magnificent frigate bird

MILES 0 100 200 300
KILOMETERS 0 200 400

FOLK DANCER
In Bhutan, dancers taking part in religious festivals wear ornate silk costumes and masks to represent gods and spirits.

BODHNATH STUPA
Begun in the fifth century, this huge shrine in Nepal is decorated with the all-seeing eyes of Buddha, the founder of Buddhism.

PAINTED ELEPHANT
During religious processions in India, elephants are painted and then draped in colorful silks and sparkling jewels.

Southeast Asia

SOUTHEAST ASIA IS MADE UP OF a mainland peninsula and more than 20,000 islands. Throughout this hot, humid region, rugged mountains rise steeply from wide river basins and coastal plains once covered in dense rain forests. Most people live in the river valleys or near the coast, where they fish and grow food. Rice is the most important crop. On the plains, it is planted in wide, flooded fields called rice paddies. On hills and mountains, rice is grown on terraces—narrow strips of land that climb the slopes like giant staircases. In recent years, many Southeast Asians have moved from the countryside to cities in search of work. Bangkok, Ho Chi Minh City, Manila and Jakarta are now among the most crowded and fastest-growing cities in the world. Southeast Asia has many natural resources. Malaysia is the world's leading exporter of tin, Myanmar supplies most of the world's rubies, and oil has made Brunei one of the world's richest countries. Timber is the most widespread resource, and the region's rain forests supply more than three-quarters of the world's tropical hardwoods. But so many trees are being chopped down that several countries could soon run out of forest, and many animal and plant species are now endangered. Some countries restrict logging activities and have turned large areas of forest into magnificent national parks.

BRUNEI
POPULATION: 350,898 • CAPITAL: BANDAR SERI BEGAWAN

CAMBODIA
POPULATION: 12,775,324 • CAPITAL: PHNOM PENH

EAST TIMOR
POPULATION: 952,618 • CAPITAL: DILI

INDONESIA
POPULATION: 231,328,092 • CAPITAL: JAKARTA

LAOS
POPULATION: 5,777,180 • CAPITAL: VIENTIANE

MALAYSIA
POPULATION: 22,662,365 • CAPITAL: KUALA LUMPUR

MYANMAR (BURMA)
POPULATION: 42,238,224 • CAPITAL: YANGON (RANGOON)

PHILIPPINES
POPULATION: 84,525,639 • CAPITAL: MANILA

SINGAPORE
POPULATION: 4,452,732 • CAPITAL: SINGAPORE

THAILAND
POPULATION: 62,354,402 • CAPITAL: BANGKOK

VIETNAM
POPULATION: 81,098,416 • CAPITAL: HANOI

PADAUNG WOMEN
The Padaung women of Myanmar wear large stacks of brass rings around their necks. They believe the rings will protect them against tiger attacks!

PETRONAS TOWERS
At 1,483 ft (452 m) high, the Petronas Towers in Malaysia are now the tallest office buildings in the world, beating Chicago's Sears Tower by 29 feet (9 m).

◆ LOOK AGAIN ◆

- In which country could you shop at a floating market?
- Name a weapon used by hunters in Malaysia.
- What kind of "dragon" lives on an island in Indonesia?

N W E S

SCALE

MILES

0   100   200   300   400

0   150   300   450   600

KILOMETERS

◆ PROJECT: *Erupting Volcano* ◆

Southeast Asia has more active volcanoes than any other part of the world. The island of Java alone has 50 volcanoes that could erupt at any time. Here's a volcano that will erupt whenever you want it to.

❶ On a tray, use moist soil to model a mountain.

❷ Scoop out a hole from the top of the mountain and put in a container, such as the lid from a spray can.

❸ Pour about ¼ cup warm water into the container. Now stir in 1 tablespoon baking soda, a few drops of red food coloring and a few drops of dishwashing liquid. Pour in ¼ cup vinegar and watch your volcano erupt.

Adding vinegar to the baking soda produces carbon dioxide gas. This causes pressure to build up until the volcano erupts, forcing lava suds out the top. This is similar to the pressure inside Earth's crust that causes a real volcano to erupt.

Dugongs

Jeepney bus

Luzon **Baguio**

Copper

Ⓔ Philippine eagle

Swordfish

Basket boat

Parrot fish

MANILA

Mindoro

PHILIPPINES

Pineapples *Samar*

Panay **Bacolod**

Tiger shark

Palawan Fishing with a frame-net **Cebu**

Negros Rice

South China Sea

Dayak woman

Sulu Sea

Muslim dancer

Davao

Mindanao

Legazpi

PACIFIC OCEAN

Oil

Kota Kinabalu

BANDAR SERI BEGAWAN

Mt. Kinabalu 13,455 ft (4,101 m)

Sandakan

BRUNEI *SABAH*

Celebes Sea

Sea gypsy collecting sea urchins

LOCATION

SARAWAK

Mulu Caves

Hunter with blowpipe

Diver and giant clam

Ⓔ Orangutan

Oil

Coconuts

Manado

Halmahera

Cloves

Oil

Greater bird of paradise

Banded pitta

KALIMANTAN

Borneo

Sail-tailed water lizard

Balikpapan

Proboscis monkey

Rafflesia flower

Banjarmasin

Sulawesi

Peppercorns

Ceram

Asmat tribesman

Puncak Jaya 16,535 ft (5,040 m)

Jayapura

IRIAN JAYA

Rice

Nutmeg

Buru

Tarsier

Ambon

New Guinea

Ⓔ Leatherback turtle

Ujung Pandang

Banda Sea

Kai

Aru

PAPUA NEW GUINEA

Bumblebee goby

Bananas

INDONESIA

Flores Sea

Komodo dragon

Tanimbar

Manta ray

Borobudur Temple **Surabaya**

Bali

Sumbawa

Flores

☆ **DILI EAST TIMOR**

Hammerhead shark

Arafura Sea

Tourism

Lombok Shadow puppet

Sumba

Corn

Balinese mask

Coconuts

Kupang

Timor Sea

AUSTRALIA

Eastern Asia

EASTERN ASIA INCLUDES ONE-QUARTER of the Asian mainland as well as several small islands. It is dominated by China, the third-largest (and most populous) country in the world. China is only slightly larger than the United States, but it has more than four times as many people. Eighty percent live in the eastern third of the country, where the climate is mild and wet, and most of the land is fertile. There are many large cities in eastern China, but most people live in villages where they raise pigs and chickens, and grow rice, wheat and vegetables. Western China is dry, rugged and sparsely populated. The southwestern region—Tibet—is sometimes called the "roof of the world" because it lies on the highest plateau on Earth and contains part of the tallest mountain range, the Himalayas. In the north, the barren Gobi Desert stretches into Mongolia, where many people are nomadic herders. On and around China's coast lie a number of rapidly developing countries and territories. South Korea and Taiwan have many thriving industries, including textile, car and electrical goods manufacturers. Macao, a tiny Portuguese colony on the south coast of China, reverted to Chinese rule in 1999. It is the world's most crowded place, with 57,100 people for every square mile (22,150 per sq. km). Neighboring Hong Kong, a former British territory which was given back to China in 1997, is the world's third-largest financial center. Its modern, high-rise office buildings tower over one of Asia's busiest harbors.

CHINA
POPULATION: 1,284,303,705 ∗ CAPITAL: BEIJING

MONGOLIA
POPULATION: 2,694,432 ∗ CAPITAL: ULAANBAATAR

NORTH KOREA
POPULATION: 22,224,195 ∗ CAPITAL: P'YŎNGYANG

SOUTH KOREA
POPULATION: 48,324,000 ∗ CAPITAL: SEOUL

TAIWAN
POPULATION: 22,548,009 ∗ CAPITAL: TAIPEI

◆ AMAZING FACT ◆

The Great Wall of China stretches for 2,150 miles (3,460 km) across northern China and is so large that astronauts can see it from space. It was built in the third century BC to keep out invaders from the north, and then rebuilt and expanded in the 14th century AD.

KAZAKSTAN

KYRGYZSTAN

Oil

Rice

Donkey cart

TIEN MTS.

Ürümqi

Playing the dotar

Coal

Camel train

Kashgar

Cotton

TAKLIMAKAN DESERT

TAJIKISTAN

Cotton

PAKISTAN   Apak Hoja Tomb

Jade

ALTUN MTS.

KUNLUN MTS.

INDIA   K2 28,250 ft
(8,611 m)

PLATEAU OF TIBET

Milking a yak

Snow leopard

Tibetan monks

TIBET

HIMALAYAS

NEPAL

Potala Palace

Lhasa

Xiagazê

Gyangze

Mt. Everest
29,028 ft
(8,848 m)

BHUTAN

W — E
N
S

SCALE

MILES

0   100   200   300

0   100   200   300   400   500

KILOMETERS

TERRA-COTTA WARRIORS
Chinese emperor Qin Shi Huang had more than 6,000 life-sized clay warriors built to guard his body after his death.

GIANT PANDA
There are only 1,000 giant pandas left in the wild, and they all live in bamboo forests in central China, near Chengdu.

J K L M N O P Q

RUSSIA

Lake Uvs

Lake Hövsgöl

Elk (moose)

Amur

(E) Tiger

Coal mining

Darhan

Traditional costume

Choybalsan

Qiqihar

Ice sledding

Timber

Harbin

ULAANBAATAR

Mongolian family and ger (tent)

Wild boars

Car manufacturing

Soybeans

Changchun

MONGOLIA

Wheat

Coal

Farmer carrying grain

Ch'ŏngjin

(E) Bactrian camel

GOBI DESERT

Great Wall of China

Corn

Iron and steel

Fushun

Shenyang

NORTH KOREA

Goats

Oil

Yumen

Pallas's cat

Iron and steel

Baotou

BEIJING

Temple of Heaven

Tangshan

Dalian

P'YŎNGYANG

Iron and steel

Sea of Japan (East Sea)

JAPAN

CHINA

Lake Qinghai

Chemicals

Cycling

Forbidden City

Tianjin

Taiyuan

Zibo

Fortune cookies

SEOUL

SOUTH KOREA

Textiles

Pusan

Cotton

Jinan

Wheat

Traditional costume

Korea Strait

Lanzhou

Reeves's pheasant

Terra-cotta warriors

Xi'an

Chemicals

Huang (Yellow)

Zhengzhou

Taking cabbages to market

Silk worm and cocoon

Grand Canal

Nanjing Pagoda

Yellow Sea

Cheju

(E) Giant panda

Golden snub-nosed monkey

Rice

Ping-pong

Nanjing

Chengdu

(E) Red panda

Iron and steel

Chongqing

Chang (Yangtze)

Lake Dongting

Lychees

Lake Poyang

Ming vase

Nanchang

Tai chi

Wuhan

Hangzhou

Shanghai

Container ship

LOCATION

East China Sea

Textiles

Grand Buddha

Farmhouse

Guiyang

Fishing with cormorants

Changsha

Tea

Sweet potatoes

Fuzhou

Shrimp

Chang (Yangtze)

Mekong

Kunming

Stone forest (rock formations)

Herding ducks

Limestone hills of Guilin

Rice

Bank of China

Pigs

TAIPEI

High-tech industries

TAIWAN

Taiwan Strait

Asiatic golden cat

INDIA

Nanning

Hydroelectricity

Paper

Guangzhou

Hong Kong

Macao

Chiang Kai Shek monument

PACIFIC OCEAN

MYANMAR (BURMA)

VIETNAM

LAOS

TRADITIONAL COSTUME
Most Korean men used to wear a white jacket and baggy pants, and a black horsehair hat. Now they wear these only on special occasions.

Coffee

Haikou

Hainan

South China Sea

Junk

Mandarin fish

J K L M N O

2

3

4

5

6

7

8

9

10

11

Japan

JAPAN CONSISTS OF a long chain of 4 main islands and more than 4,000 smaller islands that lies off the east coast of the Asian mainland. The northern half of Japan has a cold temperate climate with snowy winters and mild summers. In the south the weather is more tropical, with mild winters and a summer wet season. Most of the land is mountainous, and almost two-thirds is covered in forests. Earthquakes are common, and there are many active volcanoes. Japan occupies an area smaller than the U.S. state of Montana but has 150 times as many people. Three-quarters live in cities, the largest of which are located on the large island of Honshū. Japan's capital, Tokyo, sprawls across more than 80 neighboring towns, forming the biggest urban area in the world, and is home to more than 27 million people. So many workers commute to the city center each day that railroad stations employ guards known as "pushers" to cram passengers into trains. Despite having little farmland, Japan manages to produce most of its food, including large quantities of rice. Fish is the country's most important resource, and the Japanese fishing fleet is the largest in the world. Although it has few other natural resources, Japan has become a major industrial power by importing raw materials and manufacturing high-quality goods. It is the world's top car manufacturer, has the world's foremost shipbuilding industry, and is a leading exporter of electronic goods.

JAPAN
POPULATION: 126,974,628 * CAPITAL: TOKYO

◆ LOOK AGAIN ◆

- What kind of festival takes place in Sapporo?
- Name two kinds of shark found off the west coast of Honshū.
- Which famous mountain lies southwest of Japan's capital?

**Map labels:**

RUSSIA

Sea of Okhotsk

Hokkaidō

Salmon
Dairy cattle
Kushiro
Coal
Great white shark
Pollock
Mackerel

Ainu man
Brown bear
Timber
Sapporo snow festival
Asahikawa
Rice
Sapporo
Otaru
Hakodate
Wakkanai
Skiing
Rebun
Rishiri
Halibut
Serows
Japanese crane

Tsugaru Strait

Aomori
Apples
Japanese spider crab
Akita
Morioka
Macaques
Sushi
Making chopsticks
Rice
Fukushima
Niigata
Shinano
Sado
Mako shark

Kokechi doll
Shiogama festival
Sardines
Carp streamers
Sendai
Dancer in traditional costume

JAPAN

Ninja

Sea of Japan (East Sea)

RYUKYU ISLANDS

East China Sea

Rice
Long-tailed carpet shark
AMAMI ISLANDS
Karate
OKINAWA ISLANDS
Tourism
Naha
Pineapples

MILES
0   25   50   75
KILOMETERS
0   50   100   150

LOCATION

◆ PROJECT: *Origami Penguin* ◆

Origami is the ancient Japanese art of folding paper to create decorative models. Origami models usually represent animals or people and sometimes have movable parts. In ancient Japan, origami was a highly prized art form and models often consisted of hundreds of folds. You can make your own origami model of a penguin if you follow these steps.

1 Fold a square of paper in half to make a crease. Unfold.

2 Fold the bottom corner up as shown.

3 Fold the paper in half again.

4 Fold the sides in as shown, to form the wing flaps.

5 Fold the top down to make a crease. Unfold.

6 Open the paper out and pull the tip forward.

7 Close the paper again and press the "head" flat.

Your origami penguin is finished!

PACIFIC OCEAN

Honshū

TOKYO
High-tech industries
skyline
Car manufacturing
Kawasaki
Yokohama
Great Buddha
Bullet train
Solar-powered ship
Pearl divers
Tea
Mt. Fuji 12,388 ft (3,776 m)
Shizuoka
Hamamatsu
Chemicals
Horyuji Temple
Nagoya
Rice
Kabuki theater
Kanazawa
Temple of the Golden Pavilion
Ōsaka
Kyōto
Ōsaka Castle
Wakayama
Kōbe
Iron and steel
Geisha preparing tea
Mandarin oranges
Swordfish
OKI ISLANDS
Matsue
Himeji Castle
Shinto priest
Okayama
Hiroshima
Tokushima
INLAND SEA
Matsuyama
Kōchi
Shikoku
Autumn harvest festival
Bluefin tuna
White-sided dolphin
Squid
Torii Gate
Sumo wrestlers
Octopus
World War II monument
Kumamoto
Kendo
Miyazaki
Kyūshū
Sweet potatoes
Rice
Fukuoka
Tiger shark
Kitakyūshū
Shipbuilding
Kagoshima
ŌSUMI ISLANDS
TOKARA ISLANDS
Tsushima
Nagasaki
Koto player
GOTŌ ISLANDS
Traditional fishing boat
Korea Strait
Tsushima Strait
SOUTH KOREA

SCALE
MILES
0 25 50 75 100
KILOMETERS
0 50 100 150

N E S W

ŌSAKA CASTLE
Completed in AD 1584, Ōsaka Castle was the fortress of Toyotomi Hideyoshi, the general who unified feudal Japan. At the time, it was the biggest castle in Asia.

KABUKI THEATER
A blend of music, drama, acrobatics and colorful costumes, kabuki first appeared in the 17th century. All the parts—even female roles—are played by men.

Africa

THE WORLD'S SECOND-LARGEST CONTINENT, Africa is an enormous plateau surrounded by narrow coastal plains. A thick band of tropical rain forest covers much of the center of the continent. To the north and south of this forest lie grasslands, known as savannas, and deserts. The Sahara Desert, the biggest desert in the world, spans the entire width of northern Africa, from the Atlantic Ocean to the Red Sea, and covers an area almost as large as the United States. The Kalahari and Namib deserts extend across much of the southwest. In the east, the Great Rift Valley, a series of valleys formed by cracks in Earth's crust, stretches from Syria, in Asia, to Mozambique. Africa includes 53 countries ranging from vast, mainly arid Sudan to the tiny tropical islands of the Seychelles. Arab peoples form the majority of the population in the north. The south's mainly black population is made up of hundreds of native tribes.

Major Mountains and Rivers

Mount Kilimanjaro, Tanzania
19,341 ft (5,895 m)

Mount Kenya, Kenya
17,058 ft (5,199 m)

Margherita Peak, Uganda–Democratic
Republic of the Congo (Zaire)
16,763 ft (5,109 m)

Ras Dashen, Ethiopia
15,158 ft (4,620 m)

Mount Meru, Tanzania
14,954 ft (4,558 m)

Mount Toubkal, Morocco
13,665 ft (4,165 m)

Nile 4,140 miles (6,670 km)
Congo (Zaire) 2,900 miles (4,670 km)
Niger 2,595 miles (4,180 km)
Zambezi 2,200 miles (3,540 km)
Ubangi-Uele 1,400 miles (2,250 km)
Kasai 1,210 miles (1,950 km)

Political Map

MADEIRA (PORTUGAL)
MOROCCO
TUNISIA
CANARY ISLANDS (SPAIN)
ALGERIA
LIBYA
EGYPT
WESTERN SAHARA (MOROCCO)
MAURITANIA
MALI
NIGER
CHAD
SUDAN
ERITREA
CAPE VERDE ISLANDS
SENEGAL
GAMBIA
GUINEA-BISSAU
GUINEA
BURKINA FASO
BENIN
NIGERIA
DJIBOUTI
SIERRA LEONE
CÔTE D'IVOIRE
GHANA
TOGO
CAMEROON
CENTRAL AFRICAN REPUBLIC
ETHIOPIA
SOMALIA
LIBERIA
SÃO TOMÉ and PRÍNCIPE
GABON
CONGO
DEMOCRATIC REPUBLIC OF THE CONGO (ZAIRE)
UGANDA
KENYA
RWANDA
BURUNDI
EQUATORIAL GUINEA
ASCENSION (U.K.)
TANZANIA
SEYCHELLES
ANGOLA
COMOROS
MAYOTTE (FRANCE)
ST. HELENA (U.K.)
ZAMBIA
MALAWI
NAMIBIA
ZIMBABWE
MOZAMBIQUE
MAURITIUS
BOTSWANA
MADAGASCAR
RÉUNION (FRANCE)
SWAZILAND
LESOTHO
SOUTH AFRICA

Regional land area: 11,716,972 sq. miles (30,354,852 sq. km)
Regional population: 840,449,396
Independent countries: Algeria, Angola, Benin, Botswana, Burkina Faso, Burundi, Cameroon, Cape Verde Islands, Central African Republic, Chad, Comoros, Congo, Côte d'Ivoire (Ivory Coast), Democratic Republic of the Congo (Zaire), Djibouti, Egypt, Equatorial Guinea, Eritrea, Ethiopia, Gabon, Gambia, Ghana, Guinea, Guinea-Bissau, Kenya, Lesotho, Liberia, Libya, Madagascar, Malawi, Mali, Mauritania, Mauritius, Morocco, Mozambique, Namibia, Niger, Nigeria, Rwanda, São Tomé and Príncipe, Senegal, Seychelles, Sierra Leone, Somalia, South Africa, Sudan, Swaziland, Tanzania, Togo, Tunisia, Uganda, Zambia, Zimbabwe

World Records

WORLD'S LARGEST DESERT
SAHARA DESERT, NORTHERN AFRICA, 3,579,000 SQ. MILES (9,269,000 SQ. KM)

WORLD'S LONGEST RIVER
NILE RIVER, NORTHERN AFRICA, 4,140 MILES (6,670 KM)

WORLD'S LARGEST ARTIFICIAL LAKE
LAKE VOLTA, GHANA, 3,275 SQ. MILES (8,482 SQ. KM)

WORLD'S HIGHEST TEMPERATURE
AL-'AZĪZĪYA, LIBYA, SHADE TEMPERATURE OF 136°F (58°C) RECORDED ON SEPTEMBER 13, 1922

Continent Records

HIGHEST MOUNTAIN
KILIMANJARO, TANZANIA, 19,341 FT (5,895 M)

LOWEST POINT
LAKE ASSAL, DJIBOUTI, 500 FT (152 M) BELOW SEA LEVEL

LARGEST LAKE
LAKE VICTORIA, EAST AFRICA, 26,828 SQ. MILES (69,485 SQ. KM)

LARGEST COUNTRY BY AREA
SUDAN, 967,500 SQ. MILES (2,505,825 SQ. KM)

LARGEST COUNTRY BY POPULATION
NIGERIA, POPULATION 129,934,911

LARGEST CITY BY POPULATION
CAIRO, EGYPT, POPULATION 12,399,000

◆ AMAZING FACT ◆

The huge volume of water that pours over Victoria Falls, on the border between Zambia and Zimbabwe, creates a deafening roar and a cloud of spray that can be seen from more than 20 miles (32 km) away. Because of this, locals refer to the falls as "the smoke that thunders."

PHYSICAL MAP

*A*FRICA

Arctic Circle

EUROPE

ASIA

Mediterranean Sea

Strait of Gibraltar

Madeira

ATLAS MOUNTAINS

LIBYAN DESERT

Nile

CANARY
ISLANDS

▲ Mt. Toubkal

AHAGGAR
MOUNTAINS

Lake
Nasser

Tropic of Cancer

SAHARA   DESERT

NUBIAN
DESERT

Red Sea

CAPE
VERDE
ISLANDS

TIBESTI
MOUNTAINS

Senegal

Niger

Lake
Chad

S A H E L

Gulf of Aden

Socotra

▲ Ras Dashen
Lake
Assal

Lake Volta

Benue

ADAMAWA
HIGHLANDS

Blue Nile

ETHIOPIAN
PLATEAU

Bioko

Uele

Príncipe
São Tomé

Ubangi

White Nile

ATLANTIC OCEAN

Equator

Gulf of
Guinea

CONGO
BASIN

Margherita
Peak ▲

Lake
Victoria

▲ Mt. Kenya

Congo (Zaire)

Kasai

Mt. Meru ▲ ▲ Mt. Kilimanjaro

GREAT RIFT VALLEY

Zanzibar

SEYCHELLES

Ascension

Lake
Tanganyika

Lake
Nyasa

COMOROS
ISLANDS

St. Helena

Okavango

Okavango
Delta

Lake
Kariba

Zambezi

Mozambique Channel

Madagascar

Mauritius

NAMIB DESERT

KALAHARI
DESERT

Limpopo

Réunion

Tropic of Capricorn

Orange

DRAKENSBERG MTS.

INDIAN OCEAN

CAPE OF
GOOD HOPE

Antarctic Circle

Northern Africa

THE SAHARA DESERT, the largest desert in the world, covers more than half of northern Africa. On its barren, rocky plains and rolling sand dunes, the heat is fierce, water is scarce and there is little land that can be farmed. Most of the people of the Sahara are nomads, who move their camels, sheep and goats around the desert in search of water and pasture. The only usable fertile land north or east of the Sahara lies in the valleys of the Atlas Mountains and along the banks of the Nile River in Egypt. People have farmed the Nile valley for thousands of years, and it is now one of the most densely populated places on Earth. There is little farmland in Algeria and Libya, but both countries possess large oil and gas reserves which have helped them overcome serious poverty. South of the Sahara lies a wide belt of dry grasslands known as the Sahel. These grasslands suffer frequent droughts, and overfarming is turning some areas into desert. Farther south, the Sahel gives way to the tropical rain forests of central Africa. Around the Gulf of Guinea, much of the forest has been cleared to make way for farms and large plantations where cocoa beans, coffee and cotton are grown. Oil and other minerals have been discovered in a number of Gulf countries, and this has created some wealth and industries. However, only a minority of the region's huge population benefit and most people are still very poor.

ALGERIA
POPULATION: 32,277,942 * CAPITAL: ALGIERS

BENIN
POPULATION: 6,787,625 * CAPITALS: COTONOU, PORTO-NOVO

BURKINA FASO
POPULATION: 12,603,185 * CAPITAL: OUAGADOUGOU

CAMEROON
POPULATION: 16,184,748 * CAPITAL: YAOUNDÉ

CAPE VERDE ISLANDS
POPULATION: 408,760 * CAPITAL: PRAIA

CENTRAL AFRICAN REPUBLIC
POPULATION: 3,642,739 * CAPITAL: BANGUI

CHAD
POPULATION: 8,997,237 * CAPITAL: N'DJAMENA

CÔTE D'IVOIRE (IVORY COAST)
POPULATION: 16,804,784 * CAPITALS: ABIDJAN, YAMOUSSOUKRO

DJIBOUTI
POPULATION: 472,810 * CAPITAL: DJIBOUTI

EGYPT
POPULATION: 70,712,345 * CAPITAL: CAIRO

EQUATORIAL GUINEA
POPULATION: 498,144 * CAPITAL: MALABO

ERITREA
POPULATION: 4,465,651 * CAPITAL: ASMARA

ETHIOPIA
POPULATION: 67,673,031 * CAPITAL: ADDIS ABABA

GAMBIA
POPULATION: 1,455,842 * CAPITAL: BANJUL

GHANA
POPULATION: 20,244,154 * CAPITAL: ACCRA

GUINEA
POPULATION: 7,775,065 * CAPITAL: CONAKRY

GUINEA-BISSAU
POPULATION: 1,345,479 * CAPITAL: BISSAU

LIBERIA
POPULATION: 3,288,198 * CAPITAL: MONROVIA

LIBYA
POPULATION: 5,368,585 * CAPITAL: TRIPOLI

MALI
POPULATION: 11,340,480 * CAPITAL: BAMAKO

MAURITANIA
POPULATION: 2,828,858 * CAPITAL: NOUAKCHOTT

MOROCCO
POPULATION: 31,167,783 * CAPITAL: RABAT

NIGER
POPULATION: 10,639,744 * CAPITAL: NIAMEY

NIGERIA
POPULATION: 129,934,911 * CAPITAL: ABUJA

SENEGAL
POPULATION: 10,589,571 * CAPITAL: DAKAR

SIERRA LEONE
POPULATION: 5,614,743 * CAPITAL: FREETOWN

SOMALIA
POPULATION: 7,753,310 * CAPITAL: MOGADISHU

SUDAN
POPULATION: 37,090,298 * CAPITAL: KHARTOUM

TOGO
POPULATION: 5,285,501 * CAPITAL: LOMÉ

TUNISIA
POPULATION: 9,815,644 * CAPITAL: TUNIS

SPAIN

ALGIERS

Sardines | Tangier | Ceuta (SPAIN)

RABAT | Fès | Melilla (SPAIN) | Oran

Casablanca

MADEIRA (PORTUGAL)

Roman arch

MOROCCO | Wheat

Kouttoubia Mosque minaret | Marrakech

Dyeing wool for carpets

Mt. Toubkal 13,665 ft (4,165 m) ▲ | ATLAS MTS.

CANARY ISLANDS (SPAIN)

Sheep

El Aaiún | Tindouf

ALGERIA

WESTERN SAHARA (MOROCCO)

Nomads carrying water

Scorpion

Dolphin

Nomad with camel

Chinguetti man making tea

SAH

Woman carrying goods to market | Tamanrasset

AHAGGAR MTS.

Imraguen fisherman

MAURITANIA

MALI

Hippopotamus

ATLANTIC OCEAN

Secretary bird

NOUAKCHOTT

Tombouctou (Timbuktu)

Ostrich

Pounding millet

Senegal

Niger | SAHEL

DAKAR | SENEGAL

Fishing traps

Ségou

BURKINA FASO

Bororro man

BANJUL

GAMBIA | BAMAKO

NIAMEY | Marad

BISSAU

OUAGADOUGOU

Fishing hut

GUINEA-BISSAU | GUINEA

Ivorian carrying palm wine

Cotton

Bauxite (aluminum)

CONAKRY | Diana monkey

Cocoa | BENIN

FREETOWN | Yams

Diamonds

CÔTE D'IVOIRE (IVORY COAST) | Lake Volta | GHANA | NI

SIERRA LEONE | YAMOUSSOUKRO | TOGO | Bananas

Cassava | ABUJ

MONROVIA | Coffee | LOMÉ | Ibadan

COTONOU

LIBERIA | ACCRA | Lagos

Bananas | ABIDJAN | PORTO-NOVO | Oil

Pea

Bioko

Gulf of Guinea

OSTRICH
The largest bird in the world, the ostrich is unable to fly but can run at up to 40 miles per hour (65 kph).

CAPE VERDE ISLANDS

Santo Antão
Mindelo
São Vicente
São Nicolau
Sal
Bananas
Boa Vista
São Tiago
Maio
African fish eagle
Brava
Fogo
PRAIA

MILES
0   50   100   150
0   100   200
KILOMETERS

PROJECT: *Khamsa Hand*

A *khamsa* is a Moroccan good luck charm in the form of a hand. A *khamsa* with spread fingers is said to keep away bad luck. A *khamsa* with closed fingers is supposed to bring good luck. Some *khamsas* are worn as pendants, but you can hang this *khamsa* on the door of your house or bedroom.

❶ Trace around your hand onto a piece of cardboard and cut out the shape.

❷ Glue sequins, buttons and shapes cut from colored paper or foil onto the hand shape.

❸ When you are happy with your design, leave it to dry and then hang it on your door. If you want to carry your good luck with you, make a tiny *khamsa* and thread it on a string to make a necklace.

SCALE
MILES
0   100   200   300   400   500
0   200   400   600   800
KILOMETERS

N W E S

LOCATION

Map labels

TUNIS
ITALY
Constantine
TUNISIA
MALTA
Tripoli
Misrātah
Benghazi
Musicians
Ghadāmis
Oil
Oil
Leptis Magna
LIBYA
LIBYAN DESERT
Dama gazelle
Gerboa
Natural gas
Oil
Mediterranean Sea
GREECE
TURKEY
CYPRUS
SYRIA
LEBANON
ISRAEL
Port Said
Oil
Alexandria
CAIRO
Suez
Giza pyramids
Suez Canal
Nile
Collecting water
EGYPT
Cotton
Luxor
Aswān
Sphinxes at Temple of Karnak
Lake Nasser
Hydroelectricity
Feluccas (traditional boats)
Red Sea
SAUDI ARABIA
A D E S E R T
TIBESTI MTS.
Lappet-faced vulture
NUBIAN DESERT
CHAD
SUDAN
Port Sudan
Lyre-tailed goldfish
YEMEN
Tuaregs
NIGER
Porcupine
Zinger
Lake Chad
Goatherd
N'DJAMENA
Cotton
Two Niles Mosque
KHARTOUM
El Obeid
Nile
White Nile
Blue Nile
Blue Nile falls
Kassala
ERITREA
ASMARA
Ras Dashen 15,158 ft (4,620 m)
Castle at Gondar
Gulf of Aden
Storage bales
Traditional house
Giraffes
Sarh
CENTRAL AFRICAN REPUBLIC
Cotton
Chari
Tapping a rubber tree
Kano Mosque
CAMEROON
Cocoa
YAOUNDÉ
Cotton
Coffee
Crocodile
ETHIOPIAN PLATEAU
ADDIS ABABA
Statue of the Lion
DJIBOUTI
DJIBOUTI
Berbera
Hoopoe
Dire Dawa
Donkeys
SOMALIA
Grinding grain
ⓔ Elephants
ⓔ Rhinoceroses
Juba
Dinka herdsman
ETHIOPIA
Lions
Zebra
MOGADISHU
RIA
Kano
BANGUI
Clay house
HALABO
EQUATORIAL GUINEA
GABON
CONGO
DEMOCRATIC REPUBLIC OF THE CONGO (ZAIRE)
UGANDA
KENYA
Bananas
ⓔ Zebra
Kismaayo
INDIAN OCEAN

BORORRO MAN

The Bororro people in Niger hold beauty contests—for men! They wear makeup and fine clothes, and the winner is selected by female judges.

GIZA PYRAMIDS

The Giza pyramids were built about 4,500 years ago as tombs for Egyptian kings. The largest pyramid is made of two million blocks of stone.

Southern Africa

IN THE NORTHWESTERN PART of this region, the Congo River and its many tributaries flow through immense tropical rain forests. Crocodiles swim the waterways, and the jungles are home to chimpanzees, gorillas and tropical birds. Most of the local people live in villages near the rivers and grow their own food on small plots of cleared land. The rain forests stretch eastward across the continent toward the Great Rift Valley, a chain of dramatic, steep-sided valleys that runs down the eastern side of Africa. Within these valleys lie many deep lakes as well as a number of volcanoes, including Mount Kilimanjaro, Africa's highest mountain. On the valley floors and across the surrounding grassland plateaus, enormous herds of zebras, wildebeests and antelopes are hunted by lions, cheetahs and other predators. To protect the region's wildlife, many countries have created nature preserves, which attract tourists from all over the world. From the southern end of the Rift Valley, in Mozambique, high grasslands known as the Veld spread westward toward the Kalahari and Namib deserts. In South Africa the Veld is an important farming region that is also rich in mineral resources including copper, gold and diamonds. Off the coast of Mozambique lies Madagascar, the world's fourth-largest island. Madagascar is famous for its unique wildlife, which includes many species of lemurs, unusual relatives of monkeys.

ANGOLA
POPULATION: 10,593,171 • CAPITAL: LUANDA

BOTSWANA
POPULATION: 1,591,232 • CAPITAL: GABORONE

BURUNDI
POPULATION: 6,373,002 • CAPITAL: BUJUMBURA

COMOROS
POPULATION: 614,382 • CAPITAL: MORONI

CONGO
POPULATION: 2,958,448 • CAPITAL: BRAZZAVILLE

DEMOCRATIC REPUBLIC OF THE CONGO (ZAIRE)
POPULATION: 55,225,478 • CAPITAL: KINSHASA

GABON
POPULATION: 1,233,353 • CAPITAL: LIBREVILLE

KENYA
POPULATION: 31,138,735 • CAPITAL: NAIROBI

LESOTHO
POPULATION: 2,207,954 • CAPITAL: MASERU

MADAGASCAR
POPULATION: 16,473,477 • CAPITAL: ANTANANARIVO

MALAWI
POPULATION: 10,701,824 • CAPITAL: LILONGWE

MAURITIUS
POPULATION: 1,200,206 • CAPITAL: PORT LOUIS

MOZAMBIQUE
POPULATION: 19,607,519 • CAPITAL: MAPUTO

NAMIBIA
POPULATION: 1,820,916 • CAPITAL: WINDHOEK

RWANDA
POPULATION: 7,398,074 • CAPITAL: KIGALI

SÃO TOMÉ AND PRÍNCIPE
POPULATION: 170,372 • CAPITAL: SÃO TOMÉ

SEYCHELLES
POPULATION: 80,098 • CAPITAL: VICTORIA

SOUTH AFRICA
POPULATION: 43,647,658 • CAPITALS: BLOEMFONTEIN, CAPE TOWN, PRETORIA

SWAZILAND
POPULATION: 1,123,605 • CAPITAL: MBABANE

TANZANIA
POPULATION: 37,187,939 • CAPITALS: DAR ES SALAAM, DODOMA

UGANDA
POPULATION: 24,699,073 • CAPITAL: KAMPALA

ZAMBIA
POPULATION: 9,959,037 • CAPITAL: LUSAKA

ZIMBABWE
POPULATION: 11,376,676 • CAPITAL: HARARE

SCALE

MILES
0   100   200   300   400

0   100   200   300   400   500   600
KILOMETERS

J K L M N O P Q

AFRICAN REPUBLIC

Tapping a
rubber tree

African
fish eagle

SUDAN

Samburu
women

ETHIOPIA

SOMALIA

Uele

Ⓔ Gorilla

Ankole cattle

Leopard

Herding
cattle

UGANDA

⭐ **KAMPALA**

*Lake
Turkana*

DEMOCRATIC
REPUBLIC OF
THE CONGO
(ZAIRE)

Margherita Peak
16,763 ft
(5,109 m) ▲

Ivory
mask

Tea

*Lake
Victoria*

KENYA

Mt. Kenya
17,058 ft
(5,199 m) ▲

Marabou
stork

RWANDA

⭐ **KIGALI**

Bananas

Masai
dancer

🕌 **NAIROBI**

Coffee

Ladataba

Lomami

Diamonds

BURUNDI

⭐ **BUJUMBURA**

Mwanza

Lions

Ninga
drummers

*Lake
Tanganyika*

Mt. Kilimanjaro
19,341 ft (5,895 m) ▲

● **Mombasa**

📷 Tourism

● **Mbuji-Mayi**

nanga

TANZANIA

Acacia tree

⭐ **DODOMA**

Zanzibar

Cheetah

⭐ **DAR ES SALAAM**

Mafia

Coffee

Open-cast copper mining

Crowned
crane

Likasi

Wildebeest

Ⓔ Elephants

Cashew
nuts

COMOROS

⭐ **MORONI**

Lubumbashi

Ruvuma

Aardvark

**MAYOTTE
(FRANCE)**

Cassava

Copper

Ndola

*Lake
Nyasa*

MALAWI

⭐ **LILONGWE**

Coconuts

ZAMBIA

Lozi royal
barge

⭐ **LUSAKA**

Fishing boat

Tea

Nampula

Zambezi

Victoria Falls

Hydroelectricity

Zambezi

Black
mamba

 ⭐ **HARARE**

Gold

Zebra

ZIMBABWE

*Lake
Kariba*

Ⓔ Coelacanth

Ⓔ Indri

Ⓔ Ruffed
lemur

Rice

📷 Tourism

● **Toamasina**

Giraffes

● **Bulawayo**

Ⓔ Zebra

Beira

Ring-tailed
lemur

Francistown

Ruined town
of Great
Zimbabwe

MOZAMBIQUE

⭐ **ANTANANARIVO**

MADAGASCAR

MAURITIUS

⭐ **PORT LOUIS**

BOTSWANA

Diamonds

Cape
buffalo

Coffee

Streaked
tenrec

**RÉUNION
(FRANCE)**

⭐ **GABORONE**

Rugby

Limpopo

Chameleon

Sugarcane

⭐ **PRETORIA**

Ndundza
woman

⭐ **MAPUTO**

Johannesburg

⭐ **MBABANE**

Gold

Zulus

SWAZILAND

Vaal

⭐ **BLOEMFONTEIN**

⭐ **MASERU**

Durban

LESOTHO

on ore

DRAKENSBERG MTS.

📷 Tourism

**East
London**

ape
ting
ogs

● **Port
Elizabeth**

I N D I A N   O C E A N

Victoria ⭐

Magnificent
frigate bird

SEYCHELLES

Great white shark

LOCATION

Mozambique Channel

AMAZING FACT

Over a short distance, the cheetah
is the fastest animal in the world. As
it pursues wildebeest, antelope and
other prey across the savanna, it can
reach speeds
of more than
60 miles per
hour (100 kph).

GIRAFFES
Giraffes grow to a height of
18 feet (6 m)—taller than a
single-story house. Their height
allows them to feed on leaves
that other animals can't reach.

ZULUS
The Zulu people have the
largest population of any African
group. In the 19th century, their
kingdom covered much of what
is now South Africa.

J K L M N O P Q

Australia and Oceania

STRETCHING FROM THE INDIAN OCEAN to the center of the Pacific Ocean, Australia and Oceania cover a vast area of the globe. But because most of this region is ocean, it has a relatively small population. Australia is by far the largest landmass. This island is so big that it is considered a continent. Oceania consists of thousands of much smaller islands that are scattered across the Pacific Ocean to the east of Australia. They are divided into three groups: Micronesia, Melanesia, and Polynesia, which includes the large islands of New Zealand. There are two main types of Pacific island: high, rugged islands that are the peaks of undersea volcanoes and submerged mountain ranges; and coral atolls—low, sandy islands formed by coral reefs growing on the tops of undersea mountains. Many of the Pacific islands are so small that they do not appear on regular maps.

Continent Facts

Regional land area: 3,283,993 sq. miles (8,507,753 sq. km)
Regional population: 30,885,204
Independent countries: Australia, Federated States of Micronesia, Fiji, Kiribati, Marshall Islands, Nauru, New Zealand, Palau, Papua New Guinea, Samoa, Solomon Islands, Tonga, Tuvalu, Vanuatu

World Records

WORLD'S LONGEST CORAL REEF
THE GREAT BARRIER REEF, AUSTRALIA, 1,260 MILES (2,025 KM)

WORLD'S LARGEST ROCK
ULURU (AYERS ROCK), AUSTRALIA, 1,143 FT (348 M) HIGH; 1.5 MILES (2.5 KM) LONG; 1 MILE (1.6 KM) WIDE

WORLD'S LARGEST SAND ISLAND
FRASER ISLAND, AUSTRALIA, 75 MILES (120 KM) LONG

Continent Records

HIGHEST MOUNTAIN
MOUNT WILHELM, PAPUA NEW GUINEA, 14,762 FEET (4,500 M)

LOWEST POINT
LAKE EYRE, AUSTRALIA, 52 FT (16 M) BELOW SEA LEVEL

LARGEST LAKE
LAKE EYRE, AUSTRALIA, 3,600 SQ. MILES (9,324 SQ. KM)

LONGEST RIVER
MURRAY-DARLING, AUSTRALIA, 2,330 MILES (3,750 KM)

LARGEST COUNTRY BY AREA
AUSTRALIA, 2,967,909 SQ. MILES (7,686,884 SQ. KM)

LARGEST COUNTRY BY POPULATION
AUSTRALIA, POPULATION 19,546,792

LARGEST CITY BY POPULATION
SYDNEY, AUSTRALIA, POPULATION 4,175,000

Major Mountains and Rivers

Mount Wilhelm, Papua New Guinea 14,762 ft (4,500 m)

Mount Victoria, Papua New Guinea 13,363 ft (4,073 m)

Mount Cook, New Zealand 12,349 ft (3,764 m)

Mount Tasman, New Zealand 11,475 ft (3,498 m)

Mount Balbi, Papua New Guinea 8,999 ft (2,743 m)

Mount Kosciuszko, Australia 7,310 ft (2,228 m)

Murray-Darling 2,330 miles (3,750 km)
Darling 1,905 miles (3,070 km)
Murray 1,600 miles (2,575 km)
Murrumbidgee 1,050 miles (1,690 km)
Lachlan 922 miles (1,484 km)
Sepik 600 miles (965 km)

Political Map

WAKE ISLAND (U.S.A.)

NORTHERN MARIANA ISLANDS (U.S.A)

GUAM (U.S.A)

MARSHALL ISLANDS

PALAU

FEDERATED STATES of MICRONESIA

PAPUA NEW GUINEA

NAURU

KIRIBATI

SOLOMON ISLANDS

TUVALU

TOKELAU (N.Z.)

SAMOA

WALLIS and FUTUNA (FRANCE)

AMERICAN SAMOA (U.S.A.)

VANUATU

TONGA

NIUE (N.Z.)

COOK ISLANDS (N.Z.)

FRENCH POLYNESIA (FRANCE)

NEW CALEDONIA (FRANCE)

FIJI

PITCAIRN ISLANDS (U.K.)

AUSTRALIA

NORFOLK ISLAND (AUSTRALIA)

KERMADEC ISLANDS (N.Z.)

NEW ZEALAND

CHATHAM ISLANDS (N.Z.)

Physical Map

ASIA

NORTH AMERICA

Arctic Circle

PACIFIC OCEAN

Tropic of Cancer

HAWAIIAN
ISLANDS

MARIANA
ISLANDS

MARSHALL
ISLANDS

CAROLINE ISLANDS

M I C R O N E S I A

LINE ISLANDS

M E L A N E S I A

Equator

GILBERT
ISLANDS

PHOENIX
ISLANDS

MARQUESAS
ISLANDS

Nauru

New
Guinea
Mt.
Wilhelm

Sepik

New
Britain

SOLOMON ISLANDS

Mt.
Balbi

Tokelau

COOK ISLANDS

P O L Y N E S I A

TUAMOTU
ARCHIPELAGO

Arafura
Sea

Torres Strait

Mt.
Victoria

Tuvalu

CAPE
YORK
PENINSULA

Great Barrier Reef

Coral Sea

Vanuatu

FIJI
ISLANDS

SAMOA ISLANDS

SOCIETY
ISLANDS

GREAT
SANDY
DESERT

GREAT DIVIDING RANGE

MACDONNELL
RANGES

Australia

New
Caledonia

Tonga

PITCAIRN
ISLANDS

Tropic of Capricorn

GREAT VICTORIA
DESERT

Lake
Eyre

Fraser
Island

Great
Australian
Bight

Darling

Lachlan

Murrumbidgee

Murray

Lord Howe
Island

Norfolk
Island

KERMADEC
ISLANDS

Mt.
Kosciuszko

Tasmania

Tasman
Sea

New
Zealand

North
Island

CHATHAM
ISLANDS

Mt.
Tasman

Mt. Cook

South
Island

Macquarie
Island

Stewart
Island

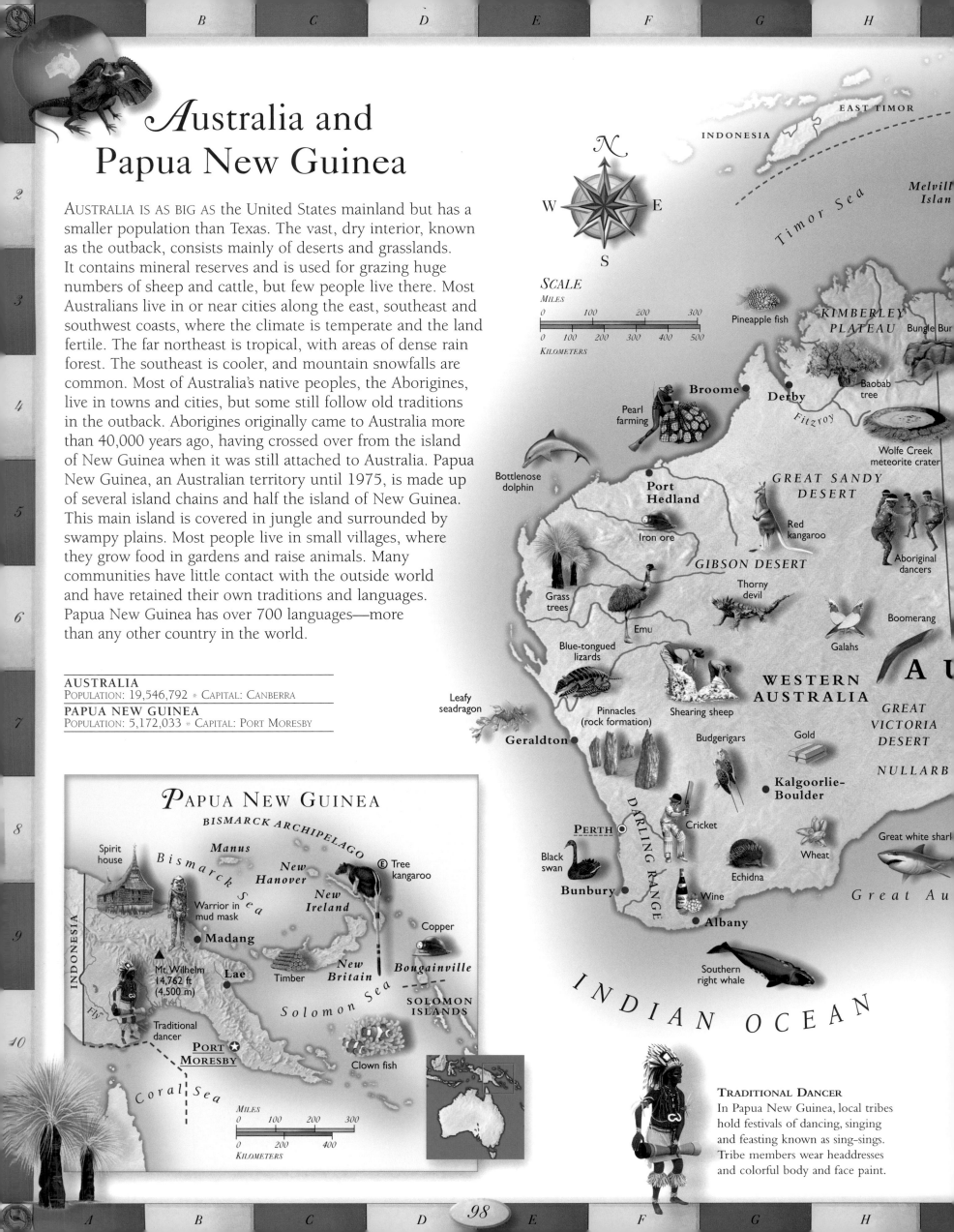

Australia and Papua New Guinea

AUSTRALIA IS AS BIG AS the United States mainland but has a smaller population than Texas. The vast, dry interior, known as the outback, consists mainly of deserts and grasslands. It contains mineral reserves and is used for grazing huge numbers of sheep and cattle, but few people live there. Most Australians live in or near cities along the east, southeast and southwest coasts, where the climate is temperate and the land fertile. The far northeast is tropical, with areas of dense rain forest. The southeast is cooler, and mountain snowfalls are common. Most of Australia's native peoples, the Aborigines, live in towns and cities, but some still follow old traditions in the outback. Aborigines originally came to Australia more than 40,000 years ago, having crossed over from the island of New Guinea when it was still attached to Australia. Papua New Guinea, an Australian territory until 1975, is made up of several island chains and half the island of New Guinea. This main island is covered in jungle and surrounded by swampy plains. Most people live in small villages, where they grow food in gardens and raise animals. Many communities have little contact with the outside world and have retained their own traditions and languages. Papua New Guinea has over 700 languages—more than any other country in the world.

AUSTRALIA
POPULATION: 19,546,792 • CAPITAL: CANBERRA
PAPUA NEW GUINEA
POPULATION: 5,172,033 • CAPITAL: PORT MORESBY

SCALE
MILES
0   100   200   300
0   100   200   300   400   500
KILOMETERS

EAST TIMOR
INDONESIA
Timor Sea
Melvill
Islan

Pineapple fish
KIMBERLEY PLATEAU
Bungle Bur
Baobab tree
Broome
Derby
Fitzroy
Pearl farming
Wolfe Creek meteorite crater

Bottlenose dolphin
GREAT SANDY DESERT
Red kangaroo
Port Hedland
Iron ore
Aboriginal dancers
GIBSON DESERT
Thorny devil
Boomerang
Grass trees
Emu
Galahs
Blue-tongued lizards
WESTERN AUSTRALIA
A U
Leafy seadragon
Pinnacles (rock formation)
Shearing sheep
GREAT VICTORIA DESERT
NULLARB
Geraldton
Budgerigars
Gold
Kalgoorlie-Boulder
Cricket
Great white shark
PERTH
Black swan
DARLING RANGE
Wheat
Bunbury
Echidna
Wine
Great Au
Albany
Southern right whale

INDIAN OCEAN

PAPUA NEW GUINEA
BISMARCK ARCHIPELAGO

Spirit house
Manus
Bismarck Sea
New Hanover
Tree kangaroo
Warrior in mud mask
New Ireland
Madang
Copper
Mt. Wilhelm 14,762 ft (4,500 m)
Lae
Timber
New Britain
Bougainville
INDONESIA
Fly
Solomon Sea
SOLOMON ISLANDS
Traditional dancer
PORT MORESBY
Clown fish
Coral Sea
MILES
0   100   200   300
0   200   400
KILOMETERS

TRADITIONAL DANCER
In Papua New Guinea, local tribes hold festivals of dancing, singing and feasting known as sing-sings. Tribe members wear headdresses and colorful body and face paint.

SOLOMON ISLANDS

House on stilts

Choiseul

Santa Isabel
Spotted cuscus

MILES
0   100   200
0 100 200 300
KILOMETERS

NEW GEORGIA ISLANDS

Malaita

HONIARA

Guadalcanal
Timber

San Cristóbal
Bananas

Harlequin tuskfish

Rennell

Coral Sea

SANTA CRUZ ISLANDS

SAMOA ISLANDS

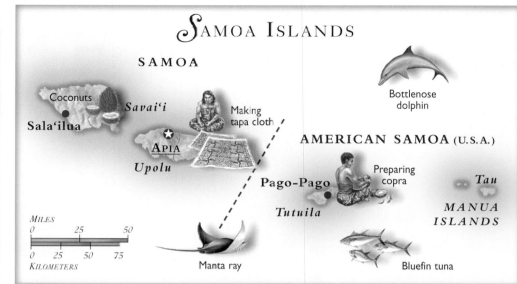

SAMOA

Coconuts

Savai'i

Sala'ilua

Making tapa cloth

APIA

Upolu

Bottlenose dolphin

AMERICAN SAMOA (U.S.A.)

Pago-Pago

Preparing copra

Tau

MANUA ISLANDS

Tutuila

MILES
0   25   50
0   25   50   75
KILOMETERS

Manta ray

Bluefin tuna

VANUATU AND NEW CALEDONIA

VANUATU

BANKS ISLANDS

Espíritu Santo

Palm trees

Maéwo

Luganville

Aoba

Great white shark

Pentecost

Ambrim

Malekula

Epi

Efate

Coral Sea

PORT VILA

Scuba diving

NEW CALEDONIA (FRANCE)

Windsurfing

Erromango

Tanna

Butterfly fish

LOYALTY ISLANDS

Yasur volcano

Coconuts

Nickel

Pouembout

Noumèa

Tourism

MILES
0   100   200
0 100 200 300
KILOMETERS

SOLOMON ISLANDS

FIJI

SAMOA ISLANDS

VANUATU AND NEW CALEDONIA

TONGA

SOCIETY ISLANDS

NEW ZEALAND

FIJI

Sugarcane

Vanua Levu

Taveuni

Koro
Tourism

Cocoa

Viti Levu

Walking on hot coals

Koro Sea

LAU GROUP

SUVA

Gau

Lakeba

Moala

Magnificent frigate bird

Coconuts

Kandavu

MILES
0   25 50 75
0   50   100   150
KILOMETERS

Angelfish

LOCATION

TONGA

TONGATAPU GROUP

HA'APAI GROUP
NOMUKA GROUP
VAVA'U GROUP

NUKU'ALOFA

Coral reef

Tongatapu

Fua'amotu

Royal Palace

Ohonua

Tourism

'Eua

Bananas

Swordfish

MILES
0   10   20
0   10   20   20
KILOMETERS

SOCIETY ISLANDS

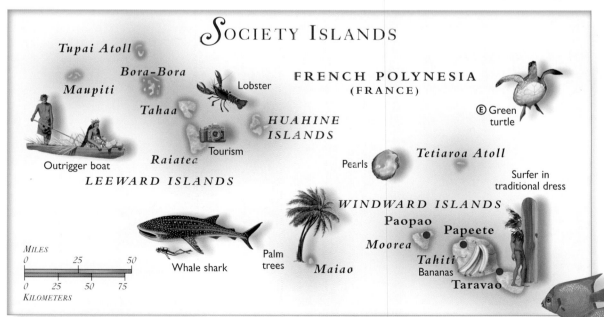

Tupai Atoll

Bora-Bora

Lobster

FRENCH POLYNESIA (FRANCE)

Maupiti

Tahaa

HUAHINE ISLANDS

Green turtle

Raiatea

Tourism

Tetiaroa Atoll

Pearls

Outrigger boat

LEEWARD ISLANDS

Surfer in traditional dress

WINDWARD ISLANDS

Paopao

Moorea

Papeete

Whale shark

Palm trees

Maiao

Tahiti
Bananas

Taravao

MILES
0   25   50
0   25   50   75
KILOMETERS

The Polar Regions

THE REGIONS THAT SURROUND the North and South poles are the coldest and windiest parts of our planet. Both are permanently covered in snow and ice, and during winter months there is little or no daylight. Antarctica is a frozen continent surrounded by ocean. The Arctic is an area of frozen ocean surrounded by continents. In winter, the Arctic ice spreads southward, reaching North America, Europe and Asia. The northern fringes of these continents are home to native peoples who have adapted to Arctic life. They include the Saami (Lapps) of Scandinavia and the Inuit of Canada, Alaska, Greenland and Russia. A Danish territory, Greenland is the world's largest island. Most of it lies under a thick sheet of ice. Antarctica is the only continent with no permanent population. Scientists spend part of the year at research stations, but many leave Antarctica before the cold, dark winter sets in. The continent is covered by a vast ice sheet which is two miles (3 km) thick in some places. Along the coast, the ice sheet forms huge ice shelves over the ocean. Giant blocks of ice break off and float away as icebergs. Some icebergs are as large as small countries and take years to melt. There is little life in the Antarctic interior, but whales, seals and fish swim just offshore, and during the summer enormous colonies of seabirds nest along the coast and on nearby islands.

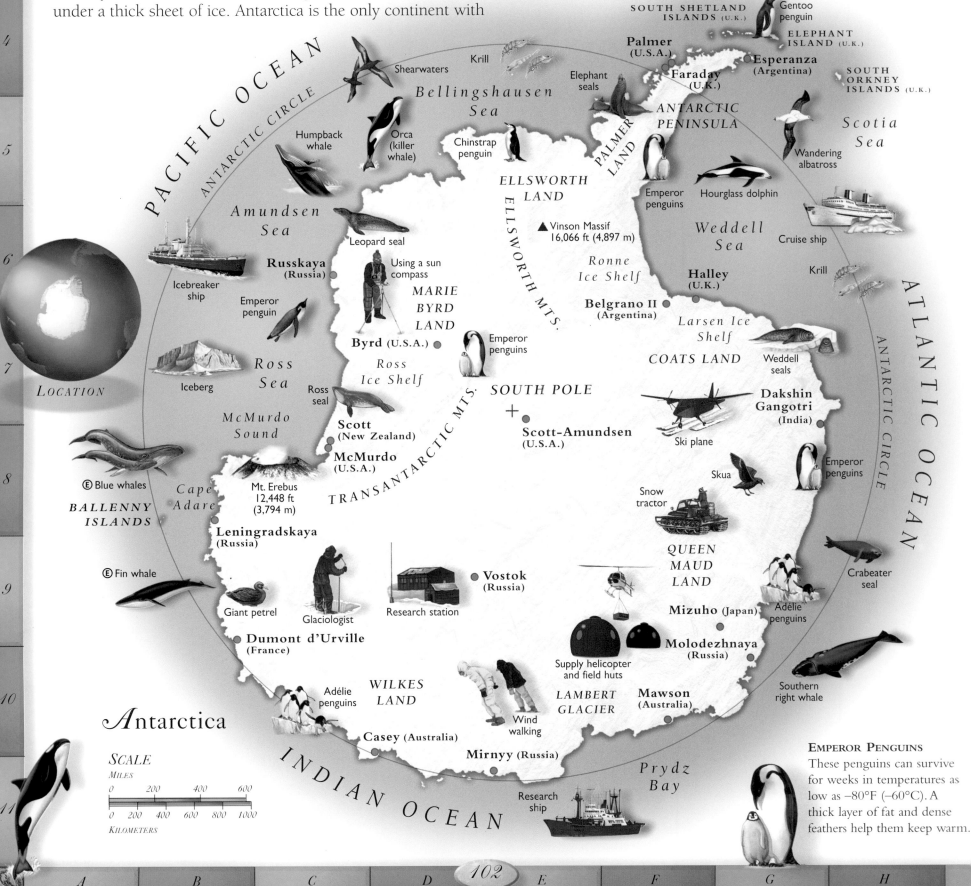

EMPEROR PENGUINS
These penguins can survive for weeks in temperatures as low as −80°F (−60°C). A thick layer of fat and dense feathers help them keep warm.

The Arctic

SCALE

MILES

0   200   400   600

0   200   400   600   800   1000

KILOMETERS

· LOOK AGAIN ·

- Name four kinds of penguins that live in Antarctica.
- Which minerals are mined on Banks Island in Canada?
- What kind of whale lives in the Barents Sea?

Icebreaker ship

Reindeer

Chukchi hunter

ALASKA (U.S.A.)

Arctic hare

Oil

Bering Strait

ARCTIC CIRCLE

Pevek

Ambarchik

Chukchi Sea

Wrangel Island

East Siberian Sea

CANADA

Prudhoe Bay

Barrow

Narwhal

Arctic tern

NEW SIBERIAN ISLANDS

Walrus

Snow goose

Beaufort Sea

Banks Island

Musk-ox

Zinc and lead

Skua

Polar bears

Gray whale

Lena

Ptarmigan

Yakut woman and children

RUSSIA

Victoria Island

Snowmobile

Snowy owl

Walrus

ARCTIC OCEAN

Laptev Sea

Nordvik

Kittiwake

Wolf

QUEEN ELIZABETH ISLANDS

SEVERNAYA ZEMLYA

Arctic fox

ARCTIC CIRCLE

Hudson Bay

Resolute

NORTH POLE
+

Beluga whale

Dudinka

Baffin Island

Ellesmere Island

Kara Sea

FRANZ JOSEF LAND

Natural gas

LOCATION

Inuit fishing through ice

Walrus tusk carvings

Thule

Jakobshavn houses

Hooded seal

Harp seals

NOVAYA ZEMLYA

CANADA

Baffin Bay

Upernavik

Svalbard reindeer

Haddock

Nenet woman

Davis Strait

GREENLAND (DENMARK)

SVALBARD (NORWAY)

Longyearbyen

Barents Sea

Nar'yan-Mar

Tourism

Inuit hunter

Spitsbergen

Musk-ox

Snowmobile

Bowhead whale

Harbor seals

NORTH CAPE

Murmansk

Nuuk

Cod

Orca (killer whale)

Hammerfest

Iceberg

Tourism

Mt. Gunnbjorn 12,139 ft (3,700 m)

FINLAND

Julianehåb

Denmark Strait

Norwegian Sea

Puffins

Sami (Lapp) man

SWEDEN

CAPE FAREWELL

ICELAND

NORWAY

CHUKCHI HUNTER
Traditionally, Chukchi people hunted seals, walruses and whales from kayaks, using ivory-tipped harpoons. Now most hunters use rifles and travel in motorboats.

REINDEER
Huge herds of reindeer roam over the tundra in search of food. Their large hooves prevent them from sinking into the snow and help them dig through to reach plants and lichens.

World Fact File

NORTH AMERICA

CANADA

PRONUNCIATION: KA-nuh-duh
AREA: 3,851,809 sq. miles (9,976,185 sq. km)
POPULATION: 31,902,268
CAPITAL: Ottawa
CURRENCY: 100 cents = 1 Canadian dollar (Can$)
OFFICIAL LANGUAGES: English, French
MAIN RELIGION: Christianity 82%
EXPORTS: Newsprint, wood pulp, timber, crude petroleum, machinery, natural gas, aluminum, motor vehicles and parts, telecommunications equipment, electricity

UNITED STATES OF AMERICA

PRONUNCIATION: yoo-NEYE-tuhd STAYTS of uh-MEHR-uh-kuh
AREA: 3,717,800 sq. miles (9,629,091 sq. km)
POPULATION: 280,562,489
CAPITAL: Washington, D.C.
CURRENCY: 100 cents = 1 United States dollar (US$)
OFFICIAL LANGUAGE: English
OTHER LANGUAGE: Spanish
MAIN RELIGIONS: Christianity 84%, Judaism 2%
EXPORTS: Motor vehicles, raw materials, consumer goods, agricultural products, industrial supplies

MEXICO

PRONUNCIATION: MEK-si-koh
AREA: 761,600 sq. miles (1,972,544 sq. km)
POPULATION: 103,400,165
CAPITAL: Mexico City
CURRENCY: 100 centavos = 1 Mexican peso (Mex$)
OFFICIAL LANGUAGE: Spanish
OTHER LANGUAGES: Regional languages
MAIN RELIGION: Christianity 95%
EXPORTS: Crude oil, oil products, coffee, silver, engines, motor vehicles, cotton, electronic goods

GUATEMALA

PRONUNCIATION: gwah-tuh-MAH-luh
AREA: 42,042 sq. miles (108,889 sq. km)
POPULATION: 13,314,079
CAPITAL: Guatemala
CURRENCY: 100 centavos = 1 Guatemalan quetzal (Q)
OFFICIAL LANGUAGE: Spanish
OTHER LANGUAGES: Quiche, Cakchiquel, Kekchi, and other regional languages
MAIN RELIGIONS: Christianity 99%, traditional Mayan religions
EXPORTS: Coffee, bananas, cotton, sugar, minerals, textiles, petroleum

BELIZE

PRONUNCIATION: buh-LEEZ
AREA: 8,867 sq. miles (22,966 sq. km)
POPULATION: 262,999
CAPITAL: Belmopan
CURRENCY: 100 cents = 1 Belizean dollar (Bz$)
OFFICIAL LANGUAGE: English
OTHER LANGUAGES: Spanish, Maya, Garifuna, Creole
MAIN RELIGION: Christianity 92%
EXPORTS: Sugar, molasses, citrus fruit, bananas, clothing, fish products, timber

HONDURAS

PRONUNCIATION: hahn-DER-uhs
AREA: 43,277 sq. miles (112,087 sq. km)
POPULATION: 6,560,608
CAPITAL: Tegucigalpa
CURRENCY: 100 centavos = 1 lempira (L)
OFFICIAL LANGUAGE: Spanish
OTHER LANGUAGES: Regional languages
MAIN RELIGION: Christianity 97%
EXPORTS: Sugar, coffee, textiles, clothing, timber and timber products

EL SALVADOR

PRONUNCIATION: el SAL-vuh-dor
AREA: 8,260 sq. miles (21,393 sq. km)
POPULATION: 6,353,681
CAPITAL: San Salvador
CURRENCY: 100 centavos = 1 Salvadoran colón (C)
OFFICIAL LANGUAGE: Spanish
OTHER LANGUAGE: Nahua
MAIN RELIGION: Christianity 92%
EXPORTS: Coffee, sugarcane, shrimp, raw materials

NICARAGUA

PRONUNCIATION: ni-kuh-RAH-gwuh
AREA: 49,998 sq. miles (129,494 sq. km)
POPULATION: 5,023,818
CAPITAL: Managua
CURRENCY: 100 centavos = 1 gold cordoba (C$)
OFFICIAL LANGUAGE: Spanish
OTHER LANGUAGES: English, regional languages
MAIN RELIGION: Christianity 100%
EXPORTS: Coffee, cotton, sugar, bananas, seafood, gold, beef, tobacco

COSTA RICA

PRONUNCIATION: kaws-tuh REE-kuh
AREA: 19,652 sq. miles (50,899 sq. km)
POPULATION: 3,834,934
CAPITAL: San José
CURRENCY: 100 centimos = 1 Costa Rican colón (C)
OFFICIAL LANGUAGE: Spanish
OTHER LANGUAGE: English
MAIN RELIGION: Christianity 92%
EXPORTS: Coffee, bananas, sugar, textiles, pineapples

PANAMA

PRONUNCIATION: PA-nuh-mah
AREA: 33,659 sq. miles (87,177 sq. km)
POPULATION: 2,882,329
CAPITAL: Panama
CURRENCY: 100 centesimos = 1 balboa (B)

PRONUNCIATION KEY

"a" sounds		"i" sounds		"u" sounds		zh	as in measure
a	as in pat	i	as in pit	uh	as in but and comma	s	as in set
ah	as in father	eye	as in bite			ch	as in chase
ar	as in dark	ihr	as in hear	u	as in put and book	j	as in jug
ay	as in bay					g	as in game
air	as in pair	"o" sounds		oo	as in boot	ng	as in sing
		o	as in pot	yoo	as in music		
"e" sounds		oh	as in boat			Emphasize the part
e	as in pet	aw	as in paw	other sounds		of the word that
ee	as in feet	or	as in poor	th	as in thin and then	is written in
er	as in pert	ow	as in how			**BOLD CAPITAL**
ehr	as in Sierra	oy	as in boy	sh	as in show	**LETTERS**

OFFICIAL LANGUAGE: Spanish
OTHER LANGUAGES: English, regional languages
MAIN RELIGION: Christianity 100%
EXPORTS: Bananas, shrimp, sugar, coffee, clothing

THE BAHAMAS
PRONUNCIATION: the buh-HAH-muhz
AREA: 5,386 sq. miles (13,950 sq. km)
POPULATION: 300,529
CAPITAL: Nassau
CURRENCY: 100 cents = 1 Bahamian dollar (B$)
OFFICIAL LANGUAGE: English
OTHER LANGUAGE: Bahamian creole
MAIN RELIGION: Christianity 95%
EXPORTS: Pharmaceuticals, cement, rum, crayfish, refined petroleum products

CUBA
PRONUNCIATION: KYOO-buh
AREA: 42,804 sq. miles (110,862 sq. km)
POPULATION: 11,224,321
CAPITAL: Havana
CURRENCY: 100 centavos = 1 Cuban peso (Cu$)
OFFICIAL LANGUAGE: Spanish
MAIN RELIGION: Christianity 85%
EXPORTS: Sugar, fish and shellfish, citrus fruit, coffee, tobacco, nickel, medical products

JAMAICA
PRONUNCIATION: juh-MAY-kuh
AREA: 4,243 sq. miles (10,990 sq. km)
POPULATION: 2,680,029
CAPITAL: Kingston
CURRENCY: 100 cents = 1 Jamaican dollar (J$)
OFFICIAL LANGUAGE: English
OTHER LANGUAGE: Jamaican creole
MAIN RELIGION: Christianity 65%
EXPORTS: Bauxite, sugar, bananas, rum, alumina

HAITI
PRONUNCIATION: HAY-tee
AREA: 10,714 sq. miles (27,749 sq. km)
POPULATION: 7,063,722
CAPITAL: Port-au-Prince
CURRENCY: 100 centimes = 1 gourde (G)
OFFICIAL LANGUAGES: French, Haitian creole
MAIN RELIGION: Christianity 96%
EXPORTS: Clothing, coffee, sugar, manufactured goods, oils, mangoes

DOMINICAN REPUBLIC
PRONUNCIATION: duh-MI-ni-kuhn ri-PUH-blik
AREA: 18,657 sq. miles (48,322 sq. km)
POPULATION: 8,721,594
CAPITAL: Santo Domingo
CURRENCY: 100 centavos = 1 Dominican peso (RD$)
OFFICIAL LANGUAGE: Spanish
MAIN RELIGION: Christianity 95%
EXPORTS: Minerals, coffee, cocoa, gold, tobacco

ANTIGUA AND BARBUDA
PRONUNCIATION: an-TEE-guh and bar-BOO-duh
AREA: 171 sq. miles (443 sq. km)
POPULATION: 67,448
CAPITAL: St. John's
CURRENCY: 100 cents = 1 East Caribbean dollar (EC$)
OFFICIAL LANGUAGE: English
OTHER LANGUAGES: Regional languages
MAIN RELIGIONS: Christianity 97%, indigenous religions 3%
EXPORTS: Petroleum products, manufactured goods, machinery and transportation equipment, food and livestock

ST. KITTS–NEVIS
PRONUNCIATION: saynt KITS NEE-vuhs
AREA: 104 sq. miles (269 sq. km)
POPULATION: 38,736
CAPITAL: Basseterre
CURRENCY: 100 cents = 1 East Caribbean dollar (EC$)
OFFICIAL LANGUAGE: English
MAIN RELIGION: Christianity 86%
EXPORTS: Machinery, food, beverages, electronics, tobacco

DOMINICA
PRONUNCIATION: dah-muh-NEE-kuh
AREA: 289 sq. miles (749 sq. km)
POPULATION: 70,158
CAPITAL: Roseau
CURRENCY: 100 cents = 1 East Caribbean dollar (EC$)
OFFICIAL LANGUAGE: English
OTHER LANGUAGE: French patois
MAIN RELIGION: Christianity 92%
EXPORTS: Bananas, grapefruit, oranges, vegetables, soap, bay oil

ST. LUCIA
PRONUNCIATION: saynt LOO-shuh
AREA: 238 sq. miles (616 sq. km)
POPULATION: 160,145
CAPITAL: Castries
CURRENCY: 100 cents = 1 East Caribbean dollar (EC$)
OFFICIAL LANGUAGE: English
OTHER LANGUAGE: French patois
MAIN RELIGION: Christianity 100%
EXPORTS: Bananas, clothing, cocoa, coconut oil, fruit and vegetables

BARBADOS
PRONUNCIATION: bar-BAY-dohs
AREA: 166 sq. miles (430 sq. km)
POPULATION: 276,607
CAPITAL: Bridgetown
CURRENCY: 100 cents = 1 Barbadian dollar (Bds$)
OFFICIAL LANGUAGE: English
OTHER LANGUAGE: Barbadian creole
MAIN RELIGION: Christianity 71%
EXPORTS: Sugar and molasses, rum, chemicals, foods and beverages, electrical components, clothing

ST. VINCENT AND THE GRENADINES
PRONUNCIATION: saynt VIN-suhnt and the gren-uh-DEENZ
AREA: 150 sq. miles (389 sq. km)
POPULATION: 116,394
CAPITAL: Kingstown
CURRENCY: 100 cents = 1 East Caribbean dollar (EC$)
OFFICIAL LANGUAGE: English
OTHER LANGUAGE: French patois
MAIN RELIGION: Christianity 75%
EXPORTS: Bananas, taro, tennis rackets, arrowroot

GRENADA
PRONUNCIATION: gruh-NAY-duh
AREA: 133 sq. miles (344 sq. km)
POPULATION: 89,211
CAPITAL: St. George's
CURRENCY: 100 cents = 1 East Caribbean dollar (EC$)
OFFICIAL LANGUAGE: English
OTHER LANGUAGE: French patois
MAIN RELIGION: Christianity 100%
EXPORTS: Bananas, fruit and vegetables, cocoa, nutmeg, clothing, mace

TRINIDAD AND TOBAGO
PRONUNCIATION: TRI-nuh-dad and tuh-BAY-goh
AREA: 1,980 sq. miles (5,128 sq. km)
POPULATION: 1,163,724
CAPITAL: Port-of-Spain
CURRENCY: 100 cents = 1 Trinidad and Tobago dollar (TT$)
OFFICIAL LANGUAGE: English
OTHER LANGUAGES: Hindi, French, Spanish, Chinese
MAIN RELIGIONS: Christianity 44%, Hinduism 24%, Islam 6%
EXPORTS: Petroleum and petroleum products, chemicals, steel products, fertilizer, sugar, cocoa, coffee, citrus fruit, flowers

SOUTH AMERICA

COLOMBIA

PRONUNCIATION: kuh-LUHM-bee-uh
AREA: 439,735 sq. miles
(1,138,914 sq. km)
POPULATION: 41,008,227
CAPITAL: Bogota
CURRENCY: 100 centavos = 1 Colombian
peso (Col$)
OFFICIAL LANGUAGE: Spanish
MAIN RELIGION: Christianity 90%
EXPORTS: Petroleum, coffee, coal, bananas, flowers

VENEZUELA

PRONUNCIATION: ve-nuh-ZWAY-luh
AREA: 352,143 sq. miles
(912,050 sq. km)
POPULATION: 24,287,670
CAPITAL: Caracas
CURRENCY: 100 centimos = 1 bolivar (Bs)
OFFICIAL LANGUAGE: Spanish
OTHER LANGUAGES: Regional languages
MAIN RELIGION: Christianity 98%
EXPORTS: Petroleum, bauxite and aluminum,
steel, chemicals, agricultural products, basic
manufactured goods

GUYANA

PRONUNCIATION: geye-AH-nuh
AREA: 83,000 sq. miles
(214,970 sq. km)
POPULATION: 698,209
CAPITAL: Georgetown
CURRENCY: 100 cents = 1 Guyanese dollar (G$)
OFFICIAL LANGUAGE: English
OTHER LANGUAGES: Local languages, Hindi, Urdu
MAIN RELIGIONS: Christianity 50%,
Hinduism 33%, Islam 9%
EXPORTS: Sugar, molasses, bauxite, rice, shrimp

SURINAME

PRONUNCIATION: SUR-uh-nah-muh
AREA: 63,039 sq. miles
(163,270 sq. km)
POPULATION: 436,494
CAPITAL: Paramaribo
CURRENCY: 100 cents = 1 Surinamese guilder or
florin (Sf)
OFFICIAL LANGUAGE: Dutch
OTHER LANGUAGES: English, Sranang Tongo,
Hindustani, Javanese
MAIN RELIGIONS: Christianity 48%,
Hinduism 27%, Islam 20%, regional religions 5%
EXPORTS: Aluminum, fish,
shrimp, timber, rice,
bananas, crude oil

ECUADOR

PRONUNCIATION: E-kwuh-dor
AREA: 109,483 sq. miles
(283,561 sq. km)
POPULATION: 13,447,494
CAPITAL: Quito
CURRENCY: 100 cents = 1 United States dollar (US$)
OFFICIAL LANGUAGE: Spanish
OTHER LANGUAGES: Quechua, other regional
languages
MAIN RELIGION: Christianity 95%
EXPORTS: Petroleum, bananas, shrimp, cocoa,
coffee, flowers, fish

PERU

PRONUNCIATION: puh-ROO
AREA: 496,222 sq. miles
(1,285,215 sq. km)
POPULATION: 27,949,639
CAPITAL: Lima
CURRENCY: 100 centimos = 1 nuevo sol (S/.)
OFFICIAL LANGUAGES: Spanish, Quechua
OTHER LANGUAGE: Aymara
MAIN RELIGION: Christianity 90%
EXPORTS: Copper, zinc, petroleum products, lead,
coffee, cotton, fish and fish products, sugar

BRAZIL

PRONUNCIATION: bruh-ZIL
AREA: 3,286,470 sq. miles
(8,511,965 sq. km)
POPULATION: 176,029,560
CAPITAL: Brasília
CURRENCY: 100 centavos = 1 real (R$)
OFFICIAL LANGUAGE: Portuguese
OTHER LANGUAGES: Spanish, English, French
MAIN RELIGION: Christianity 80%
EXPORTS: Iron ore, soybean bran, coffee, sugar,
footwear, manufactured goods

BOLIVIA

PRONUNCIATION: buh-LI-vee-uh
AREA: 424,162 sq. miles
(1,098,579 sq. km)
POPULATION: 8,445,134
CAPITALS: La Paz (seat of government),
Sucre (legal and judicial)
CURRENCY: 100 centavos = 1 boliviano ($B)
OFFICIAL LANGUAGES: Spanish, Quechua, Aymara
MAIN RELIGION: Christianity 100%
EXPORTS: Natural gas, soybeans, zinc, gold
jewelry, timber

CHILE

PRONUNCIATION: CHI-lee
AREA: 292,257 sq. miles
(756,946 sq. km)
POPULATION: 15,498,930
CAPITAL: Santiago
CURRENCY: 100 centavos = 1 Chilean peso (Ch$)
OFFICIAL LANGUAGE: Spanish
OTHER LANGUAGES: Regional languages
MAIN RELIGION: Christianity 99%
EXPORTS: Copper, metals and minerals, timber
products, fish, fruit, chemicals

PARAGUAY

PRONUNCIATION: PAR-uh-gweye
AREA: 157,043 sq. miles
(406,741 sq. km)
POPULATION: 5,884,491
CAPITAL: Asunción
CURRENCY: 100 centimos = 1 guarani (G)
OFFICIAL LANGUAGES: Spanish, Guarani
MAIN RELIGION: Christianity 97%
EXPORTS: Cotton, soybeans, timber, vegetable
oils, meat products, coffee, electricity, feed
for livestock

ARGENTINA

PRONUNCIATION: ar-juhn-TEE-nuh
AREA: 1,068,296 sq. miles
(2,766,884 sq. km)
POPULATION: 37,812,817
CAPITAL: Buenos Aires
CURRENCY: 100 centavos = 1 Argentine peso (ARS)
OFFICIAL LANGUAGE: Spanish
OTHER LANGUAGES: English, Italian,
German, French
MAIN RELIGIONS: Christianity 92%, Judaism 2%
EXPORTS: Manufactured goods, meat, wheat, corn,
vegetable oil, fuel and energy

URUGUAY

PRONUNCIATION: OOR-uh-gweye
AREA: 68,039 sq. miles
(176,221 sq. km)
POPULATION: 3,386,575
CAPITAL: Montevideo
CURRENCY: 100 centesimos = 1 Uruguayan peso
($Ur)
OFFICIAL LANGUAGE: Spanish
OTHER LANGUAGE: Brazilero
MAIN RELIGIONS: Christianity 68%, Judaism 1%
EXPORTS: Wool, textiles, beef and other animal
products, leather, rice

EUROPE

UNITED KINGDOM

PRONUNCIATION: yoo-NEYE-tuhd king-duhm
AREA: 94,525 sq. miles (244,820 sq. km)
POPULATION: 58,836,700
CAPITAL: London
CURRENCY: 100 pence = 1 British pound (£)
OFFICIAL LANGUAGE: English
OTHER LANGUAGES: Welsh, Scottish Gaelic, Irish Gaelic
MAIN RELIGIONS: Christianity 90%, Islam 3%, Sikh 1%, Hinduism 1%, Judaism 1%
EXPORTS: Manufactured goods, machinery, fuels, chemicals, food and beverages, tobacco

IRELAND
PRONUNCIATION: EYER-luhnd
AREA: 26,600 sq. miles (68,894 sq. km)
POPULATION: 3,883,159
CAPITAL: Dublin
CURRENCY: 100 cents = 1 euro (€)
OFFICIAL LANGUAGES: English, Irish (Gaelic)
MAIN RELIGION: Christianity 94%
EXPORTS: Chemicals, data processing equipment, industrial machinery, livestock, animal products, pharmacueticals

PORTUGAL
PRONUNCIATION: POR-chi-guhl
AREA: 35,383 sq. miles (91,642 sq. km)
POPULATION: 10,084,245
CAPITAL: Lisbon
CURRENCY: 100 cents = 1 euro (€)
OFFICIAL LANGUAGE: Portuguese
MAIN RELIGION: Christianity 98%
EXPORTS: Clothing, footwear, machinery, cork, paper products, animal hides, chemicals

SPAIN
PRONUNCIATION: spayn
AREA: 194,881 sq. miles (504,742 sq. km)
POPULATION: 40,077,100
CAPITAL: Madrid
CURRENCY: 100 cents = 1 euro (€)
OFFICIAL LANGUAGE: Castilian Spanish
OTHER LANGUAGES: Catalan, Galician, Basque
MAIN RELIGION: Christianity 99%
EXPORTS: Motor vehicles, manufactured goods, food, machinery, consumer goods

ANDORRA
PRONUNCIATION: an-DOR-uh
AREA: 180 sq. miles (482 sq. km)
POPULATION: 68,403
CAPITAL: Andorra la Vella
CURRENCIES: 100 cents = 1 euro (€)
OFFICIAL LANGUAGE: Catalan
OTHER LANGUAGES: French, Castilian Spanish
MAIN RELIGION: Christianity 95%
EXPORTS: Electricity, tobacco products, timber, furniture

FRANCE
PRONUNCIATION: frans
AREA: 211,209 sq. miles (547,030 sq. km)
POPULATION: 59,765,983
CAPITAL: Paris
CURRENCY: 100 cents = 1 euro (€)
OFFICIAL LANGUAGE: French
OTHER LANGUAGES: Occitan, Breton, Catalan, Basque, Arabic, Corsican, Flemish, Alsatian
MAIN RELIGIONS: Christianity 92%, Judaism 1%, Islam 3%
EXPORTS: Machinery and transportation equipment, chemicals, food, agricultural products, iron and steel, textiles, clothing, pharmacueticals

MONACO
PRONUNCIATION: MAH-nuh-koh
AREA: 0.58 sq. miles (1.5 sq. km)
POPULATION: 31,987
CAPITAL: Monaco
CURRENCY: 100 cents = 1 euro (€)
OFFICIAL LANGUAGE: French
OTHER LANGUAGES: English, Italian, Monégasque
MAIN RELIGION: Christianity 95%
EXPORTS: Pharmaceuticals, perfumes, clothing

THE NETHERLANDS
PRONUNCIATION: the NE-ther-luhndz
AREA: 16,033 sq. miles (41,525 sq. km)
POPULATION: 16,067,754
CAPITALS: Amsterdam; The Hague (judicial)
CURRENCY: 100 cents = 1 euro (€)
OFFICIAL LANGUAGE: Dutch
MAIN RELIGIONS: Christianity 52%, Islam 4%
EXPORTS: Metal products, chemicals, processed food, tobacco, agricultural products, machinery and equipment

BELGIUM
PRONUNCIATION: BEL-juhm
AREA: 11,781 sq. miles (30,513 sq. km)
POPULATION: 10,274,595
CAPITAL: Brussels
CURRENCY: 100 cents = 1 euro (€)
OFFICIAL LANGUAGES: Dutch (Flemish), French
OTHER LANGUAGE: German
MAIN RELIGION: Christianity 100%
EXPORTS: Iron and steel, machinery and equipment, chemicals, diamonds, petroleum products

LUXEMBOURG
PRONUNCIATION: LUK-suhm-berg
AREA: 999 sq. miles (2,587 sq. km)
POPULATION: 429,100
CAPITAL: Luxembourg
CURRENCY: 100 cents = 1 euro (€)
OFFICIAL LANGUAGES: Luxembourgish (Letzeburgesh), German, French
OTHER LANGUAGE: English
MAIN RELIGIONS: Christianity 99%, Judaism 1%
EXPORTS: Steel products, chemicals, rubber products, glass, aluminum, machinery and equipment

GERMANY
PRONUNCIATION: JER-muh-nee
AREA: 137,735 sq. miles (356,734 sq. km)
POPULATION: 83,251,851
CAPITAL: Berlin
CURRENCY: 100 cents = 1 euro (€)
OFFICIAL LANGUAGE: German
MAIN RELIGIONS: Christianity 72%, Islam 2%
EXPORTS: Machines and machine tools, chemicals, motor vehicles, iron and steel products, textiles, agricultural products, raw materials

SWITZERLAND
PRONUNCIATION: SWIT-suhr-luhnd
AREA: 15,941 sq. miles (41,287 sq. km)
POPULATION: 7,301,994
CAPITAL: Bern
CURRENCY: 100 centimes = 1 Swiss franc (CHF)
OFFICIAL LANGUAGES: German, French, Italian
OTHER LANGUAGE: Romansch
MAIN RELIGION: Christianity 86%
EXPORTS: Machinery, precision instruments, metal products, food, textiles, chemicals

LIECHTENSTEIN
PRONUNCIATION: LIK-tuhn-shteyen
AREA: 62 sq. miles (161 sq. km)
POPULATION: 32,842
CAPITAL: Vaduz
CURRENCY: 100 centimes = 1 Swiss franc (CHF)
OFFICIAL LANGUAGE: German
MAIN RELIGION: Christianity 87%
EXPORTS: Machinery, dental products, stamps, hardware, pottery

AUSTRIA

PRONUNCIATION: AWS-tree-uh
AREA: 32,375 sq. miles
(83,851 sq. km)
POPULATION: 8,169,929
CAPITAL: Vienna
CURRENCY: 100 cents = 1 euro (€)
OFFICIAL LANGUAGE: German
MAIN RELIGION: Christianity 82%
EXPORTS: Machinery, electrical equipment,
iron and steel, lumber, textiles, paper and
paper products, chemicals, foodstuffs,
metal goods

ITALY

PRONUNCIATION: IT-uh-lee
AREA: 116,313 sq. miles
(301,251 sq. km)
POPULATION: 57,715,625
CAPITAL: Rome
CURRENCY: 100 cents = 1 euro (€)
OFFICIAL LANGUAGE: Italian
OTHER LANGUAGES: German, French, Slovene
MAIN RELIGION: Christianity 98%
EXPORTS: Textiles, clothing, machinery, motor
vehicles, transportation equipment, chemicals,
food products, minerals

SAN MARINO

PRONUNCIATION: san muh-REE-noh
AREA: 24 sq. miles (62 sq. km)
POPULATION: 27,730
CAPITAL: San Marino
CURRENCY: 100 cents = 1 euro (€)
OFFICIAL LANGUAGE: Italian
MAIN RELIGION: Christianity 95%
EXPORTS: Building stone, lime, timber, chestnuts,
wheat, wine, baked goods, animal skins, ceramics

VATICAN CITY

PRONUNCIATION: VA-ti-kuhn city
AREA: 0.17 sq. miles (0.44 sq. km)
POPULATION: 900
CAPITAL: Vatican City
CURRENCY: 100 cents = 1 euro (€)
OFFICIAL LANGUAGES: Italian, Latin, French
MAIN RELIGION: Christianity 100%
EXPORTS: None

MALTA

PRONUNCIATION: MAWL-tuh
AREA: 122 sq. miles (316 sq. km)
POPULATION: 397,499
CAPITAL: Valletta
CURRENCY: 100 cents = 1 Maltese lira (LM)
OFFICIAL LANGUAGES: Maltese, English
MAIN RELIGION: Christianity 98%
EXPORTS: Machinery and transportation
equipment, clothing, footwear

SLOVENIA

PRONUNCIATION: sloh-VEE-nee-uh
AREA: 7,819 sq. miles (20,251 sq. km)
POPULATION: 1,932,917
CAPITAL: Ljubljana
CURRENCY: 100 stotins = 1 tolar (SIT)
OFFICIAL LANGUAGE: Slovenian
OTHER LANGUAGE: Serbo-Croatian
MAIN RELIGIONS: Christianity 72%, Islam 1%
EXPORTS: Motor vehicles, furniture, machinery,
manufactured goods, chemicals, textiles, food,
raw materials

CROATIA

PRONUNCIATION: kroh-AY-shuh
AREA: 21,829 sq. miles
(56,537 sq. km)
POPULATION: 4,390,751
CAPITAL: Zagreb
CURRENCY: 100 lipas = 1 Croatian kuna (HRK)
OFFICIAL LANGUAGE: Serbo-Croatian
MAIN RELIGIONS: Christianity 88%, Islam 1%
EXPORTS: Machinery and transportation
equipment, other manufactured goods,
chemicals, food, livestock, raw materials,
fuels, textiles

BOSNIA AND HERZEGOVINA

PRONUNCIATION: BAHZ-nee-uh and
hert-suh-goh-VEE-nuh
AREA: 19,740 sq. miles (51,129 sq. km)
POPULATION: 3,964,388
CAPITAL: Sarajevo
CURRENCY: 100 pfenniga = 1 marka (BAM)
OFFICIAL LANGUAGES: Serbo-Croatian, Bosnian
MAIN RELIGIONS: Christianity 50%, Islam 40%
EXPORTS: Timber, furniture

YUGOSLAVIA

PRONUNCIATION: yoo-goh-SLAH-vee-uh
AREA: 39,449 sq. miles (102,173 sq. km)
POPULATION: 10,656,929
CAPITAL: Belgrade
CURRENCY: 100 paras = 1 Yugoslav new dinar (YD)
OFFICIAL LANGUAGE: Serbo-Croatian
OTHER LANGUAGE: Albanian
MAIN RELIGIONS: Christianity 70%, Islam 19%
EXPORTS: Manufactured goods, raw materials, food

ROMANIA

PRONUNCIATION: roh-MAY-nee-uh
AREA: 91,699 sq. miles (237,500 sq. km)
POPULATION: 22,317,730
CAPITAL: Bucharest
CURRENCY: 100 bani = 1 leu (L)
OFFICIAL LANGUAGE: Romanian
OTHER LANGUAGES: Hungarian, German
MAIN RELIGION: Christianity 82%
EXPORTS: Metals and metal products, minerals
and fuels, textiles and footwear, electrical goods,
machinery and equipment

BULGARIA

PRONUNCIATION: buhl-GAIR-ee-uh
AREA: 42,823 sq. miles
(110,912 sq. km)
POPULATION: 7,621,337
CAPITAL: Sofia
CURRENCY: 100 stotinki = 1 lev (Lv)
OFFICIAL LANGUAGE: Bulgarian
MAIN RELIGIONS: Christianity 86%, Islam 13%,
Judaism 1%
EXPORTS: Machinery and equipment, fuels,
minerals and raw materials, metals, clothing,
footwear

ALBANIA

PRONUNCIATION: al-BAY-nee-uh
AREA: 11,100 sq. miles
(28,749 sq. km)
POPULATION: 3,544,841
CAPITAL: Tiranë
CURRENCY: 100 qintars = 1 lek (L)
OFFICIAL LANGUAGE: Albanian (Tosk dialect)
OTHER LANGUAGE: Greek
MAIN RELIGIONS: Islam 70%, Christianity 30%
EXPORTS: Asphalt, metals and metallic ores,
electricity, crude oil, fruit and vegetables, tobacco

MACEDONIA

PRONUNCIATION: ma-suh-DOH-nee-uh
AREA: 9,928 sq. miles (25,714 sq. km)
POPULATION: 2,054,800
CAPITAL: Skopje
CURRENCY: 100 deni = 1 Macedonian denar (MKD)
OFFICIAL LANGUAGE: Macedonian
OTHER LANGUAGES: Albanian, Turkish,
Serbo-Croatian
MAIN RELIGIONS: Christianity 67%, Islam 30%
EXPORTS: Manufactured goods, machinery and
transportation equipment, food, beverages,
tobacco, iron and steel

GREECE

PRONUNCIATION: grees
AREA: 50,944 sq. miles
(131,945 sq. km)
POPULATION: 10,645,343
CAPITAL: Athens
CURRENCY: 100 cents = 1 euro (€)
OFFICIAL LANGUAGE: Greek
OTHER LANGUAGES: English, French
MAIN RELIGIONS: Christianity 98%, Islam 1%
EXPORTS: Manufactured goods, food, petroleum

ESTONIA

PRONUNCIATION: e-STOH-nee-uh
AREA: 17,413 sq. miles
(45,100 sq. km)
POPULATION: 1,415,681
CAPITAL: Tallinn
CURRENCY: 100 cents = 1 Estonian kroon (EEK)
OFFICIAL LANGUAGE: Estonian
OTHER LANGUAGES: Russian, Ukrainian, English
MAIN RELIGION: Christianity 99%
EXPORTS: Textiles, food, machinery, timber

LATVIA

PRONUNCIATION: LAT-vee-uh
AREA: 24,938 sq. miles (64,589 sq. km)
POPULATION: 2,366,515
CAPITAL: Riga
CURRENCY: 100 santims = 1 Latvian lat (LVL)
OFFICIAL LANGUAGE: Latvian (Lettish)
OTHER LANGUAGES: Lithuanian, Russian
MAIN RELIGION: Christianity 100%
EXPORTS: Timber, metals, dairy products, furniture, textiles, machinery and equipment

LITHUANIA

PRONUNCIATION: li-thuh-WAY-nee-uh
AREA: 25,174 sq. miles (65,201 sq. km)
POPULATION: 3,601,138
CAPITAL: Vilnius
CURRENCY: 100 centas = 1 Lithuan litas (Lt)
OFFICIAL LANGUAGE: Lithuanian
OTHER LANGUAGES: Polish, Russian
MAIN RELIGION: Christianity 98%
EXPORTS: Machinery, minerals, chemicals, textiles and clothing, food

BELARUS

PRONUNCIATION: be-luh-ROOS
AREA: 80,154 sq. miles (207,599 sq. km)
POPULATION: 10,335,382
CAPITAL: Minsk
CURRENCY: Belarussian rubel (BR)
OFFICIAL LANGUAGE: Belarussian
OTHER LANGUAGE: Russian
MAIN RELIGION: Christianity 80%
EXPORTS: Machinery and equipment, chemicals, food, metals, textiles

POLAND

PRONUNCIATION: POH-luhnd
AREA: 120,756 sq. miles (312,758 sq. km)
POPULATION: 38,625,478
CAPITAL: Warsaw
CURRENCY: 100 groszy = 1 zloty (Zl)
OFFICIAL LANGUAGE: Polish
MAIN RELIGION: Christianity 95%
EXPORTS: Machinery and transportation equipment, manufactured goods, food and livestock, fuels

CZECH REPUBLIC

PRONUNCIATION: chek ri-PUH-blik
AREA: 30,450 sq. miles (78,866 sq. km)
POPULATION: 10,256,760
CAPITAL: Prague
CURRENCY: 100 haleru = 1 Czech koruna (CZK)
OFFICIAL LANGUAGE: Czech
MAIN RELIGION: Christianity 47%
EXPORTS: Manufactured goods, raw materials and fuels, machinery and transportation equipment, chemicals, agricultural products

SLOVAKIA

PRONUNCIATION: sloh-VAH-kee-uh
AREA: 18,923 sq. miles (49,011 sq. km)
POPULATION: 5,422,366
CAPITAL: Bratislava
CURRENCY: 100 halierov = 1 Slovak koruna (Sk)
OFFICIAL LANGUAGE: Slovak
OTHER LANGUAGE: Hungarian
MAIN RELIGION: Christianity 73%
EXPORTS: Machinery and transportation equipment, chemicals, minerals and metals, manufactured goods, agricultural products

UKRAINE

PRONUNCIATION: yoo-KRAYN
AREA: 233,089 sq. miles (603,701 sq. km)
POPULATION: 48,396,470
CAPITAL: Kiev
CURRENCY: 100 kopiykas = 1 hryvnia
OFFICIAL LANGUAGE: Ukrainian
OTHER LANGUAGES: Russian, Romanian, Polish, Hungarian
MAIN RELIGIONS: Christianity 90%, Judaism 2%
EXPORTS: Metals, chemicals, machinery and transportation equipment, grain, meat, fuel and petroleum products

HUNGARY

PRONUNCIATION: HUHNG-uh-ree
AREA: 35,919 sq. miles (93,030 sq. km)
POPULATION: 10,075,034
CAPITAL: Budapest
CURRENCY: 100 filler = 1 forint (Ft)
OFFICIAL LANGUAGE: Hungarian
MAIN RELIGION: Christianity 93%
EXPORTS: Raw materials, machinery and transportation equipment, manufactured goods, food products, agriculture, fuels, energy

MOLDOVA

PRONUNCIATION: mawl-DOH-vuh
AREA: 13,012 sq. miles (33,701 sq. km)
POPULATION: 4,434,547
CAPITAL: Chişinău
CURRENCY: Moldovan Leu (L)
OFFICIAL LANGUAGE: Moldovan
OTHER LANGUAGES: Russian, Gagauz
MAIN RELIGIONS: Christianity 98%, Judaism 2%
EXPORTS: Food, wine, tobacco, textiles, footwear, machinery, chemicals

ICELAND

PRONUNCIATION: EYES-luhnd
AREA: 39,702 sq. miles (102,828 sq. km)
POPULATION: 279,384
CAPITAL: Reykjavík
CURRENCY: 100 aurar = 1 Icelandic krona (IKr)

OFFICIAL LANGUAGE: Icelandic
MAIN RELIGION: Christianity 99%
EXPORTS: Fish and fish products, animal products, minerals

NORWAY

PRONUNCIATION: nor-way
AREA: 125,181 sq. miles (324,220 sq. km)
POPULATION: 4,525,116
CAPITAL: Oslo
CURRENCY: 100 oere = 1 Norwegian krone (NKr)
OFFICIAL LANGUAGE: Norwegian
OTHER LANGUAGES: Finnish, Sami
MAIN RELIGION: Christianity 89%
EXPORTS: Petroleum and petroleum products, metals, fish and fish products, chemicals, ships, machinery and equipment, natural gas

SWEDEN

PRONUNCIATION: SWEE-duhn
AREA: 173,665 sq. miles (449,792 sq. km)
POPULATION: 8,912,000
CAPITAL: Stockholm
CURRENCY: 100 oere = 1 Swedish krona (SKr)
OFFICIAL LANGUAGE: Swedish
OTHER LANGUAGES: Finnish, Sami
MAIN RELIGION: Christianity 96%
EXPORTS: Machinery, motor vehicles, paper products, pulp and wood, iron and steel products, chemicals, petroleum products

FINLAND

PRONUNCIATION: FIN-luhnd
AREA: 130,128 sq. miles (337,032 sq. km)
POPULATION: 5,183,545
CAPITAL: Helsinki
CURRENCY: 100 cents = 1 euro (€)
OFFICIAL LANGUAGES: Finnish, Swedish
OTHER LANGUAGES: Sami, Russian
MAIN RELIGION: Christianity 90%
EXPORTS: Paper and pulp, machinery and equipment, chemicals, metals, timber

DENMARK

PRONUNCIATION: DEN-mark
AREA: 16,629 sq. miles (43,069 sq. km)
POPULATION: 5,368,854
CAPITAL: Copenhagen
CURRENCY: 100 ore = 1 Danish krone (DKr)
OFFICIAL LANGUAGE: Danish
OTHER LANGUAGES: Faroese, Greenlandic, German
MAIN RELIGION: Christianity 98%
EXPORTS: Meat and meat products, dairy products, ships, fish, chemicals, machinery and instruments, furniture, windmills

ASIA

RUSSIA

PRONUNCIATION: RUH-shuh
AREA: 6,592,812 sq. miles
(17,075,383 sq. km)
POPULATION: 144,978,573
CAPITAL: Moscow
CURRENCY: 100 kopecks = 1 Russian ruble (R)
OFFICIAL LANGUAGE: Russian
MAIN RELIGIONS: Christianity 75%, Islam,
Buddhism
EXPORTS: Petroleum and petroleum products,
natural gas, timber and timber products, metals,
chemicals, manufactured goods

TURKEY

PRONUNCIATION: TER-kee
AREA: 301,380 sq. miles
(780,574 sq. km)
POPULATION: 67,308,928
CAPITAL: Ankara
CURRENCY: Turkish lira (TL)
OFFICIAL LANGUAGE: Turkish
OTHER LANGUAGES: Kurdish, Arabic, Armenian
MAIN RELIGION: Islam 99%
EXPORTS: Manufactured goods, food, textiles
and clothing, transport equipment

CYPRUS

PRONUNCIATION: SEYE-pruhs
AREA: 3,572 sq. miles (9,251 sq. km)
POPULATION: 767,314
CAPITAL: Nicosia
CURRENCY: 100 cents = 1 Cypriot pound (£C);
100 kurus = 1 Turkish lira (TL)
OFFICIAL LANGUAGES: Greek, Turkish
OTHER LANGUAGE: English
MAIN RELIGIONS: Christianity 78%, Islam 18%
EXPORTS: Citrus fruit, potatoes, grapes, wine,
cement, textiles and clothing, shoes

GEORGIA

PRONUNCIATION: JOR-juh
AREA: 26,911 sq. miles
(69,699 sq. km)
POPULATION: 4,960,951
CAPITAL: T'bilisi
CURRENCY: Lari (GEL)
OFFICIAL LANGUAGE: Georgian
OTHER LANGUAGES: Russian, Armenian, Azeri
MAIN RELIGIONS: Christianity 83%, Islam 11%
EXPORTS: Citrus fruit, tea, wine, machinery,
metals, textiles, chemicals, fuel re-exports

ARMENIA

PRONUNCIATION: ar-MEE-nee-uh
AREA: 11,506 sq. miles
(29,800 sq. km)
POPULATION: 3,330,099
CAPITAL: Yerevan
CURRENCY: 100 luma = 1 dram (AMD)
OFFICIAL LANGUAGE: Armenian
OTHER LANGUAGES: Russian, Azeri
MAIN RELIGION: Christianity 94%
EXPORTS: Diamonds, scrap metal, machinery
and equipment, brandy, copper ore

AZERBAIJAN

PRONUNCIATION: a-zuhr-beye-ZHAHN
AREA: 33,436 sq. miles
(86,599 sq. km)
POPULATION: 7,798,497
CAPITAL: Baku
CURRENCY: 100 gopiks = 1 Azerbaijani manat (AzM)
OFFICIAL LANGUAGE: Azerbaijani
OTHER LANGUAGES: Russian, Armenian
MAIN RELIGIONS: Islam 94%, Christianity 5%
EXPORTS: Oil, gas, chemicals, oil field equipment,
textiles, cotton, foodstuffs

KAZAKSTAN

PRONUNCIATION: kuh-zahk-STAHN
AREA: 1,049,150 sq. miles
(2,717,300 sq. km)
POPULATION: 16,741,519
CAPITAL: Astana
CURRENCY: 100 tiyn = 1 tenge (KZT)
OFFICIAL LANGUAGES: Kazak, Russian
MAIN RELIGIONS: Islam 47%, Christianity 46%
EXPORTS: Oil, metals, chemicals, grain, wool,
cotton, machinery, ferrous and non-ferrous metals,
meat and livestock, coal

UZBEKISTAN

PRONUNCIATION: uz-be-ki-STAN
AREA: 172,741 sq. miles
(447,400 sq. km)
POPULATION: 25,563,441
CAPITAL: Tashkent
CURRENCY: Uzbekistani Sum (UKS)
OFFICIAL LANGUAGE: Uzbek
OTHER LANGUAGES: Russian, Tajik
MAIN RELIGIONS: Islam 88%. Christianity 9%
EXPORTS: Cotton, gold, natural gas, mineral
fertilizer, metals, textiles, food, automobiles

TURKMENISTAN

PRONUNCIATION: terk-me-nuh-STAN
AREA: 188,455 sq. miles
(488,098 sq. km)
POPULATION: 4,688,963
CAPITAL: Ashkhabad
CURRENCY: 100 tenesi = 1 Turkmen manat (TMM)
OFFICIAL LANGUAGE: Turkmen
OTHER LANGUAGES: Russian, Uzbek
MAIN RELIGIONS: Islam 89%, Christianity 9%
EXPORTS: Natural gas, cotton, petroleum products,
textiles, carpets

KYRGYZSTAN

PRONUNCIATION: kihr-gi-STAN
AREA: 76,641 sq. miles
(198,500 sq. km)
POPULATION: 4,822,166
CAPITAL: Bishkek
CURRENCY: 100 tyiyn = 1 Kyrgyzstani som (KGS)
OFFICIAL LANGUAGES: Kyrgyz (Kirghiz), Russian
MAIN RELIGIONS: Islam 75%, Christianity 20%
EXPORTS: Wool, chemicals, cotton, metals, shoes,
machinery, tobacco, potatoes, vegetables, fruits,
sheep, goats, cattle

TAJIKISTAN

PRONUNCIATION: tah-ji-ki-STAN
AREA: 55,251 sq. miles
(143,100 sq. km)
POPULATION: 6,719,567
CAPITAL: Dushanbe
CURRENCY: 100 diram = 1 somoni (SM)
OFFICIAL LANGUAGE: Tajik
OTHER LANGUAGE: Russian
MAIN RELIGION: Islam 85%
EXPORTS: Cotton, aluminum, fruits, vegetable oil,
textiles, electricity

SYRIA

PRONUNCIATION: SIHR-ee-uh
AREA: 71,498 sq. miles
(185,180 sq. km)
POPULATION: 17,155,814
CAPITAL: Damascus
CURRENCY: 100 piastres = 1 Syrian pound (£S)
OFFICIAL LANGUAGE: Arabic
OTHER LANGUAGES: Kurdish, Armenian, Aramaic,
Circassian, French, English
MAIN RELIGIONS: Islam 90%, Christianity 10%
EXPORTS: Petroleum, textiles, raw cotton, fruit
and vegetables, live sheep, phosphates

IRAQ

PRONUNCIATION: i-RAHK
AREA: 168,927 sq. miles
(437,521 sq. km)
POPULATION: 24,001,816
CAPITAL: Baghdad
CURRENCY: 1,000 fils = 1 Iraqi dinar (ID)
OFFICIAL LANGUAGES: Arabic, Kurdish
(in Kurdish regions)
OTHER LANGUAGES: Assyrian, Armenian
MAIN RELIGIONS: Islam 97%, Christianity 3%
EXPORTS: Crude oil and refined products,
fertilizer, sulfur

IRAN

PRONUNCIATION: i-RAHN
AREA: 635,932 sq. miles
(1,647,064 sq. km)
POPULATION: 66,622,704
CAPITAL: Tehran
CURRENCY: 100 dinars = 1 Iranian rial (R)
OFFICIAL LANGUAGE: Farsi (Persian)
OTHER LANGUAGES: Turkic, Kurdish, Luri
MAIN RELIGION: Islam 99%
EXPORTS: Petroleum, carpets, fruit, nuts, iron
and steel, chemicals

LEBANON

PRONUNCIATION: LE-buh-nuhn
AREA: 3,949 sq. miles (10,228 sq. km)
POPULATION: 3,677,780
CAPITAL: Beirut
CURRENCY: 100 piastres = 1 Lebanese pound (£L)
OFFICIAL LANGUAGE: Arabic
OTHER LANGUAGES: Armenian, English, French
MAIN RELIGIONS: Islam 70%, Christianity 30%
EXPORTS: Agricultural products, chemicals, paper,
textiles, metals, jewelry, electrical products

ISRAEL

PRONUNCIATION: IZ-ray-uhl
AREA: 7,992 sq. miles (20,699 sq. km)
POPULATION: 6,029,529
CAPITAL: Jerusalem
CURRENCY: 100 new agorot = 1 new Israeli
shekel (ILS)
OFFICIAL LANGUAGES: Hebrew, Arabic
OTHER LANGUAGE: English
MAIN RELIGIONS: Judaism 80%, Islam 15%,
Christianity 2%
EXPORTS: Machinery, cut diamonds, chemicals,
textiles, agricultural products, metals, software

JORDAN

PRONUNCIATION: JOR-duhn
AREA: 35,637 sq. miles
(92,300 sq. km)
POPULATION: 5,307,470
CAPITAL: Amman
CURRENCY: 1,000 fils = 1 Jordanian dinar (JD)
OFFICIAL LANGUAGE: Arabic
OTHER LANGUAGE: English
MAIN RELIGIONS: Islam 92%, Christianity 6%
EXPORTS: Phosphates, fertilizer, potash,
agricultural products, manufactured goods

SAUDI ARABIA

PRONUNCIATION: SOW-dee
uh-RAY-bee-uh
AREA: 756,981 sq. miles (1,960,582 sq. km)
POPULATION: 23,513,330
CAPITAL: Riyadh
CURRENCY: 100 halalas = 1 Saudi riyal (SR)
OFFICIAL LANGUAGE: Arabic
MAIN RELIGION: Islam 100%
EXPORTS: Petroleum and petroleum products

KUWAIT

PRONUNCIATION: koo-WAYT
AREA: 6,880 sq. miles (17,819 sq. km)
POPULATION: 2,111,561
CAPITAL: Kuwait
CURRENCY: 1,000 fils = 1 Kuwaiti dinar (KD)
OFFICIAL LANGUAGE: Arabic
OTHER LANGUAGE: English
MAIN RELIGIONS: Islam 85%, Christianity 8%,
Hinduism and Parsi 2%
EXPORTS: Oil and refined products, fertilizers

BAHRAIN

PRONUNCIATION: bah-RAYN
AREA: 255 sq. miles (661 sq. km)
POPULATION: 656,397
CAPITAL: Manama
CURRENCY: 1,000 fils = 1 Bahraini dinar (BD)
OFFICIAL LANGUAGE: Arabic
OTHER LANGUAGES: English, Farsi, Urdu
MAIN RELIGION: Islam 100%
EXPORTS: Petroleum and petroleum
products, aluminum

QATAR

PRONUNCIATION: KAH-tuhr
AREA: 4,400 sq. miles (11,395 sq. km)
POPULATION: 793,341
CAPITAL: Doha
CURRENCY: 100 dirhams = 1 Qatari rial (QR)
OFFICIAL LANGUAGE: Arabic
OTHER LANGUAGE: English
MAIN RELIGION: Islam 95%
EXPORTS: Petroleum products, steel, fertilizer

UNITED ARAB EMIRATES

PRONUNCIATION: yoo-NEYE-tuhd
A-ruhb EM-uh-ruhts
AREA: 32,000 sq. miles (82,880 sq. km)
POPULATION: 2,445,989
CAPITAL: Abu Dhabi
CURRENCY: 100 fils = 1 Emirati dirham (Dh)
OFFICIAL LANGUAGE: Arabic
OTHER LANGUAGES: Persian, English, Hindi, Urdu
MAIN RELIGION: Islam 96%
EXPORTS: Crude oil, natural gas, dried fish, dates

OMAN

PRONUNCIATION: oh-MAHN
AREA: 82,000 sq. miles
(212,380 sq. km)
POPULATION: 2,713,462
CAPITAL: Muscat
CURRENCY: 1,000 baiza = 1 Omani rial (RO)
OFFICIAL LANGUAGE: Arabic
OTHER LANGUAGES: English, Baluchi, Urdu,
Indian languages
MAIN RELIGIONS: Islam 86%, Hinduism 13%
EXPORTS: Petroleum, fish, metals, textiles

YEMEN

PRONUNCIATION: YE-muhn
AREA: 203,849 sq. miles
(527,969 sq. km)
POPULATION: 18,701,257
CAPITAL: Sanaa
CURRENCY: Yemeni rial (YRI)
OFFICIAL LANGUAGE: Arabic
MAIN RELIGION: Islam 99%
EXPORTS: Crude oil, cotton, coffee, animal skins,
vegetables, dried and salted fish

AFGHANISTAN

PRONUNCIATION: af-GA-nuh-stan
AREA: 250,775 sq. miles
(649,507 sq. km)
POPULATION: 27,755,775
CAPITAL: Kabul
CURRENCY: 100 puls = 1 afghani (AF)
OFFICIAL LANGUAGES: Afghan, Persian (Dari), Pashtu
OTHER LANGUAGES: Uzbek, Turkmen, Balochi
MAIN RELIGIONS: Islam 99%, Hinduism and Judaism 1%
EXPORTS: Opium, fruit, nuts, handwoven carpets, wool, cotton, animal skins, precious and semiprecious gemstones

PAKISTAN

PRONUNCIATION: pa-ki-STAN
AREA: 310,403 sq. miles
(803,944 sq. km)
POPULATION: 147,663,429
CAPITAL: Islamabad
CURRENCY: 100 paisa = 1 Pakistani rupee (PRe)
OFFICIAL LANGUAGES: Urdu, English
OTHER LANGUAGES: Punjabi, Sindhi, Siraiki Pashtu, Balochi, Hindko
MAIN RELIGION: Islam 97%
EXPORTS: Cotton, textiles, clothing, rice, yarn leather, carpets, agricultural products

INDIA

PRONUNCIATION: IN-dee-uh
AREA: 1,269,338 sq. miles
(3,287,590 sq. km)
POPULATION: 1,045,845,226
CAPITAL: New Delhi
CURRENCY: 100 paise = 1 Indian rupee (Re)
OFFICIAL LANGUAGES: Hindi, English, Bengali, Telugu, Marathi, Tamil, Urdu, Gujarati, Malayalam, Kannada, Oriya, Punjabi, Assamese, Kashmiri, Sindhi, Sanskrit
OTHER LANGUAGES: Hindustani, Rajasthani
MAIN RELIGIONS: Hinduism 81%, Islam 12%, Christianity 2%, Sikh 2%
EXPORTS: Clothing and textiles, gemstones and jewelry, engineering equipment, chemicals, leather goods, cotton yarn, fabric

NEPAL

PRONUNCIATION: nuh-PAHL
AREA: 54,362 sq. miles
(140,798 sq. km)
POPULATION: 25,873,917
CAPITAL: Kathmandu
CURRENCY: 100 paisa = 1 Nepalese rupee (NR)
OFFICIAL LANGUAGE: Nepali
MAIN RELIGIONS: Hinduism 86%, Buddhism 8%, Islam 4%
EXPORTS: Carpets, clothing, leather goods, jute goods, grain

BHUTAN

PRONUNCIATION: boo-TAHN
AREA: 18,147 sq. miles
(47,000 sq. km)
POPULATION: 2,094,176
CAPITAL: Thimphu
CURRENCY: 100 chetrums = 1 ngultrum (Nu); Indian currency is also legal tender
OFFICIAL LANGUAGE: Dzongkha
OTHER LANGUAGES: Tibetan and Nepali
MAIN RELIGIONS: Buddhism 75%, Hinduism 25%
EXPORTS: Timber, handicrafts, cement, fruit, electricity, gemstones, spices, gypsum

BANGLADESH

PRONUNCIATION: bahng-gluh-DESH
AREA: 55,598 sq. miles
(144,000 sq. km)
POPULATION: 133,376,684
CAPITAL: Dhaka
CURRENCY: 100 paisa = 1 taka (Tk)
OFFICIAL LANGUAGE: Bengali (Bangla)
OTHER LANGUAGE: English
MAIN RELIGIONS: Islam 83%, Hinduism 16%,
EXPORTS: Clothing and textiles, jute and jute goods, leather, frozen fish and seafood, agricultural products

MALDIVES

PRONUNCIATION: MAWL-deevz
AREA: 115 sq. miles (298 sq. km)
POPULATION: 320,165
CAPITAL: Male
CURRENCY: 100 laari = 1 rufiyaa (Rf)
OFFICIAL LANGUAGE: Maldivian Dhivehi
OTHER LANGUAGE: English
MAIN RELIGION: Islam 100%
EXPORTS: Fish, clothing

SRI LANKA

PRONUNCIATION: sree LAHNG-kuh
AREA: 25,332 sq. miles
(65,610 sq. km)
POPULATION: 19,576,783
CAPITAL: Colombo
CURRENCY: 100 cents = 1 Sri Lankan rupee (SLRe)
OFFICIAL LANGUAGES: Sinhala, Tamil
OTHER LANGUAGE: English

MAIN RELIGIONS: Buddhism 70%, Hinduism 15%, Christianity 8%, Islam 7%
EXPORTS: Textiles, tea, diamonds and other precious gemstones, petroleum products, rubber products, agricultural products, marine products

MYANMAR (BURMA)

PRONUNCIATION: MYAHN-mar (BER-muh)
AREA: 261,789 sq. miles
(678,034 sq. km)
POPULATION: 42,238,224
CAPITAL: Yangon (Rangoon)
CURRENCY: 100 pyas = 1 kyat (K)
OFFICIAL LANGUAGE: Burmese
OTHER LANGUAGE: ethnic languages
MAIN RELIGIONS: Buddhism 89%, Christianity 4%, Islam 4%, animist 1%
EXPORTS: Clothing, foodstuffs, rice, precious stones, timber

LAOS

PRONUNCIATION: lows
AREA: 91,428 sq. miles
(236,799 sq. km)
POPULATION: 5,777,180
CAPITAL: Vientiane
CURRENCY: 100 at = 1 kip (LAK)
OFFICIAL LANGUAGE: Lao
OTHER LANGUAGES: French, English, local dialects
MAIN RELIGIONS: Buddhism 60%, animism 34%, Christianity 2%
EXPORTS: Electricity, timber products, coffee, tin, textiles and clothing

VIETNAM

PRONUNCIATION: vee-et-NAHM
AREA: 127,243 sq. miles
(329,560 sq. km)
POPULATION: 81,098,416
CAPITAL: Hanoi
CURRENCY: 100 xu = 1 new dong (D)
OFFICIAL LANGUAGE: Vietnamese
OTHER LANGUAGES: French, Chinese languages, English, Khmer, tribal languages
MAIN RELIGIONS: Buddhism 55%, Christianity 7%, Taoism, indigenous religions, Islam
EXPORTS: Crude oil, rice, clothing and footwear, rubber, tea, marine products, coffee

THAILAND

PRONUNCIATION: TEYE-land
AREA: 198,455 sq. miles
(513,998 sq. km)
POPULATION: 62,354,402
CAPITAL: Bangkok
CURRENCY: 100 satang = 1 baht (B)
OFFICIAL LANGUAGE: Thai
OTHER LANGUAGES: English, Chinese languages, Malay, regional languages
MAIN RELIGIONS: Buddhism 95%, Islam 4%
EXPORTS: Computers and parts, textiles, integrated circuits, rice

CAMBODIA

PRONUNCIATION: kam-BOH-dee-uh
AREA: 69 898 sq. miles
(181,036 sq. km)
POPULATION: 12,775,324
CAPITAL: Phnom Penh
CURRENCY: 100 sen = 1 new riel (CR)
OFFICIAL LANGUAGE: Khmer
OTHER LANGUAGES: French, English
MAIN RELIGIONS: Buddhism 95%, Islam 2%
EXPORTS: Timber, rubber, clothing, rice, fish

MALAYSIA
PRONUNCIATION: muh-LAY-zhuh
AREA: 127,316 sq. miles
(329,750 sq. km)
POPULATION: 22,662,365
CAPITAL: Kuala Lumpur
CURRENCY: 100 sen = 1 ringgit (MYR)
OFFICIAL LANGUAGE: Malay (Bahasa Melayu)
OTHER LANGUAGES: English, Chinese languages,
Tamil, Telugu, regional languages
MAIN RELIGIONS: Islam 53%, Buddhism 17%,
Confucianism 12%, Christianity 9%,
Hinduism 7%
EXPORTS: Electronic equipment, petroleum,
liquified natural gas, palm oil, timber and timber
products, rubber, textiles

PHILIPPINES
PRONUNCIATION: FI-luh-peenz
AREA: 115,651 sq. miles
(299,536 sq. km)
POPULATION: 84,525,639
CAPITAL: Manila
CURRENCY: 100 centavos = 1 Philippine peso (P)
OFFICIAL LANGUAGES: Filipino, English
OTHER LANGUAGES: Regional languages
MAIN RELIGIONS: Christianity 92%, Islam 5%,
Buddhism 3%
EXPORTS: Electronics, machinery and transport
equipment, textiles, coconut products, copper, fish

SINGAPORE
PRONUNCIATION: SING-uh-por
AREA: 200 sq. miles (648 sq. km)
POPULATION: 4,452,732
CAPITAL: Singapore
CURRENCY: 100 cents = 1 Singapore dollar (S$)
OFFICIAL LANGUAGES: Chinese, Malay, Tamil,
English
MAIN RELIGIONS: Buddhism 28%, Islam 15%,
Christianity 13%, Taoism 13%, Hinduism 5%
EXPORTS: Computer equipment, chemicals,
mineral fuels, telecommunications equipment

BRUNEI
PRONUNCIATION: broo-NEYE
AREA: 2,226 sq. miles
(5,765 sq. km)
POPULATION: 350,898
CAPITAL: Bandar Seri Begawan
CURRENCY: 100 cents = 1 Bruneian dollar (B$)
OFFICIAL LANGUAGE: Malay
OTHER LANGUAGES: English, Chinese
MAIN RELIGIONS: Islam 67%, Buddhist 13%,
Christianity 10%, indigenous religions
EXPORTS: Crude oil, liquefied natural gas,
petroleum products

INDONESIA
PRONUNCIATION: in-duh-NEE-zhuh
AREA: 741,096 sq. miles
(1,919,440 sq. km)
POPULATION: 216,109,000
CAPITAL: Jakarta
CURRENCY: 100 sen = 1 Indonesian rupiah (IDR)
OFFICIAL LANGUAGE: Bahasa Indonesia
OTHER LANGUAGES: English, Dutch, Javanese,
regional languages
MAIN RELIGIONS: Islam 88%, Christianity 8%,
Hinduism 2%, Buddhism 1%
EXPORTS: Manufactured goods, oil and gas,
textiles, rubber, plywood

EAST TIMOR
PRONUNCIATION: EEST TEE-mor
AREA: 7,000 sq. miles (19,000 sq.km)
POPULATION: 952,618
CAPITAL: Dili
CURRENCY: 100 cents = 1 United States dollar (US$)
OFFICIAL LANGUAGE: Tetum, Portuguese
OTHER LANGUAGES: Bahasa Indonesia, English
MAIN RELIGION: Christianity 93%, Islam 4%
EXPORTS: Coffee, sandalwood, marble

CHINA
PRONUNCIATION: CHEYE-nuh
AREA: 3,705,386 sq. miles
(9,596,960 sq. km)
POPULATION: 1,284,303,705
CAPITAL: Beijing
CURRENCY: 10 jiao = 1 yuan (Y)
OFFICIAL LANGUAGE: Mandarin
OTHER LANGUAGES: Cantonese, Shanghaiese,
Fuzhou, Hokkien-Taiwanese, regional languages
MAIN RELIGIONS: Daoism (Taoism) 20%,
Buddhism 6%, Islam 3%, Christianity 1%
EXPORTS: Textiles and clothing, shoes, toys,
machinery and equipment, mineral fuels

MONGOLIA
PRONUNCIATION: mahn-GOHL-yuh
AREA: 604,247 sq. miles
(1,565,000 sq. km)
POPULATION: 2,694,432
CAPITAL: Ulaanbaatar
CURRENCY: 100 mongos = 1 togrog/tugrik (Tug)
OFFICIAL LANGUAGE: Khalkha Mongol
OTHER LANGUAGES: Turkic, Russian, Chinese

MAIN RELIGIONS: Buddhism 95%, Islam 4%
EXPORTS: Copper, livestock, animal products,
cashmere, wool, animal skins, non-ferrous metals

NORTH KOREA
PRONUNCIATION: north kuh-REE-uh
AREA: 46,609 sq. miles
(120,717 sq. km)
POPULATION: 22,224,195
CAPITAL: P'yŏngyang
CURRENCY: 100 chon = 1 North Korean
won (Wn)
OFFICIAL LANGUAGE: Korean
MAIN RELIGIONS: Chondogyo 14%, Buddhism 2%,
Christianity 1%
EXPORTS: Minerals, metal products, agricultural
and fishery products, manufactured goods

SOUTH KOREA
PRONUNCIATION: sowth kuh-REE-uh
AREA: 38 022 sq. miles
(98,477 sq. km)
POPULATION: 48,324,000
CAPITAL: Seoul
CURRENCY: 100 chon = 1 South Korean won (W)
OFFICIAL LANGUAGE: Korean
OTHER LANGUAGE: English
MAIN RELIGIONS: Christianity 49%, Buddhism
47%, Confucianism 3%
EXPORTS: Electronic and electrical equipment,
machinery, steel, motor vehicles, ships, textiles,
clothing, shoes, fish

TAIWAN

PRONUNCIATION: TEYE-WAHN
AREA: 13,887 sq. miles
(35,967 sq. km)
POPULATION: 22,548,009
CAPITAL: Taipei
CURRENCY: 100 cents = 1 New Taiwan dollar
(NT$)
OFFICIAL LANGUAGE: Mandarin
OTHER LANGUAGES: Taiwanese, Hakka dialects
MAIN RELIGIONS: Buddhism 43%, Daoism
(Taoism) 21%, Christianity 5%, Confucianism
EXPORTS: Electrical machinery, electronic goods,
textiles, metals, plastics, chemicals

JAPAN
PRONUNCIATION: juh-PAN
AREA: 145,882 sq. miles
(377,835 sq. km)
POPULATION: 126,974,628
CAPITAL: Tokyo
CURRENCY: 100 sen = 1 yen (¥)
OFFICIAL LANGUAGE: Japanese
MAIN RELIGIONS: Shinto and Buddhism 84%,
Christianity 1%
EXPORTS: Machinery, motor vehicles,
consumer electronics, chemicals,
semiconductors

AFRICA

MOROCCO

PRONUNCIATION: muh-RAH-koh
AREA: 172,413 sq. miles
(446,550 sq. km)
POPULATION: 31,167,783
CAPITAL: Rabat
CURRENCY: 100 centimes = 1 Moroccan
dirham (DH)
OFFICIAL LANGUAGE: Arabic
OTHER LANGUAGES: French, Berber dialects
MAIN RELIGIONS: Islam 99%, Christianity 1%
EXPORTS: Food, beverages, consumer goods,
phosphates and fertilizers, minerals

ALGERIA

PRONUNCIATION: al-JIHR-ee-uh
AREA: 919,590 sq. miles
(2,381,740 sq. km)
POPULATION: 32,277,942
CAPITAL: Algiers
CURRENCY: 100 centimes = 1 Algerian dinar (DA)
OFFICIAL LANGUAGE: Arabic
OTHER LANGUAGES: French, Berber dialects
MAIN RELIGIONS: Islam 99%, Christianity
and Judaism 1%
EXPORTS: Petroleum products, natural gas

TUNISIA

PRONUNCIATION: too-NEE-zhuh
AREA: 63,378 sq. miles
(164,149 sq. km)
POPULATION: 9,815,644
CAPITAL: Tunis
CURRENCY: 1,000 millimes = 1 Tunisian dinar (TD)
OFFICIAL LANGUAGE: Arabic
OTHER LANGUAGE: French
MAIN RELIGIONS: Islam 98%, Christianity 1%,
Judaism 1%
EXPORTS: Agricultural products, chemicals,
textiles, mechanical goods, phosphates

LIBYA

PRONUNCIATION: LI-bee-uh
AREA: 679,360 sq. miles
(1,759,540 sq. km)
POPULATION: 5,368,585
CAPITAL: Tripoli

CURRENCY: 1,000 dirhams =
1 Libyan dinar (LD)
OFFICIAL LANGUAGE: Arabic
OTHER LANGUAGES: Italian,
English
MAIN RELIGION: Islam 97%
EXPORTS: Crude oil, refined
petroleum products

CAPE VERDE ISLANDS

PRONUNCIATION: kayp VAIRD islands
AREA: 1,557 sq. miles (4,033 sq. km)
POPULATION: 408,760
CAPITAL: Praia
CURRENCY: 100 centavos = 1 Cape Verdean
escudo (CVE)
OFFICIAL LANGUAGE: Portuguese
OTHER LANGUAGE: Cape Verde creole (Crioulo)
MAIN RELIGION: Christianity 97%
EXPORTS: Fish, bananas, animal skins, clothing, fuel

EGYPT

PRONUNCIATION: EE-juhpt
AREA: 386,660 sq. miles
(1,001,450 sq. km)
POPULATION: 70,712,345
CAPITAL: Cairo
CURRENCY: 100 piasters = 1 Egyptian pound (£E)
OFFICIAL LANGUAGE: Arabic
OTHER LANGUAGES: English, French
MAIN RELIGIONS: Islam 94%, Christianity 6%
EXPORTS: Crude oil and petroleum products,
cotton, textiles, metal products, chemicals

MAURITANIA

PRONUNCIATION: maw-ruh-TAY-nee-uh
AREA: 397,955 sq. miles
(1,030,807 sq. km)
POPULATION: 2,828,858
CAPITAL: Nouakchott
CURRENCY: 5 khoums = 1 ouguiya (MRO)
OFFICIAL LANGUAGES: Hasaniya Arabic, Wolof
OTHER LANGUAGES: French, Pular, Soninke
MAIN RELIGION: Islam 100%
EXPORTS: Iron ore, fish and fish products, gold

MALI

PRONUNCIATION: mah-lee
AREA: 478,652 sq. miles
(1,239,709 sq. km)
POPULATION: 11,340,480
CAPITAL: Bamako
CURRENCY: 100 centimes = 1 CFA
franc (CFAF)
OFFICIAL LANGUAGE: French
OTHER LANGUAGES: Bambara, regional
languages
MAIN RELIGIONS: Islam 90%,
indigenous religions 9%,
Christianity 1%
EXPORTS: Cotton, livestock, gold

BURKINA FASO

PRONUNCIATION: ber-KEE-nuh FAH-soh
AREA: 105,869 sq. miles
(274,201 sq. km)
POPULATION: 12,603,185
CAPITAL: Ouagadougou
CURRENCY: 100 centimes = 1 CFA franc (CFAF)
OFFICIAL LANGUAGE: French
OTHER LANGUAGES: Tribal languages
MAIN RELIGIONS: Islam 50%, indigenous
religions 40%, Christianity 10%
EXPORTS: Cotton, gold, animal products

NIGER

PRONUNCIATION: NEYE-juhr
AREA: 459,073 sq. miles
(1,188,999 sq. km)
POPULATION: 10,639,744
CAPITAL: Niamey
CURRENCY: 100 centimes = 1 CFA franc (CFAF)
OFFICIAL LANGUAGE: French
OTHER LANGUAGES: Hausa, Djerma
MAIN RELIGIONS: Islam 80%, indigenous
religions 14%, Christianity 1%
EXPORTS: Uranium ore, livestock, cowpeas, onions

CHAD

PRONUNCIATION: chad
AREA: 495,752 sq. miles
(1,283,998 sq. km)
POPULATION: 8,997,237
CAPITAL: N'Djamena
CURRENCY: 100 centimes = 1 CFA franc (CFAF)
OFFICIAL LANGUAGES: French, Arabic
OTHER LANGUAGES: Sara, Sango, tribal languages
MAIN RELIGIONS: Islam 50%, Christianity 25%,
indigenous religions and animism 25%
EXPORTS: Cotton, cattle, textiles

SUDAN

PRONUNCIATION: soo-DAN
AREA: 967,500 sq. miles
(2,505,825 sq. km)
POPULATION: 37,090,298
CAPITAL: Khartoum
CURRENCY: 100 girsh = 1 Sudanese dinar (SDD)
OFFICIAL LANGUAGE: Arabic
OTHER LANGUAGES: Nubian, Ta Bedawie, Nilotic,
Nilo-Hamitic, regional languages, English
MAIN RELIGIONS: Islam 70%, indigenous
religions 25%, Christianity 5%
EXPORTS: Oil, livestock, cotton, sesame, peanuts

ERITREA

PRONUNCIATION: ehr-uh-TREE-uh
AREA: 46,842 sq. miles
(121,320 sq. km)
POPULATION: 4,465,651
CAPITAL: Asmara
CURRENCY: 100 cents = 1 nafka
OFFICIAL LANGUAGES: Arabic, Tigrinya, Tigre
OTHER LANGUAGES: Regional languages
MAIN RELIGIONS: Islam 50%, Christianity 50%
EXPORTS: Livestock, sorghum, textiles, food

ETHIOPIA

PRONUNCIATION: ee-thee-OH-pee-uh
AREA: 435,184 sq. miles
(1,127,127 sq. km)
POPULATION: 67,673,031
CAPITAL: Addis Ababa
CURRENCY: 100 cents = 1 birr (Br)
OFFICIAL LANGUAGE: Amharic, Tigrinya,
Oromigna, Guiragigna, Somali
OTHER LANGUAGES: Arabic, English
MAIN RELIGIONS: Islam 45%, Christianity 35%,
animism 12%
EXPORTS: Coffee, leather products, gold, oilseeds, qat

DJIBOUTI

PRONUNCIATION: ji-BOO-tee
AREA: 8,494 sq. miles
(22,000 sq. km)
POPULATION: 472,810
CAPITAL: Djibouti
CURRENCY: 100 centimes = 1 Djiboutian
franc (DF)
OFFICIAL LANGUAGES: French, Arabic
OTHER LANGUAGES: Somali, Afar
MAIN RELIGIONS: Islam 94%, Christianity 6%
EXPORTS: Animal skins, coffee

SOMALIA

PRONUNCIATION: soh-MAH-lee-uh
AREA: 246,154 sq. miles
(637,539 sq. km)
POPULATION: 7,753,310
CAPITAL: Mogadishu
CURRENCY: 100 cents = 1 Somali shilling (SOS)
OFFICIAL LANGUAGE: Somali
OTHER LANGUAGES: Arabic, Italian, English
MAIN RELIGION: Islam 99%
EXPORTS: Bananas, livestock, fish, animal skins

SENEGAL

PRONUNCIATION: sen-i-GAWL
AREA: 75,749 sq. miles
(196,190 sq. km)
POPULATION: 10,589,571
CAPITAL: Dakar
CURRENCY: 100 centimes = 1 CFA franc (CFAF)
OFFICIAL LANGUAGE: French
OTHER LANGUAGES: Wolof, Pulaar, Jola, Mandinka
MAIN RELIGIONS: Islam 92%, indigenous
religions 6%, Christianity 2%
EXPORTS: Fish, peanuts, petroleum products,
phosphates, cotton

GAMBIA

PRONUNCIATION: GAM-bee-uh
AREA: 4,363 sq. miles (11,300 sq. km)
POPULATION: 1,455,842
CAPITAL: Banjul
CURRENCY: 100 bututs = 1 dalasi (D)
OFFICIAL LANGUAGE: English
OTHER LANGUAGES: Mandinka, Wolof, Fula
MAIN RELIGIONS: Islam 90%, Christianity 9%,
indigenous religions 1%
EXPORTS: Peanuts, fish, palm kernels, cotton lint

GUINEA-BISSAU

PRONUNCIATION: gi-nee-bi-SOW
AREA: 13,948 sq. miles
(36,125 sq. km)
POPULATION: 1,345,479
CAPITAL: Bissau
CURRENCY: 100 centimes = 1 CFA franc (CFAF)
OFFICIAL LANGUAGE: Portuguese
OTHER LANGUAGES: Crioulo, African languages
MAIN RELIGIONS: Indigenous religions 50%,
Islam 45%, Christianity 5%
EXPORTS: Cashews, shrimp, palm kernels,
peanuts, timber

GUINEA

PRONUNCIATION: GI-nee
AREA: 94,925 sq. miles
(245,856 sq. km)
POPULATION: 7,775,065
CAPITAL: Conakry
CURRENCY: 100 centimes = 1 Guinean franc (FG)
OFFICIAL LANGUAGE: French
OTHER LANGUAGES: Tribal languages
MAIN RELIGIONS: Islam 85%, Christianity 8%,
indigenous religions 7%
EXPORTS: Bauxite, alumina, diamonds, gold,
coffee, fish, agricultural products

SIERRA LEONE

PRONUNCIATION: see-EHR-uh lee-OHN
AREA: 27,699 sq. miles
(71,740 sq. km)
POPULATION: 5,614,743
CAPITAL: Freetown
CURRENCY: 100 cents = 1 leone (Le)
OFFICIAL LANGUAGE: English
OTHER LANGUAGES: Mende, Temne, Krio
MAIN RELIGIONS: Islam 60%, indigenous
religions 30%, Christianity 10%
EXPORTS: Diamonds and other minerals, coffee,
cocoa, fish

LIBERIA

PRONUNCIATION: leye-BIHR-ee-uh
AREA: 43,000 sq. miles
(111,370 sq. km)
POPULATION: 3,288,198
CAPITAL: Monrovia
CURRENCY: 100 cents = 1 Liberian dollar (L$)
OFFICIAL LANGUAGE: English
OTHER LANGUAGES: Tribal languages
MAIN RELIGIONS: Indigenous religions 40%,
Christianity 40%, Islam 20%
EXPORTS: Iron ore, rubber, timber, coffee, diamonds

CÔTE D'IVOIRE (IVORY COAST)

PRONUNCIATION: koht dee-VWAR
AREA: 124,503 sq. miles
(322,463 sq. km)
POPULATION: 16,804,784
CAPITALS: Abidjan (seat of government),
Yamoussoukro (official)
CURRENCY: 100 centimes = 1 CFA franc (CFAF)
OFFICIAL LANGUAGE: French
OTHER LANGUAGES: Regional languages
MAIN RELIGIONS: Christianity 34%, Islam 27%,
animist 15%
EXPORTS: Cocoa, coffee, timber, petroleum, cotton,
bananas, pineapples, palm oil, fish

GHANA

PRONUNCIATION: GAH-nuh
AREA: 92,100 sq. miles
(238,539 sq. km)
POPULATION: 20,244,154
CAPITAL: Accra
CURRENCY: 100 pesewas = 1 new cedi (C)
OFFICIAL LANGUAGE: English
OTHER LANGUAGES: Regional languages
MAIN RELIGIONS: Indigenous religions 38%,
Islam 30%, Christianity 24%
EXPORTS: Cocoa, gold, timber, tuna, bauxite,
aluminum, manganese ore, diamonds

TOGO

PRONUNCIATION: TOH-goh
AREA: 21,853 sq. miles
(56,599 sq. km)
POPULATION: 5,285,501
CAPITAL: Lomé
CURRENCY: 100 centimes = 1 CFA franc (CFAF)
OFFICIAL LANGUAGE: French
OTHER LANGUAGES: Regional languages
MAIN RELIGIONS: Indigenous religions 59%,
Christianity 29%, Islam 12%
EXPORTS: Phosphates, cotton, cocoa, coffee

BENIN
PRONUNCIATION: buh-NEEN
AREA: 43,483 sq. miles
(112,621 sq. km)
POPULATION: 6,787,625
CAPITALS: Cotonou (seat of government),
Porto-Novo (official)
CURRENCY: 100 centimes = 1 CFA franc (CFAF)
OFFICIAL LANGUAGE: French
OTHER LANGUAGES: Fon, Yoruba, tribal languages
MAIN RELIGIONS: Indigenous religions 50%,
Islam 20%, Christianity 30%
EXPORTS: Cotton, crude oil, palm products, cocoa

NIGERIA
PRONUNCIATION: neye-JIHR-ee-uh
AREA: 356,669 sq. miles
(923,773 sq. km)
POPULATION: 129,934,911
CAPITAL: Abuja
CURRENCY: 100 kobo = 1 naira (₦)
OFFICIAL LANGUAGE: English
OTHER LANGUAGES: Regional languages
MAIN RELIGIONS: Islam 50%, Christianity 40%,
indigenous religions 10%
EXPORTS: Oil and petroleum products, cocoa, rubber

CAMEROON
PRONUNCIATION: ka-muh-ROON
AREA: 183,591 sq. miles
(475,501 sq. km)
POPULATION: 16,184,748
CAPITAL: Yaoundé
CURRENCY: 100 centimes = 1 CFA franc (CFAF)
OFFICIAL LANGUAGES: English, French
OTHER LANGUAGES: Regional
languages
MAIN RELIGIONS: Indigenous
religions 40%,
Christianity 40%,
Islam 20%
EXPORTS: Crude oil
petroleum products,
timber, cocoa beans,
aluminum, coffee, cotton

EQUATORIAL GUINEA
PRONUNCIATION: e-kwuh-TOR-ee-uhl
GI-nee
AREA: 10,825 sq. miles (28,037 sq. km)
POPULATION: 498,144
CAPITAL: Malabo
CURRENCY: 100 centimes = 1 CFA franc (CFAF)
OFFICIAL LANGUAGES: Spanish, French
OTHER LANGUAGES: Pidgin English, Fang, Bubi,
Ibo, other regional languages
MAIN RELIGION: Christianity 85%
EXPORTS: Timber, cocoa, petroleum

CENTRAL AFRICAN REPUBLIC
PRONUNCIATION: SEN-truhl AF-ri-kuhn
ri-PUH-blik
AREA: 240,534 sq. miles (622,984 sq. km)
POPULATION: 3,642,739
CAPITAL: Bangui
CURRENCY: 100 centimes = 1 CFA franc (CFAF)
OFFICIAL LANGUAGE: French
OTHER LANGUAGES: Sangho, Arabic, Hunsa,
Swahili
MAIN RELIGIONS: Christianity 50%,
indigenous religions 24%, Islam 15%
EXPORTS: Diamonds, timber, cotton,
coffee, tobacco

SÃO TOMÉ AND PRÍNCIPE
PRONUNCIATION: sow tuh-MAY and
PRIN-suh-pee
AREA: 372 sq. miles (963 sq. km)
POPULATION: 170,372
CAPITAL: São Tomé
CURRENCY: 100 centimos = 1 dobra (Db)
OFFICIAL LANGUAGE: Portuguese
MAIN RELIGION: Christianity 80%
EXPORTS: Cocoa, copra, coffee, palm oil

GABON
PRONUNCIATION: ga-BOHN
AREA: 103,346 sq. miles
(267,667 sq. km)
POPULATION: 1,233,353
CAPITAL: Libreville
CURRENCY: 100 centimes = 1 CFA franc (CFAF)
OFFICIAL LANGUAGE: French
OTHER LANGUAGES: Regional languages
MAIN RELIGIONS: Christianity 60%, animism 40%,
Islam 1%
EXPORTS: Crude oil, timber, manganese, uranium

CONGO
PRONUNCIATION: KAHN-goh
AREA: 132,047 sq. miles
(342,002 sq. km)
POPULATION: 2,958,448
CAPITAL: Brazzaville
CURRENCY: 100 centimes = 1 CFA franc (CFAF)
OFFICIAL LANGUAGE: French
OTHER LANGUAGES: Lingala, Monokutuba
MAIN RELIGIONS: Christianity 50%, animism 48%,
Islam 2%
EXPORTS: Petroleum, timber, sugar, cocoa,
coffee, diamonds

DEMOCRATIC REPUBLIC OF THE CONGO (ZAIRE)
PRONUNCIATION: de-muh-KRA-tik
ri-PUH-blik of the KAHN-goh
AREA: 905,356 sq. miles
(2,344,872 sq. km)
POPULATION: 55,225,478
CAPITAL: Kinshasa
CURRENCY: Congolese franc (CF)
OFFICIAL LANGUAGE: French
OTHER LANGUAGES: Lingala, Kingwana,
Kikongo, Tshiluba
MAIN RELIGIONS: Christianity 70%, Islam 10%,
Kimbanguism 10%, indigenous beliefs 10%
EXPORTS: Copper, coffee, diamonds, crude oil

UGANDA
PRONUNCIATION: yoo-GAN-duh
AREA: 91,134 sq. miles
(236,037 sq. km)
POPULATION: 24,699,073
CAPITAL: Kampala
CURRENCY: 100 cents = 1 Ugandan shilling (USh)
OFFICIAL LANGUAGE: English
OTHER LANGUAGES: Ganda or Luganda, Swahili,
other regional languages
MAIN RELIGIONS: Christianity 66%, indigenous
religions 18%, Islam 16%
EXPORTS: Coffee, cotton, tea, fish, iron and steel

KENYA
PRONUNCIATION: ken-yuh
AREA: 224,960 sq. miles
(582,646 sq. km)
POPULATION: 31,138,735
CAPITAL: Nairobi
CURRENCY: 100 cents = 1 Kenyan
shilling (KSh)
OFFICIAL LANGUAGES: English,
Kiswahili
OTHER LANGUAGES: Regional
indigenous languages
MAIN RELIGIONS: Christianity 66%,
indigenous religions 26%, Islam 7%
EXPORTS: Tea, coffee, petroleum products, fish

RWANDA
PRONUNCIATION: ruh-WAHN-duh
AREA: 10,169 sq. miles (26,338 sq. km)
POPULATION: 7,398,074
CAPITAL: Kigali
CURRENCY: 100 centimes = 1 Rwandan franc (RF)
OFFICIAL LANGUAGES: Kinyarwanda, French, English
OTHER LANGUAGE: Kiswahili
MAIN RELIGIONS: Christianity 87%,
indigenous religions 7%, Islam 2%
EXPORTS: Coffee, tea, animal skins, tin ore

BURUNDI
PRONUNCIATION: boo-RUN-dee
AREA: 10,759 sq. miles (27,866 sq. km)
POPULATION: 6,373,002
CAPITAL: Bujumbura
CURRENCY: 100 centimes = 1 Burundi franc (FBu)
OFFICIAL LANGUAGES: Kirundi, French
OTHER LANGUAGE: Swahili
MAIN RELIGIONS: Christianity 67%, indigenous
religions 23%, Islam 10%
EXPORTS: Coffee, tea, cotton, animal skins, sugar

TANZANIA
PRONUNCIATION: tan-zuh-NEE-uh
AREA: 364,900 sq. miles (945,091 sq. km)
POPULATION: 37,187,939
CAPITALS: Dar es Salaam (seat of government),
Dodoma (official)

Currency: 100 cents = 1 Tanzanian shilling (TSh)
Official Languages: Swahili, English
Other Languages: Arabic, regional languages
Main Religions: Christianity 45%, Islam 35%, indigenous religions 20%
Exports: Coffee, cotton, tobacco, cashews, minerals

ANGOLA

Pronunciation: ang-GOH-luh
Area: 481,351 sq. miles (1,246,699 sq. km)
Population: 10,593,171
Capital: Luanda
Currency: 100 lwei = 1 kwanza (NKz)
Official Language: Portuguese
Other Languages: Bantu, other regional languages
Main Religions: Christianity 53%, indigenous religions 47%
Exports: Crude oil, diamonds, refined petroleum products, gas, coffee, sisal (fiber), fish and fish products, timber, cotton

ZAMBIA

Pronunciation: zam-bee-uh
Area: 290,585 sq. miles (752,615 sq. km)
Population: 9,959,037
Capital: Lusaka
Currency: 100 ngwee = 1 Zambian kwacha (ZK)
Official Language: English
Other Languages: Regional languages
Main Religions: Christianity 62%, Islam and Hinduism 36%, indigenous religions 1%
Exports: Copper, cobalt, electricity, tobacco

ZIMBABWE

Pronunciation: zim-BAH-bway
Area: 150,820 sq. miles (390,624 sq. km)
Population: 11,376,676
Capital: Harare
Currency: 100 cents = 1 Zimbabwean dollar (Z$)
Official Language: English
Other Languages: Shona, regional languages
Main Religions: Syncretic (part Christianity, part indigenous religions) 50%, Christianity 25%, indigenous religions 24%. Islam 1%
Exports: Tobacco, manufactured goods, metals, cotton, gold

MALAWI

Pronunciation: muh-LAH-wee
Area: 45,747 sq. miles (118,485 sq. km)
Population: 10,701,824
Capital: Lilongwe
Currency: 100 tambala = 1 Malawian kwacha (MK)
Official Languages: English, Chichewa
Other Languages: Regional languages
Main Religions: Christianity 75%, Islam 20%, indigenous religions 5%
Exports: Tobacco, tea, sugar, cotton, coffee, peanuts, timber products

MOZAMBIQUE

Pronunciation: moh-zahm-BEEK
Area: 309,494 sq. miles (801,590 sq. km)
Population: 19,607,519
Capital: Maputo
Currency: 100 centavos = 1 metical (Mt)
Official Language: Portuguese
Other Languages: Regional languages
Main Religions: Indigenous religions 50%, Christianity 30%, Islam 20%
Exports: Shrimp, cashews, cotton, sugar, citrus fruit, timber, bulk electricity

NAMIBIA

Pronunciation: nuh-mi-bee-uh
Area: 318,694 sq. miles (825,418 sq. km)
Population: 1,820,916
Capital: Windhoek
Currency: 100 cents = 1 Namibian dollar (N$)
Official Language: English
Other Languages: Afrikaans, German, Herero, Oshivambo, Nama
Main Religion: Christianity 85%, indigenous religions 15%
Exports: Diamonds, metals, cattle, processed fish

BOTSWANA

Pronunciation: bawt-SWAH-nuh
Area: 231,803 sq. miles (600,370 sq. km)
Population: 1,591,232
Capital: Gaborone
Currency: 100 thebe = 1 pula (P)
Official Language: English
Other Language: Setswana
Main Religions: Indigenous religions 50%, Christianity 50%
Exports: Diamonds, copper and nickel, meat

SOUTH AFRICA

Pronunciation: sowth AF-ri-kuh
Area: 471,008 sq. miles (1,219,912 sq. km)
Population: 43,427,000
Capitals: Pretoria (administrative), Bloemfontein (judicial), Cape Town (legislative)
Currency: 100 cents = 1 rand (R)
Official Languages: Afrikaans, English, Xhosa, Zulu, other regional languages
Main Religions: Christianity 68%, Hinduism, Islam
Exports: Gold, diamonds and other minerals and metals, machinery and equipment

SWAZILAND

Pronunciation: swah-zee-land
Area: 6,705 sq. miles (17,366 sq. km)
Population: 1,123,605
Capital: Mbabane, Lobamba (royal and legislative)
Currency: 100 cents = 1 lilangeni (E)
Official Languages: English, Swazi
Main Religions: Christianity 60%, indigenous religions 30%, Islam 10%
Exports: Sugar, wood pulp, cotton, refridgerators

LESOTHO

Pronunciation: luh-SOH-toh
Area: 11,716 sq. miles (30,344 sq. km)
Population: 2,207,954
Capital: Maseru
Currency: 100 licente = 1 loti (L)
Official Languages: English, Sesotho
Other Languages: Zulu, Xhosa
Main Religions: Christianity 80%, indigenous religions 20%
Exports: Wool, mohair, food and livestock, clothing, footwear, road vehicles

COMOROS

Pronunciation: KAH-muh-rohz
Area: 719 sq. miles (1,862 sq. km)
Population: 614,382
Capital: Moroni
Currency: 100 centimes = 1 Comoran franc (CF)
Official Languages: Arabic, French
Other Language: Comoran
Main Religions: Islam 98%, Christianity 2%
Exports: Vanilla, cloves, perfume oil, copra

MADAGASCAR

Pronunciation: ma-duh-GAS-kuhr
Area: 226,657 sq. miles (587,042 sq. km)
Population: 16,473,477
Capital: Antananarivo
Currency: 100 centimes = 1 Malagasy franc (FMG)
Official Languages: French, Malagasy
Main Religions: Indigenous religions 52%, Christianity 41%, Islam 7%
Exports: Coffee, vanilla, shellfish, chromite, sugar, petroleum products, cotton cloth

SEYCHELLES

Pronunciation: say-SHELZ
Area: 176 sq. miles (455 sq. km)
Population: 80,098
Capital: Victoria
Currency: 100 cents = 1 Seychelles rupee (SRe)
Official Languages: English, French
Other Language: Seychelles creole
Main Religion: Christianity 98%
Exports: Fish, cinnamon bark, copra, petroleum products

MAURITIUS

Pronunciation: maw-ri-shuhs
Area: 720 sq. miles (1,865 sq. km)
Population: 1,200,206
Capital: Port Louis
Currency: 100 cents = 1 Mauritian rupee (MauR)
Official Language: English
Other Languages: Mauritian creole, French, Hindi, Urdu, Hakka, Bojpoori
Main Religions: Hinduism 52%, Christianity 28%, Islam 17%
Exports: Textiles and clothing, sugar, cut flowers, molasses

AUSTRALIA AND OCEANIA

AUSTRALIA

PRONUNCIATION: aw-STRAYL-yuh
AREA: 2,967,909 sq. miles
(7,686,884 sq. km)
POPULATION: 19,546,792
CAPITAL: Canberra
CURRENCY: 100 cents = 1 Australian
dollar ($A)
OFFICIAL LANGUAGE: English
OTHER LANGUAGES: Aboriginal languages
MAIN RELIGION: Christianity 76%
EXPORTS: Coal, gold, meat, wool, wheat, alumina,
iron ore, machinery and transportation equipment

PAPUA NEW GUINEA

PRONUNCIATION: PA-pyoo-uh noo
GI-nee
AREA: 178,703 sq. miles (462,840 sq. km)
POPULATION: 5,172,033
CAPITAL: Port Moresby
CURRENCY: 100 toea = 1 kina (K)
OFFICIAL LANGUAGES: English, pidgin English, Motu
OTHER LANGUAGES: Regional languages
MAIN RELIGIONS: Christianity 66%, indigenous
religions 34%
EXPORTS: Gold, copper ore, oil, lumber, palm oil,
coffee, cocoa, lobster, crayfish

NEW ZEALAND

PRONUNCIATION: noo ZEE-luhnd
AREA: 103,736 sq. miles
(268,676 sq. km)
POPULATION: 3,908,037
CAPITAL: Wellington
CURRENCY: 100 cents = 1 New Zealand dollar (NZ$)
OFFICIAL LANGUAGES: English, Maori
MAIN RELIGION: Christianity 67%
EXPORTS: Wool, lamb, mutton, beef, fish, cheese,
chemicals, forestry products, fruit and vegetables,
manufactured goods

SOLOMON ISLANDS

PRONUNCIATION: SAH-luh-muhn islands
AREA: 10,985 sq. miles (28,450 sq. km)
POPULATION: 494,786
CAPITAL: Honiara
CURRENCY: 100 cents = 1 Solomon Islands
dollar (SI$)
OFFICIAL LANGUAGE: Melanesian pidgin
OTHER LANGUAGES: English, regional languages
MAIN RELIGIONS: Christianity 96%,
indigenous religions 4%
EXPORTS: Fish, timber, palm oil,
cocoa, copra

SAMOA

PRONUNCIATION: suh-MOH-uh
AREA: 1,100 sq. miles
(2,850 sq. km)
POPULATION: 178,631
CAPITAL: Apia
CURRENCY: 100 sene = 1 tala (WS$)
OFFICIAL LANGUAGES: Samoan (Polynesian),
English
MAIN RELIGION: Christianity 99%
EXPORTS: Coconut oil and cream, taro, fish,
beer, copra

VANUATU

PRONUNCIATION: van-wah-TOO
AREA: 4,710 sq. miles (12,200 sq. km)
POPULATION: 196,178
CAPITAL: Port-Vila
CURRENCY: 100 centimes = 1 vatu (VT)
OFFICIAL LANGUAGES: English, French
OTHER LANGUAGE: Bislama (pidgin)
MAIN RELIGIONS: Christianity 77%, indigenous
religions 8%
EXPORTS: Copra, kava, beef, cocoa, timber, coffee

FIJI

PRONUNCIATION: FEE-jee
AREA: 7,055 sq. miles (18,272 sq. km)
POPULATION: 856,346
CAPITAL: Suva
CURRENCY: 100 cents = 1 Fijian
dollar (F$)
OFFICIAL LANGUAGE: English
OTHER LANGUAGES: Fijian,
Hindustani
MAIN RELIGIONS: Christianity 52%,
Hinduism 38%, Islam 8%
EXPORTS: Sugar, clothing, gold,
processed fish, timber

TONGA

PRONUNCIATION: TAHNG-guh
AREA: 270 sq. miles (699 sq. km)
POPULATION: 106,137
CAPITAL: Nuku'alofa
CURRENCY: 100 seniti = 1 pa'anga (T$)
OFFICIAL LANGUAGES: Tongan, English
MAIN RELIGION: Christianity 70%
EXPORTS: Squash, vanilla, fish, root crops,
coconut oil

KIRIBATI

PRONUNCIATION: kihr-uh-BAH-tee
AREA: 277 sq. miles (717 sq. km)
POPULATION: 96,335
CAPITAL: Tarawa
CURRENCY: 100 cents = 1 Australian dollar ($A)
OFFICIAL LANGUAGE: English
OTHER LANGUAGE: I-Kiribati
MAIN RELIGION: Christianity 94%
EXPORTS: Copra, coconuts, seaweed, fish

MARSHALL ISLANDS

PRONUNCIATION: MAR-shuhl islands
AREA: 70 sq. miles (181 sq. km)
POPULATION: 73,630
CAPITAL: Majuro
CURRENCY: 100 cents = 1 United States dollar (US$)
OFFICIAL LANGUAGE: English
OTHER LANGUAGES: Marshallese, Japanese
MAIN RELIGION: Christianity 98%
EXPORTS: Coconut oil, fish, trochus shells

FEDERATED STATES OF MICRONESIA

PRONUNCIATION: FE-der-ayt-ed STAYTS
of meye-kruh-NEE-zhuh
AREA: 266 sq. miles (689 sq. km)
POPULATION: 135,869
CAPITAL: Palikir
CURRENCY: 100 cents = 1 United States dollar (US$)
OFFICIAL LANGUAGE: English
OTHER LANGUAGES: Regional languages
MAIN RELIGION: Christianity 97%
EXPORTS: Fish, clothing, bananas, black pepper

NAURU

PRONUNCIATION: nah-OO-roo
AREA: 8.5 sq. miles (22 sq. km)
POPULATION: 12,329
CAPITAL: None. Government offices in Yaren
district
CURRENCY: 100 cents = 1 Australian dollar ($A)
OFFICIAL LANGUAGE: Nauruan
OTHER LANGUAGE: English
MAIN RELIGION: Christianity 100%
EXPORT: Phosphates

PALAU

PRONUNCIATION: puh-LOW
AREA: 191 sq. miles (495 sq. km)
POPULATION: 19,409
CAPITAL: Koror
CURRENCY: 100 cents = 1 United States dollar (US$)
OFFICIAL LANGUAGE: English
OTHER LANGUAGES: Palauan, Sonsorolese, Angaur,
Japanese, Tobi
MAIN RELIGIONS: Christianity 67%, Modekngei
religion 33%
EXPORTS: Shellfish, tuna, trochus shells, copra

TUVALU

PRONUNCIATION: too-VAH-loo
AREA: 9 sq. miles (23 sq. km)
POPULATION: 11,146
CAPITAL: Funafuti
CURRENCY: 100 cents = 1 Tuvaluan dollar ($T)
or 1 Australian dollar ($A)
OFFICIAL LANGUAGES: Tuvaluan, English
MAIN RELIGION: Christianity 98%, Baha'i 1%
EXPORTS: Copra

Territories and Dependencies

THE COUNTRIES LISTED BELOW govern land outside their national borders. These areas of land are known as territories or dependencies. Some territories are governed directly by the country to which they belong. Others receive only protection and financial assistance, and have their own governments and laws.

UNITED STATES OF AMERICA

AMERICAN SAMOA: South Pacific Ocean; 76 sq. miles (197 sq. km); population 68,688
GUAM: Western Pacific Ocean; 209 sq. miles (541 sq. km); population 160,796
MIDWAY: Central Pacific Ocean; 2 sq. miles (5 sq. km); no permanent population
NORTHERN MARIANA ISLANDS: North Pacific Ocean; 184 sq. miles (477 sq. km); population 77,311
PUERTO RICO: Caribbean Sea; 3,515 sq. miles (9,104 sq. km); population 3,888,000
VIRGIN ISLANDS OF THE UNITED STATES: Caribbean Sea; 133 sq. miles (345 sq. km); population 123,498
WAKE ISLAND: North Pacific Ocean; 3 sq. miles (7.7 sq. km); population 124

UNITED KINGDOM

ANGUILLA: Caribbean Sea; 35 sq. miles (91 sq. km); population 12,446
BERMUDA: North Atlantic Ocean; 20 sq. miles (52 sq. km); population 63,960
BRITISH INDIAN OCEAN TERRITORY: Indian Ocean; 23 sq. miles (60 sq. km); no permanent population
BRITISH VIRGIN ISLANDS: Caribbean Sea; 59 sq. miles (153 sq. km); population 21,272
CAYMAN ISLANDS: Caribbean Sea; 118 sq. miles (306 sq. km); population 36,273
FALKLAND ISLANDS AND DEPENDENCIES (SOUTH GEORGIA AND SOUTH SANDWICH ISLANDS): South Atlantic Ocean; 4,700 sq. miles (12,173 sq. km); population 2,967
GIBRALTAR: Southern Spain; 2.25 sq. miles (6 sq. km); population 27,714
GUERNSEY: English Channel; 30 sq. miles (78 sq. km); population 64587
ISLE OF MAN: Irish Sea; 221 sq. miles (572 sq. km); population 73,873
JERSEY: English Channel; 45 sq. miles (116 sq. km); population 89,775
MONTSERRAT: Caribbean Sea; 40 sq. miles (104 sq. km); population 8,437

PITCAIRN ISLANDS: South Pacific Ocean; 18 sq. miles (47 sq. km); population 47
ST. HELENA AND DEPENDENCIES (ASCENSION ISLAND AND TRISTAN DA CUNHA): South Atlantic Ocean; 158 sq. miles (410 sq. km); population 7,317
TURKS AND CAICOS ISLANDS: Caribbean Sea; 166 sq. miles (430 sq. km); population 18,738

FRANCE

FRENCH GUIANA: Northern South America; 35,126 sq. miles (90,976 sq. km); population 182,333
FRENCH POLYNESIA: South Pacific Ocean; 1,609 sq. miles (4,167 sq. km); population 257,847
GUADELOUPE: Caribbean Sea; 852 sq. miles (1,507 sq. km); population 435,739
MARTINIQUE: Caribbean Sea; 425 sq. miles (1,101 sq. km); population 422,277
MAYOTTE: Mozambique Channel, Africa; 144 sq. miles (373 sq. km); population 170,879
NEW CALEDONIA: South Pacific Ocean; 7,367 sq. miles (19,081 sq. km); population 207,858
RÉUNION: Indian Ocean; 969 sq. miles (2,510 sq. km); population 743,981
ST-PIERRE AND MIQUELON: North Atlantic Ocean; 93 sq. miles (241 sq. km); population 6,954
WALLIS AND FUTUNA ISLANDS: South Pacific Ocean; 106 sq. miles (275 sq. km); population 15,585

THE NETHERLANDS

ARUBA: Caribbean Sea; 69 sq. miles (179 sq. km); population 70,441
NETHERLANDS ANTILLES: Caribbean Sea; 371 sq. miles (961 sq. km); population 214,258

NORWAY

BOUVET ISLAND: South Atlantic Ocean; 22.6 sq. miles (58.5 sq. km); no permanent population
JAN MAYEN ISLAND: North Atlantic Ocean; 144 sq. miles (373 sq. km); no permanent population
SVALBARD: Arctic Ocean; 23,958 sq. miles (62,052 sq. km); population 2,868

DENMARK

FAROE ISLANDS: North Atlantic Ocean; 540 sq. miles (1,399 sq. km); population 46,011
GREENLAND: North Atlantic Ocean; 836,326 sq. miles (2,166,086 sq. km); population 59,900

AUSTRALIA

CHRISTMAS ISLAND: Indian Ocean; 52 sq. miles (135 sq. km); population 474
COCOS (KEELING) ISLANDS: Indian Ocean; 9 sq. miles (23 sq. km); population 632
HEARD AND MCDONALD ISLANDS: Indian Ocean; 159 sq. miles (412 sq. km); no permanent population
NORFOLK ISLAND: South Pacific Ocean; 13 sq. miles (34 sq. km); population 1,866

NEW ZEALAND

COOK ISLANDS: South Pacific Ocean; 92 sq. miles (238 sq. km); population 20,811
NIUE: South Pacific Ocean; 100 sq. miles (259 sq. km); population 2,134
TOKELAU: South Pacific Ocean; 4 sq. miles (10 sq. km); population 1,431

DISPUTED TERRITORIES

GAZA STRIP (PALESTINE): Middle East; disputed by Israel and Palestine, Palestinian interim self-government; 139 sq. miles (360 sq. km); population 1,225,911
KASHMIR: Southern Asia; disputed by India and Pakistan; 85,085 sq. miles (222,236 sq. km); population 7,718,700
TURKISH FEDERATED STATE OF CYPRUS: Mediterranean Sea; disputed by Turkey and Cyprus; 1,295 sq. miles (3,355 sq. km); population 177,120
WEST BANK (PALESTINE): Middle East; disputed by Israel and Palestine, Palestinian interim self-government; 2,263 sq. miles (5,860 sq. km); population 1,612,000
WESTERN SAHARA: Northwestern Africa; disputed by Morocco and separatist movement; 102,703 sq. miles (266,001 sq. km); population 256,177

Glossary

acid rain ~ Rain that has combined with pollution in the atmosphere to form an acid. Acid rain can kill plants and damage buildings.

adaptation ~ A change that occurs in a plant's structure or in an animal's body or behavior to allow it to cope better with its environment.

agriculture ~ The use of the land to grow crops and raise animals. Agriculture is another word for farming.

altitude ~ The height of a place or object above sea level.

ancestor ~ A member of a person's family who lived a long time ago.

Antarctic Circle ~ A line of latitude at 66.5° south which marks the boundary of Earth's southern polar region. South of this line there is continuous daylight in midsummer and continuous darkness in midwinter.

archipelago ~ A large group of islands.

Arctic Circle ~ A line of latitude at 66.5° north that marks the boundary of Earth's northern polar region. North of this line there is continuous daylight in midsummer and continuous darkness in midwinter.

arid ~ Having low rainfall and, as a result, little vegetation. Very arid areas are called deserts.

atoll ~ A low, ring-shaped, sandy island enclosing a lagoon. An atoll is usually formed by the growth of a coral reef on top of an undersea mountain.

axis ~ An imaginary line through the center of Earth around which the planet is constantly rotating.

■

basin ~ 1. A wide, bowl-shaped depression in the landscape. 2. An area of land that is drained by a river and its tributaries.

bay ~ A body of water partly enclosed by land.

bight ~ A recess in a stretch of coastline which forms a large bay.

border ~ A line that separates one country from another.

■

canal ~ An artificial waterway, normally created by digging a large ditch to carry water to an irrigation area or to create a transportation route for shipping.

canyon ~ A deep, steep-sided valley formed by a river.

cape ~ A piece of land that juts out into a lake or sea.

capital ~ The city where a state or country's government is located. Sometimes a country has more than one capital because parts of its government are located in different cities.

cartographer ~ A person who makes maps. The science of making maps is known as cartography.

channel ~ A narrow stretch of water between two landmasses.

climate ~ The pattern of weather that occurs in a place over an extended period of time. Earth can be divided into a number of climate zones.

compass ~ 1. A device that contains a magnetic needle which indicates the direction of north. 2. An arrow or similar icon that indicates the direction of north on a map.

coniferous ~ Coniferous trees are evergreen trees that produce seeds inside cones and usually have thin, needle-shaped or scaly leaves.

continent ~ One of Earth's seven major landmasses: Europe, Asia, Africa, North America, South America, Australia and Antarctica.

coral ~ A hard, rocky material formed by the skeletons of tiny creatures called coral polyps.

crop ~ A plant that is grown in large quantities by farmers. Crops include foods such as cereals and vegetables as well as other plants such as cotton and tobacco.

crust ~ The hard, thin rocky layer that covers the surface of Earth. The crust is broken into segments called plates.

culture ~ The shared traditions and way of life of a people.

currency ~ The kind of money used in a country.

■

dam ~ A wall-like barrier built to hold back the water of a river and create an artificial lake called a reservoir.

deciduous ~ Deciduous trees shed their leaves every year, usually in fall. The tree remains bare during winter but grows new leaves in spring.

deforestation ~ The cutting down of forest trees for timber, or to clear land for farming or building.

delta ~ A fan-shaped area of land formed by silt deposited by rivers where they empty into the sea.

dependency ~ A region or landmass governed by another country.

descendants ~ The offspring of a person, including his or her children, children's children, and so on.

desert ~ A dry area with low rainfall and sparse vegetation that is adapted to withstand drought.

■

earthquake ~ A shaking of the ground caused by the sudden movement of part of Earth's crust.

ecosystem ~ A community of plants and animals and the environment to which they are adapted.

endangered ~ An animal or plant species that is in danger of becoming extinct.

environment ~ The natural surroundings of a community of plants and animals, particularly the shape of the land, the climate and the soil.

equator ~ An imaginary line that circles the globe midway between the North and South poles. The equator divides the world into the Northern and Southern hemispheres.

ethnic group ~ A group of people sharing the same origin, language, nationality and lifestyle.

evergreen ~ An evergreen tree is a tree that does not shed its leaves in winter.

evolution ~ A process of gradual change, especially in living things.

exports ~ Goods that are sold to other countries.

extinct ~ An extinct species of animal or plant is one that no longer exists because all the individual animals or plants died.

■

federation ~ A union, by mutual agreement, of states or territories to form one country.

fertile ~ Fertile land is land with good soil. Plants grow well in fertile land if there is good rainfall or irrigation.

fjord ~ A deep, steep-sided valley gouged out by a glacier and later flooded by the sea to form a narrow inlet.

forestry ~ The science of making use of and managing forest resources.

fossil ~ The remains or traces of a prehistoric plant or animal, normally found between layers of rock.

fossil fuel ~ Fuel found deep underground which formed from the decayed remains of prehistoric plants and animals. The most common fossil fuels are coal, oil and natural gas.

■

gazetteer ~ An index of place names.

geyser ~ A spring that boils and emits hot water and steam.

glacier ~ A large mass of ice that moves slowly down the side of a mountain or along a valley, and is constantly replenished by snowfall at the top of the mountain.

gorge ~ A deep, steep-sided, rocky valley.

grassland ~ A large area of land covered with grass plants.

Greenwich meridian ~ An imaginary line that extends from the North Pole to the South Pole through Greenwich, England, and that marks 0° longitude.

gulf ~ A large bay.

■

hemisphere ~ One half of the world. Earth is divided into Northern and Southern hemispheres by the equator, and into Eastern and Western hemispheres by the Greenwich meridian (0°) and 180° line.

high-tech industries ~ Industries that produce electronic goods such as computers.

hydroelectricity ~ Electricity produced using the power of running water.

■

iceberg ~ A large block of ice floating in the sea. Icebergs break off the ends of glaciers and ice sheets. The part of an iceberg under the surface of the sea is usually eight times as large as the part above the surface.

ice cap ~ A sheet of ice and snow that covers an area permanently. Ice caps are found in polar regions and on some high mountaintops.

immigrant ~ A person who has come from one country to live in another.

independent ~ Not governed by another country.

inlet ~ A narrow bay.

irrigation ~ The process of providing water to farmland by artificial means, such as pumping water from rivers, lakes and dams, or diverting water through channels and pipes.

island ~ An area of land surrounded by water.

■

kingdom ~ A country whose ruler or head of state is a king or queen.

■

lagoon ~ 1. A shallow area of salt water separated from the sea by a strip of land. 2. Inland bodies of water that were previously part of a river.

landmass ~ A large area of land not covered by water.

latitude ~ Distance north or south of the equator measured in degrees.

livestock ~ Animals, such as cattle or sheep, raised by farmers.

longitude ~ Distance east or west of the Greenwich meridian measured in degrees.

■

marsh ~ An area of wet land containing plants adapted to growth in water. Also called a swamp or wetland.

manufacturing ~ The making of useful products from raw materials.

migration ~ Movement of people or animals to another country or region. Many animals migrate to find food or avoid severe weather.

mineral ~ A substance occurring naturally in Earth's crust that is neither plant nor animal. Well-known minerals include chalk, clay and many metals.

■

native people ~ The original human inhabitants of a region or country.

nomad ~ A person who does not live in one place but continually moves around. Nomads often move in search of food and water for themselves and their animals.

North Pole ~ see pole

■

oasis ~ A patch of land in a desert where there is water and more vegetation than elsewhere.

■

peninsula ~ A long strip of land that extends outward from a larger landmass and is almost surrounded by water.

plain ~ An area of flat or rolling land with shallow river valleys.

plantation ~ A piece of land where a particular tree crop is grown. Such crops include forest trees, rubber and coconut palms.

plate ~ One of the segments of Earth's crust.

plateau ~ An area of flat or rolling land with deep river valleys, gorges and canyons.

pole ~ The points on Earth's surface representing the ends of the planet's axis, around which it is constantly rotating. The North Pole is Earth's most northern point. The South Pole is the most southern point. The regions around the poles are known as the polar regions.

population ~ 1. The people who live in a place. 2. The total number of people living in a place.

populous ~ A populous country is a country with a large population.

principality ~ A country whose ruler or head of state is a prince or princess.

■

radioactive ~ Radioactive materials emit high-energy particles in the form of invisible rays. Some natural substances, such as uranium, are radioactive.

rain forest ~ A type of dense forest that grows in regions of high rainfall.

range ~ 1. A chain of mountains. 2. An area of open grassland where animals graze.

raw materials ~ Natural substances which can be turned into useful products. Examples include timber, coal and coffee beans. Raw materials are also known as resources.

reef ~ A ridge of rock, sand or coral lying just below the surface of the sea.

republic ~ A country led by an elected representative called a president.

reservoir ~ An artificial lake, usually created by building a dam across a river.

resources ~ Substances or materials that occur naturally in a place and are of value to the area's inhabitants. Resources that can never be used up, such as water and waves, are called renewable resources. Resources that will eventually be used up, such as coal and other minerals, are known as nonrenewable resources.

river basin ~ An area of land drained by a river and its tributaries.

rural ~ Relating to the countryside. Rural industry means industry located in country areas.

■

savanna ~ A type of grassland with scattered trees. Most savannas occur in tropical areas that have a distinct summer wet season.

scale ~ An indication on a map of how distances on the map relate to actual distances.

scrub ~ An area of land covered with shrubs and low trees.

sea level ~ The average height of the surface of the sea, which is used as a base point for measuring altitude.

South Pole ~ see pole

species ~ Animals or plants of the same type.

steppe ~ A type of dry grassland that covers parts of eastern Europe and central Asia.

strait ~ A narrow strip of water that connects two larger bodies of water.

swamp ~ An area of wet land containing plants adapted to growth in water. Also called a marsh or wetland.

■

technology ~ The use of scientific knowledge to carry out certain tasks or solve certain problems. Using machines in industry is an example of technology.

temperate ~ Neither hot nor cold. Most of Earth's temperate regions are located between the tropics and the polar regions.

territory ~ 1. A large area of land. 2. All the land and sea governed by a country or state. 3. A region or landmass governed by a country that is located in another part of the world.

textiles ~ Woven or knitted fabrics.

time zone ~ A region in which everyone uses the same time. The world is divided into 24 time zones. The time in each zone is usually one hour earlier than the zone to its east.

trade ~ The buying and selling of goods.

tributary ~ A stream or river that flows into a larger stream or river.

Tropic of Cancer/Capricorn ~ see tropics

tropics ~ 1. The hot, wet regions of Earth that lie near the equator. 2. Either of two lines of latitude: the Tropic of Cancer at 23.5° north and the Tropic of Capricorn at 23.5° south. Because Earth is tilted at an angle of 23.5°, these lines mark the point at which the Sun is directly overhead in summer.

tundra ~ A cold, barren area where much of the soil is frozen and the vegetation consists of only mosses, lichens and other small plants adapted to withstanding intense cold. Tundra is found near the Arctic Circle and on mountaintops.

■

urban ~ Relating to cities. A country's urban population is the number of people that live in its cities.

■

valley ~ A long, narrow depression in the land along which a river usually flows.

vegetation ~ The community of plants that is characteristic of a particular region.

volcano ~ A mountain that has been built up from molten rock erupting through a hole in Earth's crust.

■

wetland ~ An area of wet land containing plants adapted to growth in water. Also called a swamp or marsh.

woodland ~ An area of land covered with widely spaced trees and shrubs.

Index and Gazetteer

*A*cknowledgments

Weldon Owen would like to thank the following people for their assistance in the production of this book:
Helen Bateman, Anthony Burton, Alastair Campbell, Jo Collard, Melanie Corfield, Simon Corfield, Sharon Dalgleish, Libby Frederico, Kathy Gammon, Kathy Gerrard, Janine Googan, Greg Hassall, Lynn Humphries, Chris Jackson, Megan Johnston, Ralph Kelly, Jennifer Le Gras, Rosemary McDonald, Kylie Mulquin, Nicholas Rowland, Rachel Smith, Julie Stanton, Dawn Titmus, Greg Tobin, Wendy van Buuren, Michael Wyatt

Cartographic sources: U.S. Central Intelligence Agency; International Boundaries Research Unit, Durham University, United Kingdom; U.S. Geographer General

Photographic credits: 14 bottom left, **David Weintraub**/The Photo Library—Sydney; 14 bottom center, **Stephen Wilkes**/The Image Bank; 14 bottom right, **Mats Wibe Lund**/Icelandic Photo; 15 center far right, **David Hardy**/SPL/The Photo Library—Sydney; 15 bottom left, **Francois Gohier**/Ardea London; 15 bottom center, **B. McDairmant**/Ardea London; 15 bottom right, **International Photo Library**; 16 top far right, **Robert Harding** Picture Library; 16 bottom, **David W. Hamilton**/The Image Bank; 17 top left, **Jeffrey C. Drewitz**/The Photo Library—Sydney; 17 top center left, **Sobel/Klonsky**/The Image Bank; 17 top center, **Horizon International**; 17 top center right, **Staffan Widstrand**/Bruce Coleman Limited; 17 top right, **Christer Fredriksson**/Bruce Coleman Limited; 19 top center, **Alain Compost**/Bruce Coleman Limited; 27 top, **Horizon International**; 27 center, **Shone/Gamma/Picturemedia**; 27 bottom, **Witt/Sipa Press**/The Photo Library—Sydney

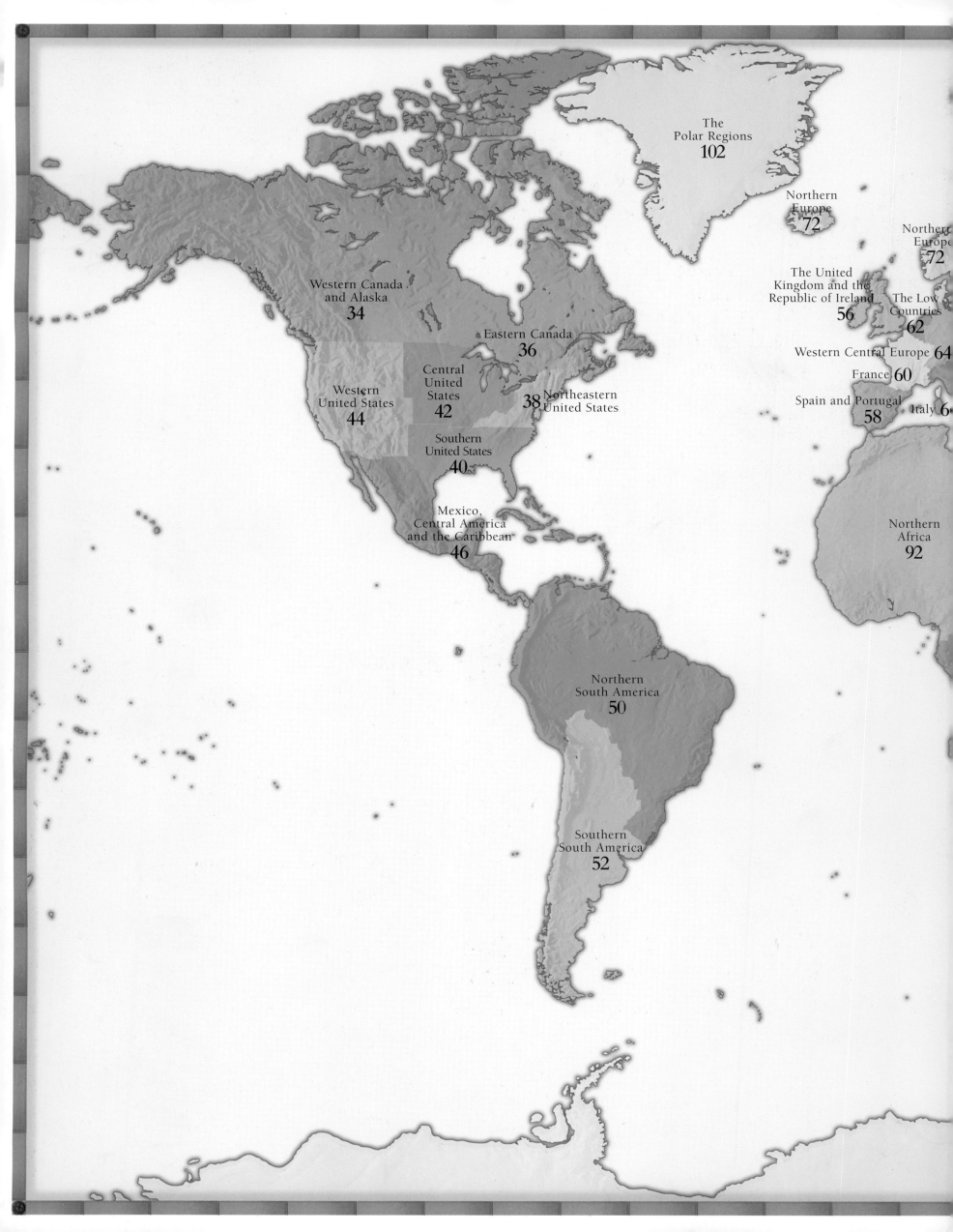

The Polar Regions
102

Northern Europe
72

Northern Europe
72

The United Kingdom and the Republic of Ireland
56

The Low Countries
62

Western Central Europe
64

Western Canada and Alaska
34

Eastern Canada
36

Central United States
42

Northeastern United States
38

France
60

Western United States
44

Spain and Portugal
58

Italy
6

Southern United States
40

Mexico, Central America and the Caribbean
46

Northern Africa
92

Northern South America
50

Southern South America
52